"I'm delighted to find this book succeeds just where so many fall short. Here is an integration of biblical-doctrinal wisdom with artistic insight which gives the arts room to be themselves without making them the touchstone of theological truth. A remarkable achievement, paving the way for a host of similar studies."

Jeremy Begbie, Thomas A. Langford Distinguished Research Professor of Theology at Duke Divinity School and coeditor of *The Art of New Creation*

"This adventurous volume evidences that theology and the arts is no longer an emerging field, but an established one—a field that sets the pace for theology as a whole."

Matthew J. Milliner, professor of art history at Wheaton College

"There are books about the Spirit. And then there are books animated by the Spirit. In *Naming the Spirit*, W. David O. Taylor and Daniel Train have brought together a collection of authors and artists who are not simply talking about the third person of the Trinity but are creating theological works that are drenched in the presence and activity of the *rûaḥ ʾĕlōhim*—the life-giving breath of God. I cannot recommend it highly enough."

Kutter Callaway, associate dean of the Center for Advanced Theological Studies at Fuller Theological Seminary and author of *Scoring Transcendence*

"This book is a rich, confident, and generous exemplification of how the discipline of theology and the arts is coming of age. Both expansive and closely attentive in its vision, it proves the value of drawing deeply on the doctrine of the Holy Spirit to frame an enlivening discourse about the life-giving power of art."

Ben Quash, director of the Centre for Arts and the Sacred at King's (ASK) and professor of Christianity and the arts at King's College London

PNEUMATOLOGY THROUGH THE ARTS

NAMING THE SPIRIT

W. DAVID O. TAYLOR &
DANIEL TRAIN, eds.

FOREWORD BY AMOS YONG

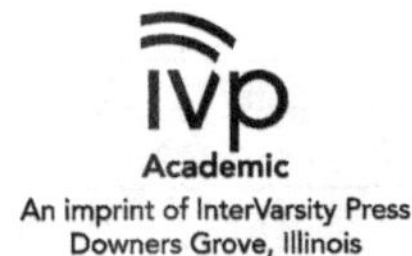

An imprint of InterVarsity Press
Downers Grove, Illinois

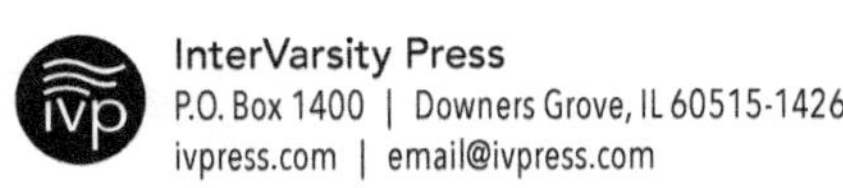

InterVarsity Press
P.O. Box 1400 | Downers Grove, IL 60515-1426
ivpress.com | email@ivpress.com

InterVarsity Press® is the publishing division of InterVarsity Christian Fellowship/USA®. For more information, visit intervarsity.org.

Cover design: Faceout Studio, Spencer Fuller
Interior design: Jeanna Wiggins

ISBN 978-1-5140-1348-9 (print) | ISBN 978-1-5140-1349-6 (digital)

Library of Congress Cataloging-in-Publication Data
A catalog record for this book is available from the Library of Congress.

31 30 29 28 27 26 25 | 13 12 11 10 9 8 7 6 5 4 3 2 1

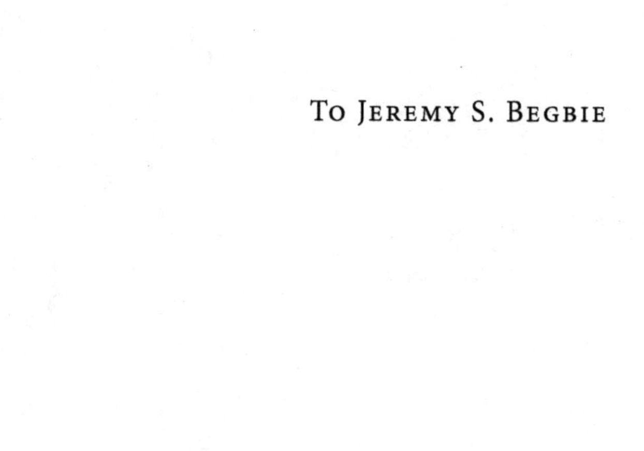

To Jeremy S. Begbie

CONTENTS

FOREWORD

AMOS YONG

As a theologian who has spent much of his vocational life attempting to trace the impossible—as Jesus himself said, "The wind blows wherever it pleases. You hear its sound, but you cannot tell where it comes from or where it is going" (Jn 3:8)—I felt empowered in this impossibility through my reading of these essays collected in the pages to come. In particular, our colleagues in the following contributions invite us to notice and then appreciate the beauty of the divine wind and breath in and through the mundane experiences of life, particularly as mediated through the arts. Let me see if I can capture some of what was stirred in me through a few brief re-readings of three familiar biblical passages.

The first comes from the opening scene of Scripture, where we are told, "In the beginning when God created the heavens and the earth, the earth was a formless void and darkness covered the face of the deep, while a wind from God swept over the face of the waters" (Gen 1:1-2 NRSVA). While a number of aspects of the Genesis narrative appear and are engaged with by some of the chapters to come (especially the one by McNutt and Vander Lugt), I was inspired by the cumulative witness to observe the beautiful workings of the divine breath in what we have usually otherwise taken for granted. Hence, this initial primeval narrative implicates the sweeping of the *rûaḥ ʾĕlōhîm* across the primordial waters, but most of us forget about this manifestation in the unfolding creational saga.

However, aren't we now invited to imagine the fluttering wind not only carrying forth the initial divine command, "Let there be light" (Gen 1:3), but also catalyzing the flickering and fluctuating of electromagnetic radiations of waves and frequencies that began illuminating the world? It is not only possible but even probable that the sweeping divine wind churns into sustained atmospheric storms of the sort that "separate[s] the waters from the waters" (Gen 1:6 NRSVUE) so that the waters above us gather—the sky!—even as the waters below also gather, thereby making a place for land (Gen 1:7-9). Isn't it? From there, does the divine wind's unpredictable blowing somehow vitalize the waters and the land in ways that prompt the emergence of self-organizing and self-metabolizing processes—single cells initially and other more complex forms of life in (agonizingly slow) tow—almost like how the Genesis narrator describes it? Doesn't this follow the divine invitational granting of permission (rather than commanding): "The earth brought forth vegetation: plants yielding seed of every kind and trees of every kind bearing fruit with the seed in it" (Gen 1:12 NRSVUE)?

Biotic life here anticipates animal life, then, which involves not only further aquatic and terrestrial responses to divine summons but also an active divine involvement:

> "*Let the waters bring forth* swarms of living creatures, and let birds fly above the earth across the dome of the sky." *So God created* the great sea monsters and every living creature that moves, of every kind, with which the waters swarm and every winged bird of every kind. And God saw that it was good. . . . "*Let the earth bring forth* living creatures of every kind: cattle and creeping things and wild animals of the earth of every kind." And it was so. *God made* the wild animals of the earth of every kind and the cattle of every kind and everything that creeps upon the ground of every kind" (Gen 1:20-21, 24-25 NRSVUE, italics added)

The latter more active divine role anticipated, it seems clear, the animation of earthly bodies with the divine breath of life (see Gen 2:7). In other words, what might elsewhere be described as mere evolutionary, geological, biological, and zoological processes come into aesthetic focus, through the traces of the witness of this volume (better seen in hindsight) of the divine wind.

The second comes from a passage core to the Pentecostal church and spirituality that nurtured me in faith and that has been the focus of much of my own efforts in theological interpretation of Scripture over decades: the Pentecost narrative in Acts 2. Although beautifully elaborated in

Anderson's chapter in what he calls the "spatialities of the Spirit," what he says there alongside a number of other considerations of Pentecost more specifically, but also of the Spirit more broadly in the rest of the book, inspire me to look again at the beauty of the Spirit precisely in the disjointed humdrum of human life. On the one hand, the beautiful Spirit's manifestation is precisely in the orchestration of the many languages of the human family; indeed, derived "from every nation under heaven" (Acts 2:5). We may not usually name the multiplicity of languages in aesthetic terms, but there is a resounding pleasantness to the richness of human language echoing in a multicultural community, even across the public square of any of our global metropolises then and now.

On the other hand, the aesthetic hermeneutic deployed for this project invites us to consider the Spirit's beautifying effects in what we might not usually so name: the din and raucousness of non-orderly human multilinguality. In this case, Luke's narration of the event, for example, "All were amazed and perplexed, saying to one another, 'What does this mean?'" (Acts 2:12 NRSVUE), is indicative not just of marvelousness and wonderment at what was being voiced but also confusion, doubt, and dissonance, the latter of which persisted also cognitively. This led to the question of significance. Herein is perhaps what scholars of religion have called the *mysterium tremendum et fascinens*, encounters of the divine that prompt both astonishment and awe-fulness (even terror). With eyes to see, ears to hear, and perceptual sensibilities attuned, then, the divine beauty emerges *for* and *to* us kinesthetically from out of the mundane cacophony of the marketplace, indeed, wherever crowds may gather (Acts 2:6), as Luke says.

Having begun with Genesis 1 and now come through the Pentecost event (so very quickly I admit on both counts), one might guess I would then go also to the final portrait, and yes, for this, I am heeding the beckoning to our final destination by the Spirit and the bride, as John of Patmos envisioned such (Rev 22:17). Now the Christian theological tradition has generally not read the final book of the biblical canon pneumatologically, or Pentecostally, not least because the references to the Spirit are less pervasive. And yet this final unveiling of Jesus Christ not only comes also in part via the divine Spirit, in fact "from the seven spirits who are before his throne" (Rev 1:4 NRSVUE; cf. 1:10, 4:2, 17:3), to be more precise, but also is the epistolary means through which the divine Spirit addressed the seven churches in Asia. More to the point, the seven divine spirits go out from the throne of God "into all the earth" (Rev 5:6), in part to renew the ends, even the "four corners of the earth" (Rev 7:1; also Rev 20:8). From this perspective, if the creation account read in light of the pneumatic—or *rûaḥ*-ic, following the transliterated Hebrew term—bookend on the Scriptural front foregrounds the beautiful creation, then the eschatological new heaven and new earth with the new Jerusalem "coming down out of heaven" (Rev 21:10) read in light of the pneumatic summons on the back end similarly elucidates the gloriously reconstructed creation.

Concretely, we surely are overwhelmed by the magnitude of the city, blinded by the brilliance of the jewels adorning its foundational walls, dazzled by the pearly gates, and mesmerized by the reflective transparencies of its divinely irradiated streets. Here, if read in light of Craft and Taylor's chapter on landscape architecture, we might see that the aesthetics of eschatological urban planning are informed by the aesthetically cultivated biosphere, with the "river of the water of life, bright as crystal, flowing from the throne of God and of the Lamb through the middle of the street of the city. On either side of the river is the tree of life with its twelve kinds of fruit, producing its fruit each month, and the leaves of the tree are for the healing of the nations" (Rev 22:2-3 NRSVUE). Might the kind of intentional cultivation of space that Craft and Taylor describe unfolding at Laity Lodge gesture toward, anticipate, or even participate in the "eschatological urban planning" we look toward? The last reference to the healing of the nations makes plain that the gorgeousness of the eschatological environment will be constituted in part also by its inhabitants—nature and culture thus blending together aesthetically—not just those from the nations or ethnic groups of the world in their distinct languages (Rev 5:9b, 7:9), but also with their cultural achievements: "the kings of the earth will bring their glory into it. . . . People will bring into it the glory and the honor of the nations" (Rev 21:24b, 26 NRSVUE). The Spirit's invitation may be received in ways that imply only that new creational beauty derives from other triune persons and we meet the divine breath as the welcoming usher. However, *Naming the Spirit: Pneumatology Through the Arts* says otherwise: the many biblical texts opened up through aesthetic lenses help us to imagine the ongoing work of the divine breath as designed to beautify our worlds and also our lives, here and in the age to come as glimpsed in the seer's visions.

David Taylor and Daniel Train and their friends begin to equip us with this gift to experience the beautiful as pneumatized. They have also assisted us in recognizing that our inhaling of the divine breath is a moment-by-moment invitation to observe the presence and activity of the beautiful God in all things, to find the spectacularity of the divine wind in the small and presumed. This latter may be the most potent enspiriting *of* and *for* our witness for all of the opportunities and challenges of our world today.

INTRODUCTION

W. DAVID O. TAYLOR AND DANIEL TRAIN

It is now common for books of this sort to begin by noting the growing interest in theology and the arts. With equal parts admiration and gratitude, these introductions often enumerate the rapid expansion within the academy (newly established degree programs, conferences, journals, publications, etc.) and the palpable interest within churches for integrating the arts into every aspect of their life (from worship to discipleship to mission and beyond). Far less common are introductions that begin with extensive apologias justifying their decision to bring two ostensibly opposed disciplines into conversation for the sake of mutually generative outcomes. These days, it is often assumed that there is an obvious relationship between theology and arts, one that will be enriching for both.

As editors of this volume, we celebrate this new state of affairs, and it prompts us to acknowledge in gratitude the debt we owe those scholars, artists, and church leaders who have made it possible for us to get on with the business, as it were, of exploring new facets of this interdisciplinary field—refining observations, deepening links, clarifying methodologies, and cultivating new partnerships, among others. There are, of course, many inspiring figures in the field without whom this present volume is unimaginable; but we are also mindful of those whose steadfastness has long been underappreciated or gone entirely unrecognized by a culture that prioritized other modes of thinking and artistic production. Their presence in local art councils, church renovation committees, and sparsely attended conference panels has born a persistent witness to the worth and promise of the field of theology and arts.

The Business of Theology and the Arts

In what way, then, does this volume aim to get on with the business? It does so by doing something surprisingly rare these days: bringing the arts into focused conversation with a specific theological locus. There is clearly a thriving theological engagement with the media of art, such as film, poetry, music, architecture, and the rest.[1] And there are a growing number of volumes that take stock of the value of art from discrete theological traditions, whether Orthodox or Reformed, or through a diversity of ecclesial traditions largely situated within a common theological one.[2] But there is much less specifically *doctrinal* engagement of ideas and practices of art. One might think of the collection of essays gathered in *Beholding the Glory: Incarnation Through the Arts*, published in 2000, or Robert K. Johnston's study in *God's Wider Presence: Reconsidering General Revelation*, published in 2014, and perhaps even Trevor Hart's exploration of the doctrine of creation in *Making Good: Creation, Creativity and Artistry*, released also in 2014.[3] But these are the exceptions, not the rule.

[1]A sample of such books includes Ben Quash and Chloë Reddaway, *Theology, Modernity and the Visual Arts* (Turnhout: Brepols, 2024); Jeremy Begbie, Daniel Train, and W. David O. Taylor, eds., *The Art of New Creation: Trajectories in Theology and the Arts* (Downers Grove, IL: IVP Academic, 2022); Robert Johnston, Craig Detweiler, and Kutter Callaway, *Deep Focus: Film and Theology in Dialogue* (Grand Rapids, MI: Baker Academic, 2019); David Brown, *Divine Generosity and Human Creativity: Theology Through Symbol, Painting and Architecture*, ed. Christopher Brewer and Robert McSwain (New York: Routledge, 2018); Jennifer Allen Craft, *Placemaking and the Arts: Cultivating the Christian Life* (Downers Grove, IL: IVP Academic, 2018); Sheona Beaumont and Madeleine Emerald Thiele, eds., *Transforming Christian Thought in the Visual Arts* (New York: Routledge, 2021); Sarah Covington and Kathryn Reklis, eds., *Protestant Aesthetics and the Arts* (New York: Routledge, 2020); Robert Covolo, *Fashion Theology* (Waco, TX: Baylor University Press, 2020); Malcolm Guite, *Faith, Hope and Poetry: Theology and the Poetic Imagination* (New York: Routledge, 2011); Murray A. Rae, *Architecture and Theology: The Art of Place* (Waco, TX: Baylor University Press, 2017); Jeremy S. Begbie, *Theology, Music and Time* (Cambridge: Cambridge University Press, 2000).

[2]For an example of the latter, see Kimberly J. Vrudny and Wilson Yates, eds., *Arts, Theology, and the Church: New Intersections* (Cleveland: Pilgrim, 2005). For an Orthodox perspective, see Michael Psellos, *Michael Psellos on Literature and Art: A Byzantine Perspective on Aesthetics* (Notre Dame, IN: University of Notre Dame Press, 2017). For a Reformed perspective, see Roger D. Henderson and Marleen Hengelaar-Rookmaaker, eds., *The Artistic Sphere: The Arts in Neo-Calvinist Perspective* (Downers Grove, IL: IVP Academic, 2024).

[3]See Jeremy Begbie, ed., *Beholding the Glory: Incarnation Through the Arts* (Grand Rapids, MI: Baker Academic, 2000); Robert K. Johnston, *God's Wider Presence: Reconsidering General Revelation*, (Grand Rapids, MI: Baker Academic, 2014); Trevor Hart, *Making Good: Creation, Creativity and Artistry* (Waco, TX: Baylor University Press, 2014). One might also put on this list Natalie Carnes, *Image and Presence: A Christological Reflection on Iconoclasm and Iconophilia* (Stanford, CA:

The reasons for this anomaly in academic theology could no doubt be parsed out at length. But for the purposes of this introduction, we simply wish to get on with the business and assume that this work, while far more challenging than we may have imagined in advance, is worth the while. Our aim here is to pursue a doctrinally rigorous engagement of the arts. Such an engagement, we believe, is best done when informed by the full resources of church tradition and a scriptural imagination, while also critically attentive to the unique challenges of the Christian faith in our contemporary times and grounded in the real-world concerns of our neighbors. Far from resulting in reductive or constricting outcomes for the arts, a specifically doctrinal, rather than broadly theological, exploration of the arts can enhance our capacities to both make and encounter artistic works. We believe likewise that the arts are not simply decorative accessories to theological labors but can play a vital role in reinvigorating the discipline of theology, our study of Holy Scripture, and our witness in the world; even more boldly, we believe that the arts can enrich our doctrinal confessions. When we do theology *through* the arts, we discover things about theology that we could not have discovered through any other means. More specifically, we discover things that enhance, clarify or, in certain cases, correct our confession in the triune God and the world that such a God makes possible. We believe, finally, that this work is best done when the distinctive modes of theology and art are respected rather than contravened.

We invited the contributors of this volume to focus on the doctrine of the person and work of the Holy Spirit and to explore how such a doctrine might both illuminate and be illuminated through a work of art. The prompt was specific, and it aimed to place constraints on the task—not in order to narrow down presumed outcomes but rather to open up a wide range of possibilities for how theology and art might be related. We asked each author to choose one of the names for the Spirit from the rich repository of Holy Scripture, to develop a brief biblical and theological account of that name, and to bring that name into conversation with a

---

Stanford University Press, 2017), and Richard Vance Goodwin, *Seeing Is Believing: The Revelation of God Through Film* (Downers Grove, IL: IVP Academic, 2022).

particular work of art. Whether they began their study with an exposition of doctrine or with a close reading of a work of art was left up to each author. In every case, we asked our authors to avoid simplistic unilateral relations between theology and art and to be open to ways in which a hermeneutical circle of sorts might come into play, whereby doctrine was further clarified by a detail-rich exegesis of the art and whereby the artwork might be allowed to become far more theologically freighted through the lens of doctrine. We also asked everyone to suggest real-world implications for their thesis. We did so not only for its practical benefit to readers but also out of the conviction that both theology and art derive their fullest meaning from the concrete conditions of our world. Last, we invited each to consider cowriting their essays. For most, this represented their first such experience.

In choosing to work with the doctrine of the Holy Spirit, we knew we entered into precarious territory. For one, Spirit language is notoriously equivocal in the field of theology and the arts. In his 1999 "Letter to Artists," for example, Pope John Paul II notes how art "must make perceptible, and as far as possible attractive, the world of the spirit, of the invisible, of God."[4] Similarly, Etienne Gilson writes, "Thanks to the fine arts, matter enters by anticipation into something like the state of glory promised to it by theologians at the end of the time, when it will be thoroughly spiritualized."[5] Wassily Kandinsky refers to the "spiritual life" as a "complex but definite movement above and beyond," while Kimberly Vrudny argues that photography possesses the capacity to capture "Spirit standing still."[6]

With such statements, it is not immediately clear how *spirit*, *spiritual*, or *spiritualize* are to be related to the *Holy* Spirit.[7] Does *spirit* stand for a

---

[4] *"Letter of His Holiness Pope John Paul II to Artists," 1999*, section 12, www.vatican.va/content/john-paul-ii/en/letters/1999/documents/hf_jp-ii_let_23041999_artists.html.

[5] Etienne Gilson, *The Arts of the Beautiful* (New York: Scribner, 1965), 33.

[6] Wassily Kandinsky, "Concerning the Spiritual in Art," in *Art, Creativity, and the Sacred: An Anthology in Religion and Art*, ed. Diane Apostolos-Cappadona (New York: Continuum, 1995), 6; Kimberly Vrudny, "Spirit Standing Still: Documenting Beauty in Photography," in *Arts, Theology, and the Church: New Intersections*, ed. Kimberly Vrudny and Wilson Yates (Cleveland: Pilgrim, 2005), 98.

[7] See Joseph Cardinal Ratzinger in *A New Song for the Lord: Faith in Christ and Liturgy Today*, trans. Martha M. Matesich (New York: Crossroad, 1996), 122.

kind of noumenal experience, a transcendental other, or a heavenly force? Does the realm of spirit rescue us from a world hopelessly corrupted by sin, or does it plunge us more deeply into such a world in divinely energized ways? The answers to these questions are rarely clear. With respect to specifically doctrinal matters, the problems that surface repeatedly are the depersonalization of the third person of the Trinity and the failure to relate the Spirit in a logically and ontologically meaningful way to the work of the Father and the Son.

For another, the language of the Bible is admittedly ambiguous in its witness to matters of the Spirit. Within the context of the Old Testament, spirit language is largely adjectival, describing usually an attribute of Yahweh—power, breath, wind, fire, and wisdom, among others. The same can be said of plenty of New Testament data (e.g., Acts 1:8; Rom 1:3-4; 1 Cor 2:6-16).[8] And while the activities that the New Testament ascribes to the Holy Spirit involve the kinds of things that only God can do, and while the *dianoia* of Scripture about the Spirit is a coherent and compelling one, church tradition has struggled to maintain a clear and consistent witness to the unique personhood of the Spirit as well as to the distinctive agency the Spirit possesses within the economy of God. In practice, Christians throughout history have often been left with a truncated Trinity (either "Father, Son, and Holy Church," or "Father, Son, and Holy Bible," or "Father, Son, and Holy Subjective Self"), and they have often reduced the Spirit to an "it," an impersonal force devoid of agency. In consequence, they have narrowly construed the ministry of the Spirit,

---

[8]Pneumatological resources that might be useful to scholars in theology and arts include Jeffery W. Barbeau and Beth Felker Jones, eds., *Spirit of God: Christian Renewal in the Community of Faith* (Downers Grove, IL: IVP Academic, 2015); David G. Firth and Paul D. Wegner, eds., *Presence, Power and Promise: The Role of the Spirit of God in the Old Testament* (Downers Grove, IL: IVP Academic, 2011); M. J. Sawyer and D. B. Wallace, eds., *Who's Afraid of the Holy Spirit?* (Dallas: Biblical Studies Press, 2005); Teresa Berger and Bryan D. Spinks, eds., *The Spirit in Worship—Worship in the Spirit* (Collegeville, MN: Liturgical Press, 2009); Graham N. Stanton, Bruce W. Longenecker, and Stephen C. Barton, eds., *The Holy Spirit and Christian Origins: Essays in Honor of James D. G. Dunn* (Grand Rapids, MI: Eerdmans, 2004); Dale M. Coulter and Amos Yong, *The Spirit, the Affections, and the Christian Tradition* (Notre Dame, IN: University of Notre Dame Press, 2016); Eugene F. Rogers Jr., *After the Spirit: A Constructive Pneumatology from Resources Outside the Modern West* (Grand Rapids, MI: Eerdmans, 2005); Anthony C. Thiselton, *The Holy Spirit—In Biblical Teaching, Through the Centuries, and Today* (Grand Rapids, MI: Eerdmans, 2013); Simeon Zahl, *The Holy Spirit and Christian Experience* (Oxford: Oxford University Press, 2020).

limiting that ministry to explicit references in the Bible (e.g., regeneration and sanctification) rather than allowing that ministry to remain as comprehensive and decisive as the ministry of Father and Son for all of creation and human history. Gaining a measure of clarity on this account was the task we entrusted to Steven Guthrie in his essay, "Remaining with a Name: The Identity of the Holy Spirit and the Posture of the Artist."

The Business of the Holy Spirit Through the Arts

The wager of this book is that the third person of the Holy Trinity is not only worthy of worship, as the divine person whom we confess in the Nicene Creed as "Lord and giver of life," but also that the distinctive work of the Spirit opens up unique possibilities for understanding, making, and receiving art. Even those who may be suspicious of anything theological will often have far fewer qualms about referencing Spirit language in relation to the arts. Take, for example, how often artists speak of being inspired without consciously reflecting on the theological implications of such experiences of inspiration. To speak of being inspired is for many a way to recognize that their work comes from beyond or above them. The contention of this book is that the beyond and above has an identifiable name, the Holy Spirit, a proper name that is revealed to us in Holy Scripture.[9] For the authors of this book, the following names become central

[9]Debates revolving around the proper way of naming the Spirit go back to the early centuries of the church and require a great deal of careful handling. At one level, the problem is a relatively straightforward one: the Holy Spirit has a name that, as Fred Sanders points out in *The Holy Spirit: An Introduction* (Wheaton, IL: Crossway, 2023), 132, "is not very name-like." At another level, there are so many names. As Lancelot Andrewes once quipped, in "Of the Sending of the Holy Ghost," in *Ninety-Six Sermons by the Right Honourable and Reverend Father in God, Lancelot Andrewes* (Oxford, UK: John Henry Parker, 1841), 3:206: "[No] person of the Three hath so many, so diverse denominations as He; and they be all to shew the manifold diversity of the gifts He bestowed on us." Beyond this, the Bible speaks of God's *rûaḥ* in largely adjectival fashion and employs three grammatical persons to identify *rûaḥ* or *pneuma*: she, he, it. The first pattern frequently leads to depersonalizing tendencies, resulting, in plenty of instances, in a projection of creaturely desires upon the Creator Spirit, while the second pattern confuses grammar for ontology, which, for many, leads to a collapsing of the Creator-creature distinction and a mapping onto the Third Person of the Trinity typically male or female characteristics. While Steve Guthrie in his chapter helpfully frames the task of naming the Spirit, it is impossible for a book like this to resolve all of the complex and complicated challenges that one faces with a subject such as this. What can be perhaps said with a measure of confidence, however, is that the many names and titles for the Holy Spirit involve an impressive chronicle of God's economy of salvation, as R. Kendall Soulen notes in his book, *The Divine Name(s) and the Holy Trinity: Distinguishing the Voices* (Louisville, KY:

to their investigations: the Spirit as Breath, the Spirit as Breadth, the outpouring Spirit, the overshadowing Spirit, the illumining Spirit, the particularizing Spirit, the Spirit as bond of peace, the comforting and disrupting Spirit, the convicting Spirit, the Spirit of shalom, and the Spirit of freedom.

While certain authors in this volume focus on what might be regarded as a proper name for the Spirit (as with "the Comforter" in Jn 15:26), others take up a key feature of the Spirit's work (such as the outpouring at Pentecost in Acts 2) and allow it to signify the Spirit's unique identity. For some, beginning with a doctrinal exposition served as the proper starting point for their investigation of a particular work of art. For others, the preferred starting point was the artwork itself, which served in turn both to frame and to inform the doctrinal exposition. For still others, the work was iterative: with theology leading to art, art leading back to theology, and at certain junctures art and theology mutually illumining each other in generative ways. For all of the authors, there was a shared conviction that the universal was to be found through the particular. Vague assertions and abstract ruminations would not do. Only the concrete would do: *this* song, enacted in *this* manner, in *this* time, in *this* place, with *these* people, resulting in *those* expected and unexpected outcomes, for instance. Julian Davis Reid's essay offers one such example of a meaningful insight into the distinctive work of the Spirit at a particular time and place with respect to a particular work of art.

The Business of Interdisciplinary Work

This in turn raised the question of method. While all the scholars here have been engaged in the field of theology and the arts for no fewer than ten years, some even approaching a quarter of a century, the choice of method proved far more difficult than may have been supposed in advance. This, we discovered, represented the unique promise and challenge of interdisciplinary work. How exactly were theology and art to be related? Simply putting two things side by side failed to clarify the task at

---

Westminster John Knox, 2011), ch. 14, and it is that good news, rooted in the good purposes of the Holy Trinity for this world, that we wish to explore in this book.

hand. Was the relation between doctrine and artwork one of correlation or causation? What verb best described their relation? Did the art illustrate a pneumatological idea, serving thereby to illumine it in some fashion? Did it clarify or complicate some aspect of the doctrine? Or did it generate constructive possibilities? And how might eisegetical tendencies be resisted, wherein the art simply reflected a priori theological judgments? More positively, on what terms might a work of visual art become a form of reasoning, as Christina Carnes Ananias shows in her essay, "The Illuminating Spirit: Seeing the Trinity in Basil of Caesarea and Olafur Eliasson's *Beauty*"? Might a renovation project in landscape architecture not merely offer fresh insight to the idea of Spirit as particularizer, as Jennifer Craft and W. David O. Taylor maintain in their joint essay, but also complexify it by showing the particularizing work of the Spirit to be far from neat and tidy?

What specific interdisciplinary skill is required, furthermore, in order to bring the doctrine of the Spirit into conversation with a poem, whose final form can be properly experienced on a printed page, as is the case with Devon Abts and Joelle Hathaway's essay, "Stewards of Breath: Poetic Imagination and the Word-Bearing Breath"? What other interdisciplinary skills are required to assess a work of art that involves multiple media working together, as with Chelle Stearns's essay, "The Overshadowing Spirit: Mary, Incarnation, and the Spirit in Olivier Messiaen's *Vingt Regards sur l'Enfant-Jésus*"? Is the overshadowing ministry of the Spirit witnessed in Messiaen's text, in Messiaen's music, or in the live performance of Messiaen's work? Or all three, even? How does one begin to convey in an essay the spiritually transformative potential of such an immersive media as film, as David W. McNutt and Wesley Vander Lugt strive to do in "Our Comforter, Our Disrupter: The Holy Spirit and Terrence Malick's *The Tree of Life*"? And what unique challenges does an author, such as Amy Krall, in "Spiritual Song: Enactment of and Participation in the Bond of Peace," face when her chosen work of art (a choral piece) cannot be properly experienced within the context of a book? A similar quandary is at work in Phil Allen and Justin Bailey's essay, "A Spacious Place: Blk Halos and the Spirit's Breadth," which examines a performance and mixed-media installation. Not all works of art, we learned afresh, are created equal, and one methodological size will not fit all interdisciplinary exercises.

In addition to this, what unique challenges face an author who relays in written form a profoundly transformative experience in the performance of his own work of music, as Reid does in "Give Us Jesus as We Cry Holy: The Holy Spirit's Convicting Use of Black Music for the New Creation"? How might such challenges compare to a project such as Shannon Sigler's "Rooted and Fixed in God: The Spirit of Freedom and an Aesthetic of Freedom," which focuses primarily on the theological work of a hymn text by Charles Wesley? To what extent is advanced graduate-level training and experience in a particular medium of art a decisive prerequisite for arriving at the rich theological insights of the sort Jonathan Anderson offers in his essay, "Outpourings: A Visual Theology of Pentecost"? Put negatively, what disadvantages might an author face in the work of interdisciplinary studies when they lack the proverbial ten thousand hours of practice that over time produce a level of expertise that increases their powers of insight, analysis, and effectual work? Might the partnership between a theologian (Taylor Worley) and a practicing artist (Erin Shaw) represent a desirable way forward, as witnessed in their coauthored essay, "The Spirit That Brings Us Home: Art, Creativity, and Native American Theologies of the Spirit"?

What the participants of this volume discovered over the course of this three-year project is what artists know better than most: that the way forward is *through* the process of work, not despite or beyond it. The end, that is, cannot be properly discerned apart from the means. While the capacity to intuit the way forward certainly increases with a depth of knowledge, intelligent practice, and the critical insights of peers in the field, a thesis at the outset of an interdisciplinary exercise may function as a kind of hypothesis, a provisional argument that could very well require adjustment after a closer study of the artwork is performed and after a doctrinal investigation is undertaken. For many, there was a genuine experience of discovery in the work of studying pneumatology and, as well as through, the arts. Assumptions held at the outset or presumed outcomes to their work were in many instances clarified and corrected *through* the work of inquiry. It was also the case that the coauthoring of essays for the authors of this volume resulted not merely in lively collaborative labors but also in a mechanism for genuine breakthroughs of insight. The ancient adage was proved right for coauthored labors: the whole was indeed greater than the sum of its parts.

The Business of the Spirit in the World at Large

In the end, the goal, we discovered, was not to be *smart* enough in order to know the answer in advance; the goal was to do the work *well enough* in order that the answer might clearly and convincingly emerge from methodological models and practices that *befit* the object of study. Under this light, the project of this book ended up involving multiple experiments. One experiment was the decision to meet in person several times over the course of three years—at a retreat center in central Texas, in the lecture halls at Duke Divinity School, within the space of an art museum at Belmont University—rather than relying only on email correspondence to get the job done. This experiment was without a doubt worth doing, for we discovered things through in-person dialogue and debate, conversation over meals, and times set aside for question and answer that could not have been discovered over email and phone calls.

A second experiment was the choice to invite coauthored essays. Five of the essays in this volume are explicitly coauthored, but all of them are collaborative in the sense that they are the product of multiple rounds of sharing drafts, comments, and revisions within focused small groups. While many of us may feel more at home writing on our own, the experience of collaboration, while at times tedious and frustrating, resulted in outcomes that exceeded our best expectations, not just in terms of their relational benefits but also in terms of the quality of the work. If the Spirit of God is in the business of forming a community that bears witness to the life, death, and resurrection of Jesus Christ, then the *manner* of our work aimed to instantiate that particular ministry of the third person of the Trinity. The result was deepened habits of generosity, moments of serendipitous insight, strengthened bonds of friendship, and generative labors that bore witness to the surplus of God's economy, where there is always more than enough.

The basic contention of this book, with all of the above in mind, is that art can become a form of constructive and critical engagement with doctrine, enriching and enlarging our confession in the triune God. Art can do so because it functions as a distinctive mode of intelligence or reasoning—of visual-spatial reasoning, kinetic reasoning, and dramatic reasoning, among others—and thereby enable us to know God and the manifold things of God's world through imaginative, sensory, affective, and metaphoric means. Art can likewise enable us to perceive connections in and across Scripture, as the essays do in spades, that we might not perceive through the usual analytical and discursive means of exegetical or systematic study. And art can attune us to the unique ways in which the Spirit not only forms a people to bear Christ's image in the world but also is always and already at work in the world at large, tending and mending, illumining and reconciling, sustaining and perfecting this world that God so loves. All of this, in short, is a way to do pneumatology *through* the arts, as our subtitle proposes.

Altogether, the essays of this book present a kind of kaleidoscopic vision of the Spirit's comprehensive work in the world. Nothing, we found yet again, is left untouched by the Spirit's work. And while much more could have been said and done here, our hope is that this volume might inspire readers to pick up where we have left off and venture into new territories, showing how the work of theology and the arts not only serves to benefit academy and church but also participates in the Spirit's healing of the world.

1

REMAINING WITH A NAME

THE IDENTITY OF THE HOLY SPIRIT AND THE POSTURE OF THE ARTIST

Steven R. Guthrie

On the first day of class; at parties and committee meetings; when entering a room or legal agreement; before the baptismal font; with one's betrothed at the altar in a wedding ceremony—in all these moments we declare our names or others declare them over us. Far from being a mere formality, in a remarkable way these syllables serve as the password by which we gain entrance to another's company. A name opens out onto further understanding, deeper knowledge, and greater intimacy. Conversely, a lost name is an obstacle to entrance as real as a lost key or a forgotten combination. We leave the party by another door, or at the very least avoid conversation, because we cannot remember the name of a friend who has just entered the room. We see the hurt on the face of a former student when we greet him by the wrong name. We experience a particularly poignant grief when a family member's dementia finally places our name beyond her reach.

What, we might ask then, *is involved in learning the name of the Holy Spirit?* Or, perhaps even more fundamentally: *Is "Holy Spirit" a name?* Thomas Aquinas begins his discussion of the Holy Spirit with just this question: "Next we have to consider the things that pertain to the person of the Holy Spirit, who is called not only the Holy Spirit, but also the Love of God, and the Gift of God. On the topic of the name 'Holy Spirit' there are four questions. [The first of which is:] (1) Is the name 'Holy Spirit' a proper name of a divine person?"[1] The issue of what constitutes a proper name, Aquinas recognizes, is important with respect to the Holy Spirit. First, consider proper names in a more mundane context:

> The Guthrie family has a pet cat.
>
> The name of that cat is Gretl (sometimes referred to in more formal settings as "Gretl the cat").

Pet is a common noun (originating, I have just learned, from a dialect in Scotland and northern England around the fifteenth century and meaning "tame animal"). *Cat* is likewise a common noun and (like all common nouns) a kind of name, in this case the name of the members of the species *Felis catus*. The common name *cat* of course, includes not only our family's cat but all the estimated seven hundred million cats in the world, as well as all the countless cats that have been or are yet to be. *Cat* is both (and equally) an aging European shorthair living in a Brussels alleyway in 1847 and a three-year-old Abyssinian enjoying the penthouse apartment of a Korean billionaire in the year 2165. *Gretl*, on the other hand, as a proper name, points to *this particular cat*, to wit: *"Gretl the cat. A shy but affectionate black-and-white shorthaired tuxedo, who will turn five next month; chosen by Lucy Guthrie and paid for with the money she had saved herself; the runt of a litter of seven kittens named after the Von Trapp children; presently residing in Nashville, Tennessee."* A proper name, then, specifies the individual who bears it and allows us to say something meaningful about the history and character of the bearer.

Is "Holy Spirit" a name in that sort of way, Aquinas wonders? Does it tell us something meaningful about the person and work of the Holy Spirit? Well, according to Aquinas, *yes and no*. Negatively, he explains, *God* (not only the third person) is Spirit, and *God* (not only the third person) is holy. Therefore, he concludes, "The expression 'holy spirit' is common to the whole Trinity."[2] In that sense, Aquinas, like Augustine

[1]Thomas Aquinas, *Summa Theologica* Ia, question 36, answer 1. Translated by the English Dominican Friars, 2nd rev. ed. (Los Angeles: Viewforth Press, 2012), 168.
[2]Aquinas, *Summa Theologica* Ia, question 36, reply to objection 1.

before him, decides that "Holy Spirit" cannot be considered the proper name of the third person of the Trinity. Instead (as we see in the quotation above), Aquinas focuses on two other names: "the Love of God" and "the Gift of God."

But there also is a sense in which "Holy Spirit" *is* a proper name. Aquinas goes on to note: "If Holy Spirit is taken as one word" (rather than divided up into *Holy* and *Spirit*), it is the "expression in the usage of the Church . . . [that signifies] one of the three persons."[3] Not only that, but Aquinas recognizes a connection between the lexical meaning of *spirit* (*spiritus* in Latin) and the activity of the third person of the Trinity. He points out, "The name *spirit* in things corporeal seems to signify impulse and motion; for we call the breath and the wind by the term spirit."[4]

This last observation is an acknowledgment of the semantic range of the word *spirit*. The biblical words that are most often translated "spirit" (*rûaḥ* in Hebrew and *pneuma* in Greek) can also be translated "wind" or "breath." The same is true of the Latin *spiritus*. Scripture does not treat these multiple meanings of *pneuma* and *rûaḥ* as an etymological quirk but as significant. Jesus tells Nicodemus (Jn 3:5-8) that the movement and activity of the *Pneuma*/Spirit of God is like the movement and activity of the *pneuma*/wind. Psalm 104, similarly, traces a path from the *rûaḥ*/breath that fills our lungs to the *Rûaḥ*/Spirit that is sent forth from God: "When you take away [creatures'] breath [*rûaḥ*], they die and return to their dust. When you send forth your spirit [*rûaḥ*], they are created" (Ps 104:29-30 NRSVUE). In light of passages such as these, Etienne Vetö argues that Aquinas is more reticent than he need be about using *Spirit* as a proper name. We can learn a great deal, he says, by "remembering something as simple as the fact that the Scriptures do have a concrete name for the mysterious third person: *Ruah* and *Pneuma*." "Of course," he adds, "breath or wind is a metaphor, but it is the least inadequate one we have, and it is provided by the Scriptures."[5]

---

[3]Aquinas, *Summa Theologica* Ia, question 36, reply to objection 1.

[4]Aquinas, *Summa Theologica* Ia, question 36, answer 1.

[5]Etienne Vetö, *The Breath of God: An Essay on the Holy Spirit in the Trinity* (Eugene, OR: Cascade Books, 2019), xxiv, xxiii.

What, if anything, is at stake in all of this? A great deal.

First, Aquinas's discussion draws our attention to the fact that *spirit* is both a common and a proper name. This is an especially helpful reminder when as theologians we undertake conversations across disciplines. In Christian life and worship, "the Spirit" is the Holy Spirit: the third person of the Trinity, the empowering presence of God, who indwells Christians to remake them in the image of Jesus Christ, who aids us in our prayers, who is included in the name into which Christians are baptized. At the same time, the word *spirit* is regularly used in other ways—to designate some ineffable property of an individual or a group, for instance, or to speak of nonhuman sentient beings, such as angels or demons. Aquinas's query, then, encourages us to give careful attention to whether *spirit* is being used as a common or a proper name when people speak about *spiritual experiences* or *spirituality*.[6] Not every cat is Gretl; nor is Gretl every cat.

Under this light, Aquinas reminds us that we look to both common and proper names for information about the bearer of that name. Knowing that Gretl is a *cat* clarifies the statement "Gretl cuddled up in bed with me last night" in really important ways. Yet, a common name can only tell you so much. With only *cat* to go on, you could not hope to pick out *Gretl* from the other felines at the local pet store. Both the common and the proper name are important. Again, this is helpful in undertaking an interdisciplinary reflection on the Holy Spirit. One mistake would be to translate every possible use of *spirit* as "Holy Spirit" without remainder. At the same time, however, it would be a mistake to neglect the wider connotations of *spirit*. That *spirit* can also mean "breath" or "wind" is important and helpful, as Jesus' conversation with Nicodemus highlights and as both Vetö and Aquinas recognize. Even more fundamentally, Aquinas's thoughtful attention to the question of naming reminds us that names are rich with meaning and worthy of careful reflection.

So, what are some ways in which the name "Holy Spirit" might be relevant to the study we are undertaking in this volume?

[6]"Since the name of spirit is given to different things, it is right to see what is that which is distinctively called the Holy Spirit. For many things are called spirits." Cyril of Jerusalem, *Catechetical Lectures* 16.13.

Pneuma: The Life-Giving Breath of God

Pneuma means "breath," and, of course, one of the things we most readily associate with breath is life. This is the first thing that the Nicene Creed emphasizes when speaking of the Spirit: "We believe in the Holy Spirit, *the Lord, the giver of life*." We encounter this intimate relation between life and God's Spirit-Breath at the very beginning of the biblical story. Genesis 2 does not use the word *rûaḥ*, but it does give us a compelling picture of the relation the Old Testament imagines between God's breath and human life. "Then the Lord God formed man from the dust of the ground, and breathed into his nostrils the breath of life; and the man became a living being" (Gen 2:7 NRSV). In the creation account, human beings do not have life as an independent possession. Rather, they are dust, held in being moment by moment by the Breath of God. Apart from God's *Breath* they "are dust, and to dust [they] shall return" (Gen 3:19 NRSV). Our life, not just its beginning but its continuation, is radically dependent on God's Spirit.

If this is so, then it is ironic that the Holy Spirit often seems the most mysterious and elusive divine person. There is a sense, nevertheless, in which the Holy Spirit is the person of God who is closest to us. The words of a contemporary worship chorus articulate this intimate dependence: "It's Your Breath in our lungs."[7] Here is God within us, whether we acknowledge God or not, each inhaled breath a renewed affirmation of the Spirit's closeness to us and provision for us (Ps 139:7-10).

Nor is the Spirit the source of only *human* life. The writer of Psalm 104 believes that the Spirit-Breath of God sustains all the extraordinary diversity of life: the wild asses, the grass, the cattle, the cedars, storks, wild goats, coneys, the moon, lions, human beings, creeping things, and even Leviathan (Ps 104:11, 14, 16-19, 21, 23, 25-26).

The Spirit is ubiquitous, in short. Within us and around us, preceding and following, the source and supply of all that is, the life of God, given to creation that it might live, sustaining all that breathes, by God's own

[7]Jason Ingram, David Leonard, and Leslie Jordan, "Great Are You Lord," Integrity's Praise! Music, Little Way Creative, 2013.

divine Breath: all of this warns us away from associating the Spirit *only* with the rarified transports of so-called mystic or miraculous wonders.[8] Indeed, because the Spirit is always and everywhere at work, giving life to creation, we may say that "in everything God is waiting for us."[9] This receptivity is in fact characteristic of much Pentecostal spirituality, particularly in the African American tradition. Estrelda Alexander writes,

> Acknowledging and engaging the presence of the Holy Spirit—is an integral part of Pentecostal living. The most mundane situations become ripe territory for the Holy Spirit's intervention. . . . The invoking of the name of the Lord, of Jesus or of the Holy Ghost is more than just a verbal gesture or a slip of the tongue. It is a confession that God's very presence and strength is required to get one through the struggle of the moment.[10]

Because all that lives from the Breath of God, we should expect to meet God in the everyday experiences of the world. This posture of careful attention, discernment, and alertness is the ground of the spiritual life; but it is likewise a posture that the arts in all their forms encourage and perhaps even require. German philosopher Josef Pieper makes the connection between art and contemplation explicit in his work Only the Lover Sings.

---

[8]Because the Spirit is the source of all life "it is . . . possible to experience God in, with and beneath each everyday experience of the world." Jürgen Moltmann, *The Spirit of Life: A Universal Affirmation*, trans. Margaret Kohl (Minneapolis: Fortress, 1991), 34.

[9]Moltmann, *Spirit of Life*, 36. Theologian Michael Welker sounds an important note of caution at this point:

> The "breathing," the sending out of God's Spirit, gives coherence, shape, and life. . . . The taking back of the *ruah* leads to death and decay. If the Spirit is held back by God, if God keeps to Godself, chaos must remain chaos. If it is recognized that the creative action of the Spirit is not self-evident, that the activity of the Spirit is not "automatic," indeterminately "everywhere," and with an arbitrarily specifiable constancy, we can begin to call into question the careless and thoughtless totalizations that have caused great difficulty for theology and piety. The abstract reference to the Spirit's "ubiquity," "universal causality," and "universal effectiveness" can be corrected and replaced. The fact that God's Spirit "has filled the world, and . . . holds all things together" (Wisd. Of Sol. 1:7, cf. Isa. 35:16) is not to be confused with abstract "ubiquity." The Spirit is present in that which is held together and enlivened by God—but not for example, in that which is decaying to dust. God is present creating life and working righteousness. But through falseness and unrighteousness human beings can grieve and banish God's Spirit. (Michael Welker, *God the Spirit* [Minneapolis: Fortress, 1994], 160-61.)

[10]Estrelda Y. Alexander, "The Spirit of God: Christian Renewal in African American Pentecostalism," in *Spirit of God: Christian Renewal in the Community of Faith*, ed. Jeffery W. Barbeau and Beth Felker Jones (Downers Grove, IL: IVP Academic, 2015), 133.

We seem, Pieper complains, less and less able to attend to the world with an attitude of receptivity, wonder, and contemplation. Though this is a spiritual malady, the "effective remedy" Pieper commends is "to be active oneself in artistic creation, producing shapes and forms for the eye to see."

> Nobody has to observe and study the visible mystery of a human face more than the one who sets out to sculpt it in a tangible medium. And this holds true not only for a manually formed image. The verbal "image" as well can thrive only when it springs from a higher level of visual perception. . . . Before you can express anything in tangible form, you first need eyes to see.[11]

Of course, any artist would agree that careful attention is vitally important. One attends to the materials employed, to the character of line, color, sound, and movement. But a conception of the world as Spirit-breathed gives this attention a distinctive texture. Indeed, one might misread Pieper as simply encouraging the artist to focus her gaze on the inert object with even greater intensity, as if the artist were simply a person uniquely gifted at extracting meaning from lifeless matter. But this is not the vision of a world held in being by God's Breath. In engaging the world, we engage what has been *given life*. This is not to suggest that we can gaze through each created object directly into the face of God, as if the material were nothing but a transparent pane opening onto the divine. No: the creation has been *given* life, which means it has its own being and character and identity. Yet it has been given *life*, which means that the artist always participates in dialogue. Our pneumatology grounds, demands, and makes sense of an engagement with art that is not only creative and attentive but responsive and receptive.

Pneuma: The Word-Bearing Breath of God

The Nicene Creed highlights another way in which the Spirit is breath-like. "We believe in the Holy Spirit, the Lord, the giver of life . . . *who has spoken* by the prophets." This line of the creed echoes the words of 2 Peter 1:21: "No prophecy ever came by human will, but men and women moved by

[11]Josef Pieper, *Only the Lover Sings: Art and Contemplation* (San Francisco: Ignatius, 1990), 35-36.

the Holy Spirit spoke from God" (NRSV). It is also an acknowledgment that one of the fundamental functions of breath is to carry word. Likewise and equally, words are in the first instance borne by breath, a fact that is too easily missed in a modern Western culture that is largely textual rather than oral and aural.[12] Eighth-century theologian John of Damascus points out that the same breath that gives life gives speech. As such, the Spirit-Breath *belongs to* the Word. "The Word must also possess Spirit. . . . For there is an attraction and movement of air which is drawn in and poured forth that the body may be sustained. And it is this which in the moment of utterance becomes the articulate word."[13] Of course, the preeminent and paradigmatic instance of the bond between Spirit and Word is the incarnation. The child to be conceived in Mary, the angel tells Joseph, "is from the Holy Spirit" (Mt 1:21) When Mary asks the angel, "How can this be, since I am a virgin?" the angel responds, "The Holy Spirit will come upon you" (Lk 1:34-35 NRSV). Breath is the bearer of the Word: not only the words of instruction, teaching, and testimony but the eternal Word of God himself.

For many of the early church fathers, this intimate relation of Word and Breath was a picture of the necessary unity of mission between the eternal Son of God and the Holy Spirit. There could be no question, then, of pitting the Spirit against the Word, of creating a dichotomy between the experience and charisms of the Spirit and the historical specificity of the Word made flesh. How could the Word sound except by Breath? And does not Breath serve to carry forth the Word?[14]

The unity of Word and Breath is worth setting alongside Jesus' conversation with Nicodemus in John 3. There Jesus emphasizes that the activity

---

[12]"No speech is possible without breath. Breathing out is necessary to make sounds. Therefore the *ruah* is already present in God's first breath. It resounds in the first word." Geiko Muller-Fahrenholz, *God's Spirit: Transforming a World in Crisis* (New York: Continuum, 1995), 13.

[13]John of Damascus, *An Exact Exposition of the Orthodox Faith*, trans. S. D. F. Salmond, in *A Select Library of Nicene and Post-Nicene Fathers of the Christian Church*, series 2, vol. 9, ed. Philip Schaff, https://ccel.org/ccel/schaff/npnf209/npnf209.iii.iv.i.vii.html.

[14]"The patristic literature," Sergius Bulgakov writes, "likened the Second hypostasis [that is, the Son] to the lips and the Third [the Holy Spirit] to the breath out of the lips, or the Second to the word and the Third to the air moving as the word sounds. . . . This dyadic union is *necessary* for the very realizability of the self-revelation." Bulgakov, *The Comforter*, trans. Boris Jakim (Grand Rapids, MI: Eerdmans, 2004), 179.

of the Spirit is elusive and mysterious. This is, in fact, Jesus says, one way in which the activity of the Spirit is wind-like. We might ask, then: How are these two held together? Is the Spirit unknowable and beyond our grasp like the wind? Or like a teacher who brings us the word? In the biblical witness, the Spirit is both. The Spirit is, on the one hand, the knowledge-bringing, word-bearing Breath of God, and, on the other hand, the mysterious, invisible, and elusive Wind of God. This double identity (much like the self-effacing character of the Spirit) is not a problem but a gift. It points us toward a more richly nuanced understanding of the relationship between mystery and knowledge.[15] The richness and complexity of the Spirit's work bars the way to a simplistic opposition of "mystery versus knowledge" or "experience versus word." If the Spirit is the giver of words and understanding, then "the spiritual" is not simply "the unknown," nor is that which is unknowable inherently spiritual. Likewise, while the Spirit is Teacher, the knowledge given by the Spirit is not absent of mystery. Spiritual wisdom is not knowledge we control or wield any more than we control or wield the wind.

All of this is helpful in any theological engagement with the arts. The theological exploration of art—employing words and concepts to engage aesthetic experience; bringing works of art to bear on theological categories—is not an attempt to mix oil and water. The activity of the Spirit teaches us that mystery, spontaneity, and creativity do not frustrate our aspirations to speech, knowledge, or understanding. Neither is it the case that our words and analyses should aim to dissolve the mystery of creativity into rational categories. Rather, the Spirit of Pentecost descends without warning and gives rise to speech; the resulting outburst of speech in turn gives rise to amazement (Acts 2:12) and awe (Acts 2:43).

The character of the Spirit's work demonstrates the potential of the sort of reflection undertaken on these pages. As much as any dimension of human experience, art and beauty testify that something can be both elusive and revelatory, both ineffable and generative of speech, both mysterious and knowledge bearing. The work of the Spirit is just so.

[15]For a fuller discussion, see Steven R. Guthrie, *Creator Spirit: The Holy Spirit and the Art of Becoming Human* (Grand Rapids, MI: Baker Academic, 2011), 12-21.

Pneuma: The Dynamic Wind of God

Whether we are inhaling a life-giving breath or projecting a Word-bearing Breath, or feeling the wind push at our backs, *pneuma* means movement. Breath apart from movement is not breath, and wind apart from movement is not wind. This is highlighted by Aquinas: "The name *spirit* in things corporeal *seems to signify impulse and motion*."[16] Movement is not only characteristic of *pneuma*; it also unites the two activities highlighted above. By the Holy Spirit, the life that is in God comes to live in us; and by the Spirit, the knowledge and wisdom that is in God is made available to the prophets. By the Spirit, God the Father moves out beyond himself in the Son.[17]

Anyone who has ever been caught in a powerful wind, however, knows that in such a situation, it is not only the wind that moves. The wind also sets other things in motion. The Nicene Creed does not say that the Holy Spirit spoke *to* the prophets but rather spoke *through* the prophets. This is not the "through" of water pouring through an empty conduit, untouched by the vessel through which it passes. Rather, the Spirit's movement sets the *prophets* in motion. The Spirit's speech causes them to speak. The movement and dynamism of the Spirit's work does not terminate in the outward movement from God to creature. The movement continues. We also can see this in another phrase of the creed: "We believe in the Holy Spirit . . . who together with the Father and the Son is worshiped and glorified." We inhale the breath of the Spirit so that we may exhale the breath of worship. The first gift brings about a second. Physiologically, the intake of breath by necessity also gives the answering exhalation. The very structure of breath reflects the generosity of God and the generative character of creation. God's intention is that we should be creatures who both inhale and exhale, who receive breath in order that we might then be givers of breath.[18]

16Aquinas, *Summa Theologica* Ia, question 36, answer 1.

17The Holy Spirit "is the capacity of God to be 'outside of himself'" (Vetö, *Breath of God*, 47, quoting H. Müllen).

18"God has already addressed man," writes Jean Louis Chrétien, "has already spoken to him before man starts to speak, *so that* [humanity] will start to speak in his turn." Jean-Louis Chrétien, *The Ark of Speech*, tr. Andrew Brown (New York: Routledge, 2004), 1 (emphasis added).

Again, all of this has enormous significance for the conversation between pneumatology and the arts. In sending forth his Life-Breath into creation, God the Father calls forth an answering breath from the creature. God gives not only breath, we might say, but *breathing*; God has not only sent forth his Word but has given creation its own distinctive voice. Creation, in other words, speaks because it has been addressed. Artistry is an enactment of this giving and receiving of breath. The created world receives God's breath of life. The answering exhalation carries not only God's breath but the voice of each creature. By its answering breath, the created world comes out to meet us. The response of the artist as she is met by stone, wood, air, or pigment is likewise testimony to the dynamic character of God's Holy Spirit. The listener, the viewer, the Christian, the theologian addressed by the created world and the artist's engagement with it, is likewise invited to respond.

At some level this dynamism can be discerned in all human endeavor and discourse, yet it is particularly evident in our engagement with art and beauty. Art foregrounds and depends on the respiratory character of a world given and held in life by God's Spirit. Artistry explicitly elicits our answering involvement. Significantly, Jean-Louis Chrétien explores the aesthetic experience in a book bearing the title *The Call and the Response* (*L'Appel et la Réponse*). "We speak," he writes, "only for having been called, called by what there is to say, and yet we learn and hear what there is to say only in speech itself. . . . The expanding diastole of beauty, in its radiant effusion, is also systole—its exodus is what allows our return."[19]

As this passage suggests, entering into this exchange—speaking about the voice that comes out to meet us—is itself a way of attending to, hearing, and understanding what has been said. The experience of art and beauty is a response to a call. And if God the Father gives his Spirit-Breath by way of his incarnate Word-Son that we might return it, enriched with our own voices, then engaging in this dialogue is one way of fulfilling our human vocation.

[19]Jean-Louis Chrétien, *The Call and the Response*, tr. Anne A. Davenport (New York: Fordham University Press, 2004), 1, 9.

Pneuma: The Enveloping Atmosphere of God

The biblical language of Spirit does not only speak of movement; it also speaks of the Spirit as the one who "comes to rest upon." We should not, in other words, imagine the *Pneuma* as (only) a stiff wind that surges past us, scattering all the lawn furniture before rushing on. Rather, Jesus tells his disciples, "I will not leave you orphaned," but "I will ask the Father, and he will give you another Advocate, *to be with you forever. . . . He abides with you, and he will be in you*" (Jn 14:16-18 NRSV). Here, alongside dynamism and movement, is being-with, abiding. The Spirit *comes* to us in order to *dwell* with us.[20]

What should we make of the apparent tension between the Holy Spirit as rushing wind and as resting, abiding presence? To some extent this tension is simply an acknowledgment that the Spirit of God will not remain within neatly drawn categories. The words of another contemporary praise chorus, however, may help us locate the "Spirit who rests upon" within the imagery of Breath and Wind:

> Holy Spirit, You are welcome here.
>
> Come flood this place and fill the atmosphere
>
> Your Glory, God, is what our hearts long for
>
> To be overcome by Your Presence, Lord[21]

The word *atmosphere* in this invitation to the Spirit is helpful, although it might be more appropriate to say that the Spirit not only *fills* but *is* the atmosphere we are invited to inhabit. Basil of Caesarea wonders at this mystery in a beautiful passage: "Although paradoxical, it is nevertheless true that Scripture frequently speaks of the Spirit in terms of *place*—a place *in* which people are made holy. . . . The Spirit is indeed the dwelling-place of the saints, and the saint is a suitable abode for the Spirit, since he or she has supplied God with a house, and is called a

---

[20]Eugene Rogers suggests that the word *rest* is especially apt in describing the activity of the Holy Spirit. Rogers, *After the Spirit: A Constructive Pneumatology from Resources Outside the Modern West* (Grand Rapids, MI: Eerdmans, 2005), 61.

[21]"Holy Spirit," by Katie Torwalt and Bryan Torwalt, 2011.

temple of God."[22] By the Spirit, Basil says, not only do we become God's dwelling but God becomes ours, the place in which we are made holy.

God sends forth his Breath, and what does this Breath carry? Word, life, wisdom, the gifts of the Spirit—yes. But the gifts of the Holy Spirit, writes Didymus, "are nothing other than the substance of the Holy Spirit. . . . [They] come to human beings from the Holy Spirit. . . . He is the substance of the goods of God."[23] Athanasius puts it forcefully: "When the Holy Spirit is given to us . . . God is in us."[24] The Spirit is not only the bearer of the gifts of God. The Holy Spirit is also the presence of God with us and in us. Likewise, God has made us those who not only receive but, having received, necessarily send forth our breath. What is borne by this breath? Words, images, stories, ideas—yes. But likewise, by our breath, we may become present to one another. We create an atmosphere in which others may dwell. Human art and creativity are a particularly rich example of this mode of shared dwelling.

In his study of African American sacred quartets, Ray Allen ties this language of sharing and exchange to both musical performance and the presence of the Holy Spirit. Allen quotes Earl Ledbetter of the Wearyland Gospel Singers: "See, the lead singer always gets the Spirit first, because he's the one leading the song. The background is just following him. But once we get into it, the background starts feeling good too. Once we start pushing him, he can really get out there and shout, do whatever he wants, he feels even better. We would push the feeling back up to him."[25] The Holy Spirit and the musical energy inspired by the Spirit are passed back and forth between lead and background singers. The singers not only sing but make it possible for others to enter into the song. The congregation, in entering into the song, expands the space, making it possible for the singers to enter in more fully. The Reverend Vernella Kelly explains:

---

[22]Basil the Great, *On the Holy Spirit*, tr. David Anderson (Crestwood, NY: St. Vladimir's Seminary Press, 2001), 62.

[23]Didymus the Blind, *On the Holy Spirit*, in *Works on the Holy Spirit: Athanasius the Great and Didymus the Blind*, tr. Andrew Radde-Gallwitz and Lewis Ayers (Yonkers, NY: St. Vladimir's Seminary Press, 2022), 157.

[24]Athanasius, *Letter to Serapion* 1.17.

[25]Ray Allen, *Singing in the Spirit: African-American Sacred Quartets in New York City* (Philadelphia: University of Pennsylvania Press, 1991), 167.

> If the congregation is pushing you and enjoying you, then that makes you enjoy more too. But if you are singing to a dead place, it looks like the Spirit doesn't come in and dwell in no dead place. . . . Any time you get support [from the congregation] it . . . . makes the Spirit come in, when they're with you. . . . Then everybody is enjoying, when the Spirit is there.[26]

Music, in this instance, is one particularly powerful way in which the character of the Holy Spirit's own life-as-shared-life is made actual in the world. It is one of the ways in which the Spirit, who gives life, reproduces in the creation the distinctive shape of that life: life as life together, life with, life as communion. There is a sense, then, in which a Christian pneumatology helps us to better account for the human experience of art and what we find meaningful about it. Artistic creation is one of the means by which human beings make themselves present to one another. So, we might say that when we dwell with one another in this way—when we extend ourselves through art or when we respond to the artist's invitation and enter into the atmosphere of the work—we are echoing something of the life of the Spirit. We are allowing breath to become shared dwelling.

The Fecundity of the Poetic Image

We have considered a few dimensions of the Spirit's work and person, all of which have been opened out and illuminated by a single image: *rûaḥ, pneuma*. The richness of the name, and the further names to which it has given rise, is its own sort of validation of the kind of dialogue undertaken in this volume. It seems significant that biblical and theological discussions of the Spirit center on *names* and *images*. In considering the Spirit, we are inevitably in the realm of the first-personal and in the region of encounter. In observing a phenomenon, we may employ concepts; but in the moment of meeting, we say a name. Likewise, the church's reflection on the Holy Spirit moves inevitably toward imagery: breath, wind, stream, fire, oil, water, and spring. Pneumatology seems to situate us, as a matter of course, in the domain of the artist

[26]Allen, *Singing in the Spirit*, 168.

and the poet. The reflection we have undertaken to this point testifies to the fecundity of attending to the image in all its named particularity. Further understanding emerges not from considering spirit as a pale noumenal abstraction but as we give sustained attention to *this* name and *this* image.

What is more, this poetic and imaginative dimension of Spirit language is not at odds with but rather is the source of further theological reflection. This is so in Ezekiel's vision of the dry bones, in Jesus' evening discourse with Nicodemus, and in the theological writings of Athanasius, John of Damascus, Aquinas, and contemporary writers. Each takes the imagery of *rûaḥ-pneuma* not merely in a decorative or illustrative manner. Instead, they derive further insight from regarding this multifaceted image from various vantage points.

"The distinctive activity of art," Rowan Williams writes, "is a departure from what is delivered by the individual sensorium: the artist projects a sensorium that has not yet been said or seen or encountered and which is not determined by what has been said, seen or encountered." This, Williams acknowledges, is what happens in every communicative act. We speak or gesture and in so doing offer a novel sensorium that must be received and interpreted by our hearer. The hearer re-creates in perception what was created in production. But the artist

> intensifies this routine process by proposing to the listener or viewer a common object that represents neither the raw givenness of the artist's individual world . . . nor the habitual shared construct of ordinary communication. We could say that the artist, by inviting some sort of recognition for what is produced in the artwork, pushes for the extension of the accepted boundaries of the common world.[27]

In this volume, artistic activity—itself an act of responsiveness—generates a further act of response in the doing of theology "through the arts." This is intended as "an extension of the boundaries" of the sort Williams describes. In some ways, this is simply another way of articulating the first

[27]Rowan Williams, *Understanding and Misunderstanding "Negative Theology"* (Milwaukee, WI: Marquette University Press, 2021), 29-30.

activity we mentioned in connection with the Spirit: the giving of life. Life *expands* and *extends*.[28] (As I write this, I think of a friend expecting her first child. Each time I see her, it is evident that the life in her has brought about greater expansion.)

There is another sort of life-giving expansion in pneumatology. Names beget names. We delight to repeat the name of our beloved, so much so that we extend that delight into additional titles, nicknames, and terms of endearment. So, in the fullness of time, Gretl has gained the further appellations: "Sweet Kitty," "Baby Girl," "Loaf," "Chonk," "Chonk-Loaf," and "Queen." Over centuries of theological reflection, the Holy Spirit has likewise accumulated additional names, mostly drawn from Holy Scripture and never drifting afar from their theological rootage in Holy Scripture. In fact, it is a commonplace in many premodern studies of the Spirit to enumerate these titles.[29]

I have said that the Spirit is both Breath and Wind, both mysterious and the giver of knowledge, both dynamic movement and abiding presence, both the one who dwells in us and the one in whom we dwell. Here, then, is one final paradox: the Spirit who is ineffable has also inspired myriad titles. The one who (at least according to some theologians) may not have a proper name is also the bearer of many names.

---

[28]Words and images matter here. There is a mode of academic theologizing that attempts not to *extend* boundaries but to *transcend* them, that aims to be not so much *expansive* as *transgressive*. The distinction is of the greatest importance. There is all the difference in the world between cherishing and extending the life one has received, on the one hand, and attempting to unmake and overturn it, on the other. In the essay quoted above, Rowan Williams continues, "The artist whose goal is purely disruptive, who is not at some level inviting recognition, cannot be recognizably an artist; they will be reducing rather than expanding the shared world because they are not producing what can be seen . . . as a shared object, a common datum for sensing and thinking" *(Understanding and Misunderstanding, 30-31)*.

[29]Calvin offers one such list:

> He is called the *"spirit of adoption"* because he is the witness to us of the free benevolence of God with which God the Father has embraced us. . . . He is called *"the guarantee and seal"* of our inheritance because from heaven he so gives life to us . . . as to assure us that our salvation is safe in God's unfailing care. He is also called *"life"* because of righteousness. By his secret watering the Spirit makes us fruitful. . . . Accordingly he is frequently called *"water."* . . . From the fact that he restores and nourishes unto vigor of life . . . he gets the names *"oil"* and *"anointing."* . . . He enflames our hearts with the love of God [and so] . . . he is justly called *"fire."* . . . He is described as the *"spring"* whence all heavenly riches flow forth to us; or as the *"hand of God"* by which he exercises his might (Calvin, *Institutes of the Christian Religion* III.1.3, tr. Ford Lewis Battles [Philadelphia: Westminster Press, 1960], 540-41. Emphasis added.)

The essays in this volume explore these names and images. They are, in fact, an invitation to dwell on the name of the one who dwells with us. "Do not leave Jerusalem," Jesus admonishes the disciples before his ascension, "but *wait* for the gift my Father promised" (Acts 1:4). In a similar way, our reflection on the verbal imagery of *Spirit* urges us to wait not only on the person of the Spirit but with *this* name and *the* image, listening and gazing attentively, that we might receive the gifts God has for us. In that sense, by engaging the arts we adopt the native tongue of pneumatology. As we inhabit the language of song and poetry and image, we take up the posture appropriate to those speaking of the Spirit: watching and listening in an attitude of attentiveness and awe, delight and love.

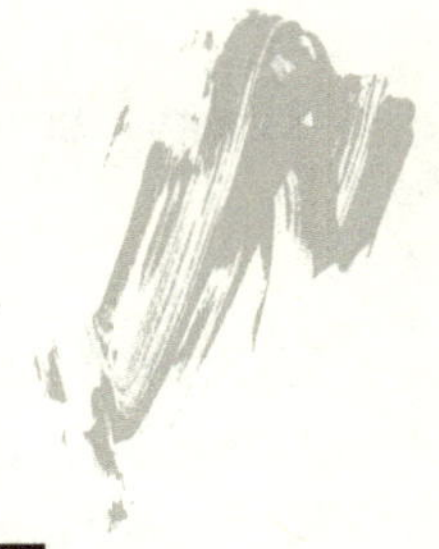

2

THE OUTPOURING SPIRIT

A VISUAL THEOLOGY OF PENTECOST

Jonathan A. Anderson

When visual artworks directly reference biblical texts—as images of Pentecost, for example, engage Acts 2—this does not mean they offer *visualizations* of those texts, in the sense of translating sentences of Scripture into visual form or depicting what this or that narrated event might have looked like. Nor do such images simply condense texts into a symbolic shorthand, providing devotional devices or visual backdrops for liturgical treatments of those texts. Rather, as Paolo Berdini argues, images that have direct scriptural referents are performing *readings* of those texts within a visual grammar, in a manner that "constitutes a form of exegesis, a visual exegesis."[1] Such visual exegesis does not (re)present the text itself but generates new sensitivities to the text made possible by forms of thinking that are integral to image making.[2]

In this way, the dense and diverse histories of Christian art are—and can more rigorously be regarded as—domains of constructive theological reasoning and biblical commentary, which operate specifically in and *as* forms of visual-spatial reasoning. Indeed, this kind of reasoning is one of the vital ways the church has done its thinking through the centuries (for better and worse). The study of the history of Christian art, therefore, must at one level be undertaken as a form of historical theology, retrieving

[1]Paolo Berdini, *The Religious Art of Jacopo Bassano: Painting as Visual Exegesis* (Cambridge: Cambridge University Press, 1997), 7.

[2]Berdini, *Religious Art of Jacopo Bassano*, 14.

some of the church's deep historical intelligence, resources, genealogies, and means by which faith seeks understanding, specifically as it pertains to a key (namely, visual) form of human intelligence. Like all forms of historical theology, such study can be both highly constructive and highly critical, with the potential to refine or reorganize what one sees as theologically meaningful and how one sees those meanings holding together, not only in the text but in one's own present.

Such retrievals and reorganizations are particularly warranted regarding images of the Holy Spirit, which have been prone to exegetical and theological reduction. Sarah Coakley whimsically refers to finding the Holy Spirit in Christian art as a matter of training one's eyes to "Hunt the pigeon!"—referring to the commonplace equation of the Spirit with a dove that is "often small, shadowy, and hard to see."[3] Her phrase is meant to highlight how diminished pneumatology tends to be in the Western visual-theological imagination (her point is well taken), but it also highlights how underinterpreted this visual-theological tradition generally is. Indeed, these are interconnected problems. While art historians have tended to be insufficiently attuned to the theological intelligence of the images they study, modern theologians have tended to be insufficiently attuned to the visual intelligence of their own traditions—mutually reinforcing tendencies that have obscured the range and depth of pneumatological reasoning within the history of Christian visual art.

This chapter seeks to retrieve and reconsider this reasoning by focusing on images of Pentecost, approached in three main movements. First, before looking at the images themselves, this chapter considers the visualities and spatialities of the Spirit's outpouring in Acts 2, the primary text to which all Pentecost imagery is tethered. Attending to the rich but enigmatic spatial frameworks in the text fosters thicker understandings of how later traditions of Christian image making constructively interpret and adapt these frameworks. Second, our inquiry turns to an illuminated page in the sixth-century Syriac *Rabbula Gospels*, attending to how its

[3]Sarah Coakley, *God, Sexuality, and the Self: An Essay "On the Trinity"* (Cambridge: Cambridge University Press, 2013), 212.

image of Pentecost engages the biblical text in exegetically and theologically significant ways. This image is important not only because of its relatively early date but because it exemplifies a compositional structure that became fundamental to subsequent traditions. Third, this case study then opens into a brief but wider consideration of Pentecost images from other times and places, highlighting significant variations within and across Christian visual traditions. These variations show how these broader traditions have extensive critical and constructive potential for a visual theology of Pentecost.

Spatialities of the Spirit

When the church speaks about the activity of the Holy Spirit in the world—in its Scriptures, doctrines, preaching, and prayers—its language is exceedingly and unavoidably spatial, even if ambiguously and allusively so. In the visual-theological traditions of Christian art, the Spirit is portrayed primarily as *descending* on persons—not only in Pentecost imagery but also across a range of subjects, from the annunciation to the eschatological new Jerusalem.

This language of the Holy Spirit's "descent" is biblical, but it is not the only language used to describe these events or their theological importance. When Peter addresses the crowds in Acts 2 to explain what is happening at the Pentecost event, he quotes Joel 2:28-29, in which God promises, "I will pour out [from] my Spirit on all people" (Acts 2:17-18).[4] The word Peter uses for "I will pour out" (ἐκχεῶ) may suggest a downward gravitational flow, but the root verb also can be translated—as can Joel's original Hebrew word (אֶשְׁפּוֹךְ)—as "pour forth," "gush," "spill," or "shed."[5] The stress of this root verb is less on downwardness than on outwardness, as when wine bursts from its container and "will be spilled out" (ἐκχυθήσεται, Lk 5:37), when blood is "shed" from a murdered body

[4]The Greek in Acts 2:17-18 literally means, "I will pour out *from* [ἀπὸ] my Spirit upon all flesh." See Gert J. Steyn, "εκχεώ άπο του πνεύματος: What Is Being Poured Out?," *Neotestamentica* 33, no. 2 (1999): 365-71.

[5]See Steyn, "What Is Being Poured Out?," esp. 367. In the Septuagint, Joel's Hebrew אֶשְׁפּוֹךְ is translated into Greek as ἐκχεῶ, which is Peter's word in Acts 2:17-18. For a similar translation, see Zech 12:10.

(ἐξεχύννετο, Acts 22:20; cf. ἐκχυννόμενον, Lk 22:20), when the entrails of a disemboweled body have "gushed out" (ἐξεχύθη, Acts 1:18), or even when people's desires have "rushed" toward vicious aims (ἐξεχύθησαν, Jude 1:11). Elsewhere in the New Testament, variations of this verb describe how the Spirit "has been poured out" (ἐκκέχυται) *upon* (ἐπὶ) Gentiles (Acts 10:45), how the love of God "has been poured out" (ἐκκέχυται) *in* (ἐν) believers' hearts through the Spirit (Rom 5:5), or how God richly "poured out" (ἐξέχεεν) the regenerating Spirit *on* (ἐφ') the church *through* (διὰ) Christ (Titus 3:6). In each instance, when placed in wider lexical contexts, this verb suggests a fluid-like displacement, not only in vertical downpour but gushing with lateral directionalities.

Elsewhere in Acts, the activity of the Spirit is described with other spatial markers, including instances in which the Spirit "fell upon" (ἐπέπεσεν ἐπὶ) people (Acts 10:44; 11:15; cf. ἐπιπεπτωκός, Acts 8:16). Here too, however, the spatiality of this term is not necessarily downward but can connote a pressing around (Mk 3:10) or an embracing of another person (Lk 15:20; Acts 20:37). More ambiguously, the Spirit is said to "come upon" (ἐπελεύσεται ἐπὶ) people in a way that is highly spatial but without clear directionality (Lk 1:35; cf. Acts 1:8; 19:6; Jn 16:7). At the end of Luke's Gospel, the giving of the Spirit is said to involve being "clothed with power from on high" (ἐνδύσησθε ἐξ ὕψους δύναμιν, Lk 24:49), whereas elsewhere people are "filled" (ἐπλήσθησαν) with the Spirit (Acts 2:4; 4:31; cf. πληροῦσθε, Eph 5:18) or simply "receive" (λήμψεσθε) the Spirit (Acts 1:8; cf. ἐλάμβανον, Acts 8:17; ἐλάβετε, Gal 3:2). Further still, Paul's imagery of the fruit of the Spirit suggests a spatiality having less to do with downwardness than slow organic growth outward and upward (Gal 5:22-23; cf. Eph 5:8-10; Jn 15:16).

All such language is visually charged, even if in underdetermined and ambiguous ways, and it thereby involves conceptualizing (the activity of) the Holy Spirit within some kind of (often implicit) spatial logic. When such spatializations become overly concrete or overly totalizing—that is, when the Spirit is imagined as a spatially constrained *something*—pernicious theological troubles emerge. But if recognized in their irreducible plurality (e.g., speaking about being clothed with the Spirit assumes a different spatiality from speaking about being filled with the Spirit, even if referring to similar phenomena), then these spatializations, and even some of the troubles they cause, can be highly productive, both theologically and exegetically.

While biblical texts speak of the Holy Spirit in visual-spatial terms, images based on these texts do something *visual* and *spatial* with these terms. Precisely in their visuality, such images extend the reading and reasoning about biblical texts in at least three ways: (1) By highlighting and rendering particular visual-spatial details in a (necessarily) selective way, they foster heightened sensitivity to the visualities of the texts themselves, sending us back into those texts for closer rereading. (2) By incorporating multiple biblical imageries or allusions into single images, they forge complex intertextual readings across the biblical canon. And (3) by organizing all these visual relations into an overall spatial structure, they initiate a critical testing and constructive reworking of the visual-spatial models that implicitly shape readers' theological and exegetical understandings, often by defamiliarizing unexamined assumptions and putting them under pressure. Theology is full of visualities and spatialities—ways of imagining the world and all manner of *relatedness* within it—and that means the arts (not only visual but musical, kinesthetic, poetic, and so on) provide vital means for sorting out, both critically and constructively, the ways Christian communities tacitly conceptualize their *relations* to God, their neighbors, themselves, their environments, and so on.

If we narrow our concentration to images of Pentecost, we find these three aspects of visual reasoning operating across multiple Christian visual traditions, generating exegetically subtle and theologically rich meditations on what it means for the Spirit to be poured out on the church. To see how this works, we now turn to an illuminated page from a sixth-century Syriac Gospel book, and then we expand outward from there, showing how such images are producing and processing visual theologies of Pentecost.

The Rabbula Pentecost

The *Rabbula Gospels* is a translation of the Gospels of Matthew, Mark, Luke, and John into Syriac, completed and signed in AD 586 by a scribe named Rabbula.[6] At some point (possibly as late as the 1460s), this manuscript was rebound with a set of fourteen illuminated folios at the beginning of the book, each with images on both sides, comprising twenty-eight illuminated pages. It is unclear which—if any—of these were in the original manuscript, but it is unlikely that all of them were, as they show signs of different artistic conventions and page formats cropped to fit the Rabbula corpus.[7] Most of these fourteen folios (2b-12b) feature Eusebian canon tables with small figurative illuminations, similar to other sixth-century Syriac manuscripts.[8] Before and after these, however, there are seven full-page images, including depictions of New Testament events—the selection of Matthias to replace Judas (1a), the crucifixion and resurrection of Christ (13a), and the ascension (13b)—as well as devotional images: the mother and child (1b), Ammonius of Alexandria and Eusebius of Caesarea (2a), and Christ in paradise surrounded by four monks (possibly Ammonius and Eusebius presenting two younger monks; 14a). The last of these illuminated pages, folio 14b, features the

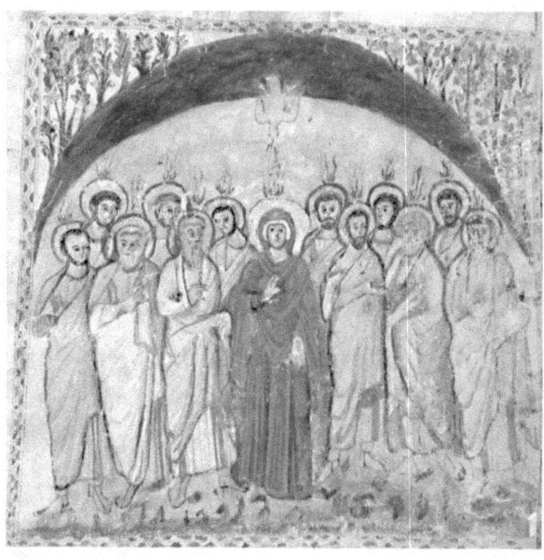

Figure 2.1. Syriac, *Pentecost*, ca. sixth century, folio 14b of Rabbula Gospels (Manuscript Plut. 1.56), 586. Biblioteca Medicea Laurenziana, Florence, Italy. Courtesy of MiC. Any further reproduction by any means is prohibited

[6]For digital images, see "Evangelia characteribus Syriacis exarata," Digitale Biblioteca Medicea Laurenziana, http://teca.bmlonline.it/ImageViewer/servlet/ImageViewer?idr=TECA0000025956&keyworks=Plut.01.56#page/1/mode/1up.

[7]See Massimo Bernabò, "The Miniatures in the Rabbula Gospels: Postscript to a Recent Book," *Dumbarton Oaks Papers* 68 (2014): 343-58; Bernabò, ed., *Il Tetravangelo di Rabbula. Firenze, Biblioteca Medicea Laurenziana, plut. 1.56: L'illustrazione del Nuovo Testamento nella Siria del VI secolo* (Rome: Edizioni di Storia e Letteratura, 2008).

[8]See Manuscript Syriac 33 (Bibliothèque nationale de France, Paris), https://gallica.bnf.fr/ark:/12148/btv1b52506821q.

outpouring of the Spirit at Pentecost (fig. 2.1). The form and format of this painted image is consistent with sixth-century Syriac illumination, but its cropping and subject matter indicate that it comes from another manuscript. (That it depicts an event narrated in Acts, rather than the Gospels, suggests it came from a New Testament manuscript or lectionary.)

Taking Pentecost as its subject, this image draws attention to several details in the biblical description of the Spirit's outpouring, but it also supplements and improvises on them, providing a synthetic theological commentary on the text more than a visualization of it. Acts, for example, specifies that the disciples were "sitting" together as fiery dividing tongues "sat" on each of them (Acts 2:2-3), yet the artist stands them upright and arranges them to face the viewer in two rows, neatly staggered like a wedding party in a photograph. This distills the literary dynamics of the text into an iconic structure, thereby suspending expectations that the image simply visualizes what the event might have looked like. Rather, the Rabbula Pentecost is a visual-theological interpretation of what the church *is* in light of the Spirit's activity in the Pentecost event.

Indeed, this image makes several striking exegetical and theological moves, precisely in how it reasons about the text in visual-spatial terms. These moves come more sharply into focus as we ask three heuristic questions about the spatial logic within which the Spirit is here poured out.

1. In what form is the Spirit poured out? The textual imagery in Acts 2:1-4 features the sudden eruption of a sound like violently rushing wind that "filled" (ἐπλήρωσεν) the house where the disciples "were sitting" (καθήμενοι) together. This sound was then accompanied by a visual appearance described as "dividing tongues as of fire" (διαμεριζόμεναι γλῶσσαι ὡσεὶ πυρός) that "sat" (ἐκάθισεν) on each person. At once, the disciples "were filled" (ἐπλήσθησαν) with the Holy Spirit and began to speak in "other tongues" (ἑτέραις γλώσσαις) as the Spirit enabled them. These recurring phrases generate an evocative interlacing of imageries—the Spirit filled the room and filled the disciples, who were seated and on whom were seated fiery phenomena, which took the form of dividing tongues and coincided with proliferating speech in many tongues. This verbal patterning is highly visual but in a way that resists visualization, and thus images "of" this text are forced to make hermeneutical decisions.

The most obvious correspondence between text and image is the association of fire with the presence of the Spirit. The Rabbula artist visually interprets the ambiguous language of "dividing tongues as of fire" by depicting a cluster of stringy red flames burning at the uppermost edge of each disciple's halo. Within the formal symmetry of the group, this creates the impression of a single multiarmed lampstand.

The artist's medium lacks the capacity to represent the tremendous *sound* of the Pentecost event. Interestingly, however, the artist shows no desire to compensate for this (as became common in later artistic convention) by converting this sound into the visual effects of an actual wind, depicted in billowing drapery, blowing hair, or angled flames. Indeed, the air in the Rabbula scene is strikingly still, with the disciples' clothing hanging directly downward and the flames burning directly upward. The movement in the image's otherwise symmetrical structure is instead concentrated in the disciples' dialogue with each other, gesticulating to each other in traditional forms of blessing. The "sound" of the image has more to do with polyphonic apostolic speech (see Acts 2:6) than with a violent rushing from heaven.

Upon further consideration, perhaps the sound that erupts "suddenly out of the heaven/sky" (Acts 2:2) is represented here after all. Rather than converting the sound into visualizable wind, the artist has rendered it in the visual form of a descending dove. In the history of Christian art (mostly unfolding in the centuries after this image), dove imagery became so pervasively associated with the Holy Spirit—not only in Pentecost but also in the annunciation, the trinitarian mercy seat, ecstatic visions of saints, and so on—that it is often simply regarded as a generic symbol for the Holy Spirit. This is regrettable insofar as it hermeneutically collapses the dense exegetical significance of such imagery. Indeed, careful viewers must not take this imagery for granted. Why is there a *dove* in this image at all?

Scripturally, the association of the Holy Spirit with a dove is principally and *specifically* anchored to the baptism of Jesus, where the Spirit descends on Jesus "in a bodily form like [or as] a dove" (σωματικῷ εἴδει ὡς περιστερὰν, Lk 3:22; cf. Mt 3:16; Mk 1:10; Jn 1:32). Like the Pentecost event, this visual appearance is accompanied by sound from above: "And a voice came from heaven [ἐξ οὐρανοῦ], 'You are my Son, the Beloved; in you I am well pleased.'" When artists depict the Spirit descending on the church *at Pentecost* in the form of a *dove*, this is not a generic symbol. It must be taken more exegetically and theologically seriously as an intertextual (or intervisual) reading of the text(s)—one that draws a highly charged link between the Spirit's anointing of Christ at his baptism and the Spirit's anointing of the church to be the body of Christ in the world.

But this link is quite subtle. The intertextual significance of this dove imagery is not merely denotative, identifying the same Spirit at work in both Pentecost and Christ's baptism. In a thicker way, putting a dove in Pentecost imagery prompts us to ask what dove imagery is doing in the baptism passages in the first place.[9] Biblical commentators have offered many possible interpretations, but when carried into the Pentecost, two have especially evocative connotations. First, in the context of the Hebrew Scriptures, many scholars see the Spirit descending like a dove as subtly alluding to the Spirit "hovering" over the face of the waters in Genesis 1:2 (see also Gen 8:10-12). In this view, placing the baptismal dove in an image of Pentecost marks the apostolic church as a site of new creation.

Second, Michael Peppard shows that, when read in the context of Roman imperial rule, the Spirit descending "like a dove" appears in direct imagistic juxtaposition to or "colonial mimicry" of the imperial Roman eagle.[10] Insofar as "the bellicose eagle was the primary symbol of Roman military might and concomitantly of the Roman imperial ideology," the dove was often held up as "a contrasting symbol of nonviolence or fear."

[9]See Leander E. Keck, "The Spirit and the Dove," *New Testament Studies* 17, no. 1 (1970): 41-67; Stephen Gero, "The Spirit as a Dove at the Baptism of Jesus," *Novum Testamentum* 18, no. 1 (1976): 17-35; Alexey Somov, "The Dove in the Story of Jesus' Baptism: Early Christian Interpretation of a Jewish Image," *The Bible Translator* 69, no. 2 (2018): 240-51.

[10]Michael Peppard, *The Son of God in the Roman World: Divine Sonship in Its Social and Political Context* (Oxford: Oxford University Press, 2011), 86-131; see also Peppard, "The Eagle and the Dove: Roman Imperial Sonship and the Baptism of Jesus (Mark 1.9-11)," *New Testament Studies* 56, no. 4 (2010): 431-51. I do not follow Peppard in seeing Christ's baptism as divine adoption, but his analysis of the text within a Roman cultural context is highly insightful.

In this context, the Gospels seem to present the baptism of Jesus as the anointing of "a counter-emperor," who "will rule not in the spirit of the bellicose eagle, but in the spirit of the pure, gentle, peaceful, and even sacrificial dove."[11] The Son of God is anointed by the Holy Spirit to reign in peace rather than violence. When artists intertextually transpose this imagery into the Pentecost event, the (true) church is implicitly but powerfully identified as a counterempire anointed by the same Holy Spirit to live in peace rather than violence.

2. To where and onto whom is the Spirit poured out? The biblical text would seem to place about 120 of Jesus' disciples (both men and women) at this Pentecost gathering (Acts 1:15), but the Rabbula image gives us only the Twelve, with Mary at their center. The formal, frontal positioning of the apostles transforms the narrative details of Acts 2 into an iconic image of the early church. But it also creates a dialogical exchange through the picture plane, turning the first-century disciples squarely to face and address the present reader(s), implying mutual acknowledgment between the apostolic church on *that* side of the parchment's picture plane and the contemporary church (whoever, wherever, and whenever they might be) on *this* side.

Mary is especially emphasized in this image, standing at the center of the composition, immediately below the outpouring of the dove. She is also visually distinguished from the rest of the group, wearing plum-colored (royal) garments and red shoes (in contrast to the apostles' pastels and sandals) with a golden halo circumscribed in red (in contrast to the apostles' transparent or flesh-toned halos trimmed in blue). A zone of red paint fills the narrow spaces between her and the other apostles, as though the spiritual fire burning above each head also burns at the Marian center of the church.[12] In these ways, Mary is presented as an archetypal embodiment of an apostolic church that has the incarnation at its heart. This, too, has an intertextual rationale, linking the overshadowing of the church

---

[11]Peppard, *Son of God*, 119, 123.

[12]See Cornelia Horn, "Ancient Syriac Sources on Mary's Role as Intercessor," in *Presbeia Theothokou: The Intercessory Role of Mary Across Times and Places in Byzantium (4th–9th Century)*, ed. Leena Mari Peltomaa, Andreas Külzer, and Pauline Allen (Vienna: Verlag der Österreichischen Akademie der Wissenschaften, 2015), 153-76.

in Acts 2 to the overshadowing of Mary in Luke 1:26-38. As she said *yes* to the overshadowing of the Holy Spirit and Christ was born into the world, so too the church must continually say *yes* to the overshadowing of the Holy Spirit and thereby *be* the body of Christ in the world.[13] As Hans Urs von Balthasar argues, the giving of the Spirit to the church means that the image of Christ takes shape in them *collectively*.[14]

3. From where is the Spirit poured out? In the Rabbula Pentecost, the descending dove-like Spirit is depicted as crossing from a spatially ambiguous dark blue canopy above into an even more ambiguous space of thinly applied rosy colors that roughly correspond to the disciples' flesh tones. In one sense, this crossing visualizes the sound that "came suddenly out of heaven/sky." Like the Greek οὐρανοῦ, this blue canopy reads ambiguously as both sky and a heavenly more-than-sky, whereas the fleshy zone beneath it is another kind of atmosphere—one that we might equally read as a wall or even the lightly altered surface of the parchment itself. In this evocative visual structure, one kind of heavens is vaulted over another without any orienting horizon other than the arched seam between them. As such, these shapes become suggestive of the low barrel vaulting common in many early churches—a suggestion that might visually link the apostolic church at Pentecost to later, far-flung Christian communities (including sixth-century Syria) that eventually worshiped in such buildings. Or, put the other way around, this vaulting over the apostles identifies them as the church—or *temple*—that persists through time and across cultures (see 1 Cor 3:16-17; 2 Cor 6:16-18; Eph 2:19-22; 1 Pet 2:4-10).[15]

Interestingly, the deep blue canopy is arched not only on its underside but on its upper edge, forming triangular compositional zones beyond the blue. In many subsequent depictions of this scene (e.g., fig. 2.5), these

[13]See Thomas A. Smail, *The Giving Gift: The Holy Spirit in Person* (London: Hodder & Stoughton, 1988), 29.

[14]Hans Urs von Balthasar, *The Glory of the Lord: A Theological Aesthetics*, vol. 1, *Seeing the Form*, ed. Joseph Fessio and John Riches, trans. Erasmo Leiva-Merikakis (San Francisco: Ignatius, 1982), 30.

[15]See G. K. Beale, *The Temple and the Church's Mission: A Biblical Theology of the Dwelling Place of God* (Downers Grove, IL: InterVarsity Press, 2004), 201-44. Several images in the Rabbula manuscript are framed by arched or domed structures suggestive of temple space (see fig. 2.2).

zones beyond this upper vault are filled with depictions of the new (or heavenly) Jerusalem. Surprisingly, here these zones do not contain further celestial or heavenly imagery (a "third heaven," so to speak; 2 Cor 12:2-4) but an abundant field of purple wildflowers. These flowers are more than ornamentation. Within the image, they contrast with the stone-colored ground beneath the disciples' feet, which is loosely dashed with green paint. This contrast identifies the space above or beyond not as ethereal but as a verdant paradise.

On the other hand, these flowers have a more specific referent in relation to the other illuminated pages in the Rabbula codex. In fact, these same flowers appear on the reverse side of this page (14a), in which Christ is portrayed enthroned on a golden, bejeweled altar-throne in a lush green field, surrounded by four monks (fig. 2.2). Christ's figuration bears similarities to Mary on the obverse side of the page: he makes a similar blessing, is clothed in the same plum-colored garments, and is crowned with a golden, red-trimmed halo. Differently from Mary, however, he appears within a brilliantly blue, egg-shaped mandorla, and he holds in his left hand a gleaming white scroll. The top edge of the green field is lined with purple flowers that directly visually rhyme the flowers above and beyond the blue canopy in the Pentecost.

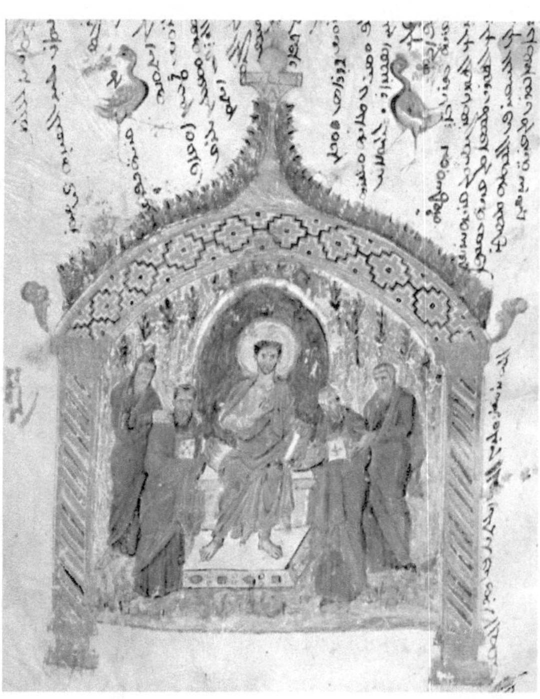

Figure 2.2. Syriac, *Christ Enthroned with Four Monks*, ca. sixth century, folio 14a of Rabbula Gospels (Manuscript Plut. 1.56), 586. Biblioteca Medicea Laurenziana, Florence, Italy. Courtesy of MiC. Any further reproduction by any means is prohibited

In this context, the "From where?" question of the Spirit in Pentecost is cast into provocatively new dimension. The deep blue canopy on 14b corresponds to the blue mandorla surrounding the enthroned Christ on 14a, and the flowered spacetime beyond the canopy corresponds to the paradisiacal—and/or eschatological—locus of Christ's enthronement. In this respect, the canopy itself is not simply the heavens in an ancient cosmological sense but the mandorla-centered place and time of Christ's glory. Indeed, this place from which the Spirit is poured out is Christ's throne, and this time is that in which "all authority in heaven and on earth" rests in him (Mt 28:18). To be sure, the corresponding flowers at the top of both images connote an earthly reality, a new creation, an eschatological reconciliation not merely of souls but of all things. This pairing of images thus seems to address the "From where?" question within a temporal aspect: the Spirit is poured out on the church at Pentecost not only from an ontologically prior elsewhere but from an eschatologically inflected *elsewhen*.

The implications of this are deepened when this dialogue between the front and back of folio 14 is extended to the immediate prior page, 13b, which features a full-page image of Christ's ascension (fig. 2.3).[16] These folios originally come from different sources, but ever since a later compiler brought them into immediate proximity, these ascension and Pentecost images (13b and 14b, respectively) speak to each other and hermeneutically modify the "From where?" question in highly generative ways. This becomes especially clear if one takes the same spatio-structural questions of how the Spirit is poured out (Acts 2:17) in the Pentecost image and reframes them to ask how Christ is taken up (Acts 1:9) in the ascension image: (1) *In what form* is Christ taken up? (2) *From where and from whom* is Christ taken up? (3) *To where* is Christ taken up? These questions can be pursued in detail and open into significant insights, but for our purposes (focused on a visual theology of Pentecost), it suffices to say that in the Rabbula ascension, the resurrected Jesus of Nazareth ascends *as* a man *from* his disciples *into* the throne of God (here

[16]Bernabò convincingly argues that folios 13 and 14 come from different manuscripts and were bound with the Rabbula Gospels sometime later (see "Miniatures in the Rabbula Gospels"). Thus, any intervisual dialogue between these folios is attributable not to artistic intention but to later compilers' activities (and perhaps to general visual-theological traditions).

unmistakably identified with Ezekiel's visions of God in Ezek 1:4-28; 10:1-22), from which the Spirit is poured out at Pentecost.[17]

Indeed, the Rabbula ascension strongly implies the outpouring of the Spirit at Pentecost, not only in its biblical logic (e.g., Jn 16:7; Lk 24:49-51) but in its visual structure, as it places Christ in the pictorial, compositional position from which he is the living head of the church and from which the Spirit is poured out as the anointing, enflaming presence of Christ in the church.[18] The open human hand emerging from below the four creatures might follow Ezekiel's descriptions of these creatures (Ezek 1:8; 10:8, 21) or allude to Ezekiel's preface, in which "the hand of the LORD came upon him" (Ezek 1:3 NASB). But in this particular placement between Christ and the church, it more directly anticipates the giving of the Spirit to Mary and the disciples, who (but for the

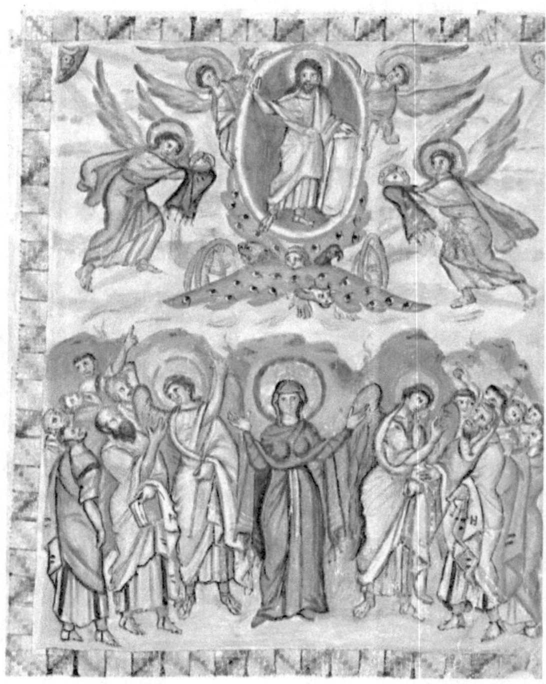

Figure 2.3. Syriac(?), *Ascension of Christ*, unknown date, folio 13b of Rabbula Gospels (MS Plut. 1.56), 586. Biblioteca Medicea Laurenziana, Florence, Italy. Courtesy of MiC. Any further reproduction by any means is prohibited

[17]In the Rabbula ascension, Christ is taken up not simply into the "sky" but into a deep blue oval that is unmistakably identified with Ezekiel's "visions of God" (Ezek 1:1), in which the prophet sees "something like a throne, in appearance like sapphire" (Ezek 1:26 NRSV; cf. Ezek 10:1), encircled with a radiant rainbow (Ezek 1:28; cf. Ex 24:10), above four mysterious "living creatures" with four eye-covered wings and faces of a man, lion, ox, and eagle, each accompanied by "a wheel within a wheel" (Ezek 1:4-25; 10:1-22; cf. Rev 4:2–6:8; 7:11; 14:3; 15:7; 19:4). In adapting this imagery, the Rabbula page interprets the ascension as Christ being taken into the throne of God, where he is "at the right hand of the power of God" (Lk 22:69; cf. Mt 26:64; Acts 7:56; Rom 8:34; Eph 1:20; Col 3:1; Heb 8:1; 12:2; 1 Pet 3:22).

[18]On the biblical pattern of descent and ascent, see Douglas Farrow, *Ascension and Ecclesia: On the Significance of the Doctrine of the Ascension for Ecclesiology and Christian Cosmology* (Grand Rapids, MI: Eerdmans, 1999).

angels in their midst) stand in the same compositional zone as in the Pentecost. In fact, precisely such a hand appears in many subsequent images of Pentecost (fig. 2.5), and the seven flames fanning outward below this hand are suggestive not only of the "fire flashing forth" in Ezekiel's vision (Ezek 1:4 NRSV) but of the fiery tongues of Pentecost manifesting the seven gifts of the Spirit (Is 11:2; see fig. 2.4).

Furthermore, the depiction of the apostles below these flames strongly implies the post-Pentecost church. The apostle Peter stands beside the angel on the right, while *Paul* accompanies the angel on the left, though the ascension occurred several years before his conversion (Acts 9). This is not an exegetical misstep by the artist but a visual-theological linking of Christ's ascension to the ongoing life of the transtemporal church in radical openness both to Jews (Peter) and to Gentiles (Paul), with the outpouring of the Spirit as that animating link.

Outpourings of the Spirit

The visual-theological reasoning of the Rabbula Pentecost (and its neighboring folios) is embedded in the broader, deeper, diverse histories of Christian art, in which this kind of reasoning moves across a range of approaches to the same topic. As one becomes sensitized to how the Rabbula imagery operates, both as a visual exegesis of Acts 2 and as a visual theology of Pentecost, this inquiry opens into (and already relies on) a wider visual-theological tradition surrounding this subject. Indeed, by briefly situating Rabbula in relation to significant variations within these traditions, we can draw out the extensive critical and constructive potential of this broader image tradition. Returning to our three orienting questions, a range of possibilities emerges.

1. In what form is the Spirit poured out? In some rare instances, Pentecost images depict the outpouring of the Spirit with not one but *seven* doves (fig. 2.4), which intertextually links the Pentecost event not only back to Christ's baptism but also, further back, to the messianic seven gifts of the Holy Spirit identified in Isaiah 11:1-3.[19] By contrast, many Pentecost

[19]The lettering above the seven doves in *Gospels of Henry the Lion* (fig. 2.4) follows the Latin translation of Is 11:2.

images do not include any dove at all and thus withhold any clear intertextual links to Christ's baptism. In the Russian icon tradition, for example, it is common for this outpouring to be depicted only by sharp, short beams of golden (or occasionally dark) light radiating from the top edge of the image, representing the uncreated "trinitarian energies" manifested in the giving of the Holy Spirit.[20] Alternatively, this outpouring is visually interpreted in thin streams of red (fire or lifeblood?), light blue (water or wind?), gold (luminous presence of God), or even green (verdant life), which either span generally over the apostles or connect to each individually (see figs. 2.4, 2.6).[21]

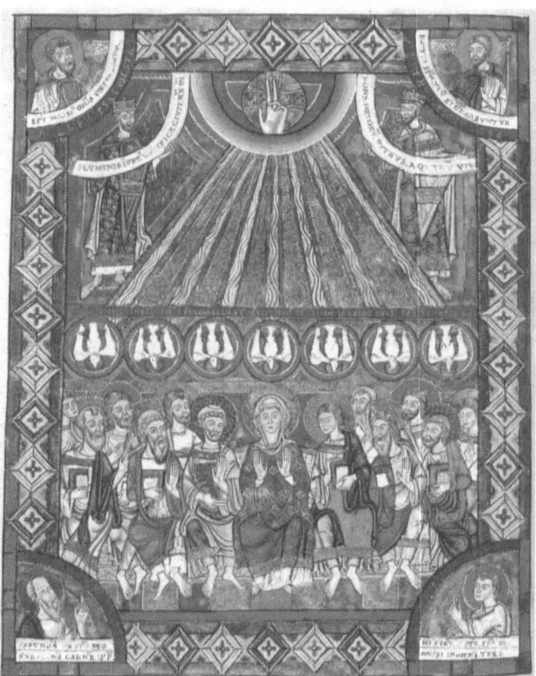

Figure 2.4. German, *Pentecost*, folio 112v of Gospels of Henry the Lion (Codex Guelf. 105 Noviss. 2), ca. 1173–1188. Herzog August Bibliothek, Wolfenbüttel, Germany

When artists render the "dividing tongues as of fire" as discrete flames, they variously identify them with the tops of the heads, the eyes, or the mouths of the disciples. The *Benedictional of Archbishop Robert* (fig. 2.5), for example, emphasizes the play of tongues in Acts 2 by depicting a blast of fire from the *mouth* of the descending dove that divides into fourteen flames touching the *mouths* of all twelve disciples (with two additional flames touching the foreheads of the

[20]See Paul Evdokimov, *The Art of the Icon: A Theology of Beauty*, trans. Steven Bigham (Redondo Beach, CA: Oakwood, 1990), 341. For Western works without dove imagery, see folio 115v of *Reichenau Sacramentary*, Manuscript Canonici Liturgical 319 (Bodleian Library, Oxford), ca. 1000–1025; folio 20v of Manuscript Ludwig V 2 (83.MF.77; Getty Center, Los Angeles), ca. 1025–1050.

[21]For red, see folio 87r of *Missal of Limoges*, Manuscript Latin 9438 (Bibliothèque nationale de France, Paris), twelfth century. For blue, see folio 143r of *Irmengard Codex*, Manuscript 125 (2023.6; Getty Center, Los Angeles), ca. 1053–1060.

centermost apostles: Peter and maybe Paul). In his *Pentecost* (1997), contemporary Thai artist Sawai Chinnawong instead emphasizes the tongues sitting on each of the seated disciples. He adapts visual language from Theravada Buddhism to depict the Spirit not as a dove but as a massive holy flame at the center of the church, which is visually rhymed in smaller versions of this flame above each disciple.[22] Indian artist P. Solomon Raj pushes this idea further in his *Pentecost* (1980), wherein dozens of yellow flames fill the space above the seated disciples as the entire room is immersed in red flame. Raj thereby forges a further intertextual link, depicting the church as a burning bush that is ablaze with the presence of the Spirit but not consumed (see Ex 3).

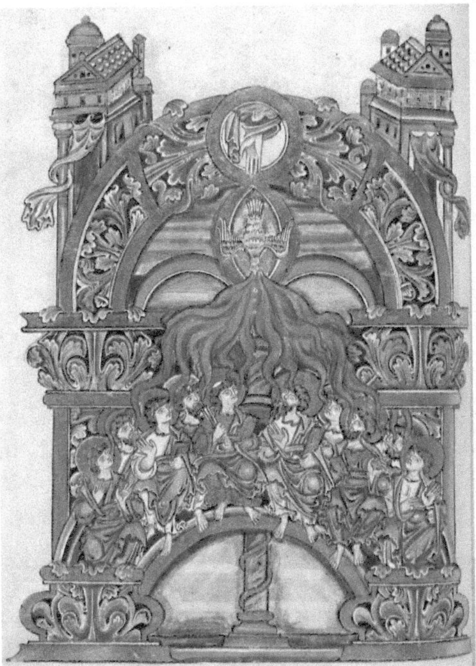

Figure 2.5. Attributed to Godeman (Anglo-Saxon), *Pentecost*, folio 29v of Benedictional of Archbishop Robert (or Winchester Pontifical; Manuscript 369 (Y-7)), ca. late tenth century. Bibliothèque Municipale, Rouen, France

2. To where and onto whom is the Spirit poured out? Whereas Mary is the central figural embodiment of the church in the Rabbula Pentecost (and ascension), she is altogether absent in many other Pentecost images, and thus the charged central vertical axis of the church gets structured in various other ways. Peter sometimes occupies this position, especially in the West in the centuries following the Great Schism in 1054.[23] In other instances, artists leave an open seam along this axis (fig. 2.5), marking a Spirit-enlivened dialogical space *between* the apostles in which they gesture toward each other in speech

[22]See Amos Yong and Jonathan A. Anderson, "Painting Pentecost: The Spirit-Filled Art of Sawai Chinnawong," *The Christian Century* 131, no. 11 (2014): 30-33.

[23]See folio 79v of *Lectionnaire de Cluny*, NAL 2246 (Bibliothèque nationale de France, Paris), ca. 1090–1110; folio 117v of *Stammheim Missal*, Manuscript 64 (97.MG.21; Getty Center, Los Angeles), ca. 1170s.

and affection, sometimes holding up a Gospel book (fig. 2.6) or a eucharistic chalice on this central axis.[24] It is not uncommon for Mark, Luke, and/or Paul to be included in such images, though none is among the Twelve in Acts 2—thereby theologically reading the Pentecost event as about the *church* more than a discrete occurrence. In several Eastern icon traditions, this central seam opens into a wide, dark semicircle at the bottom of the composition, where Cosmos—a kingly figure personifying all peoples of the earth who "sit in darkness and in the shadow of death" (Lk 1:79 NRSV)—is portrayed holding either the wisdom of the nations or the teachings of the apostles.[25] Whereas the Rabbula Pentecost conspicuously emphasizes a Marian/incarnational center in its depiction of the church, with the surface of the earth firmly beneath its feet, these other images develop various other ways of conceptualizing the transtemporal church in relation to the world.

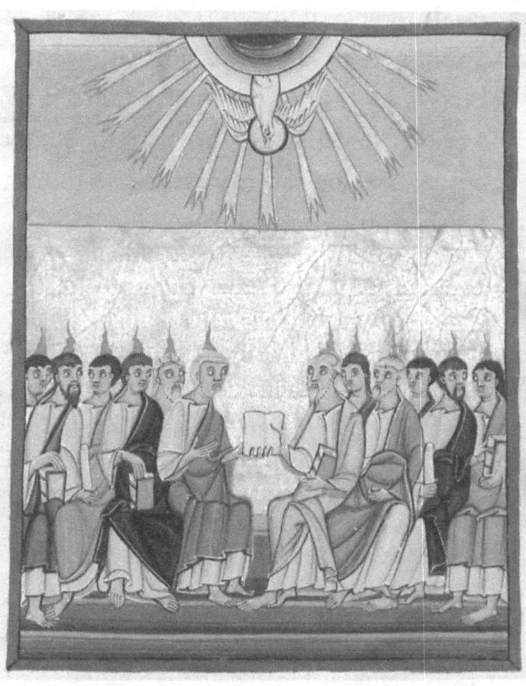

Figure 2.6. German, *Pentecost*, folio 73r of Bamberg Apocalypse (Msc. Bibl. 140), ca. 1010. Staatsbibliothek Bamberg, Bamberg, Germany

3. From where is the Spirit poured out? In the Rabbula Pentecost, this question is answered only implicitly in dialogue with surrounding pages. Subsequent image traditions sometimes follow this modest (even apophatic) approach (fig. 2.6), but often they

[24]To see an image with a space between the apostles, see folio 6r of Armenian Gospel Book by Youhannès de Berkri (Armenian Museum at Vank Cathedral, Isfahan), 1362. For an image with a Gospel book held up, see folio 14r of Armenian Gospel Book, Manuscript Ludwig II 6 (83. MB.70; Getty Center, Los Angeles), 1386. For an image with a eucharistic chalice held up, see Armenian manuscript by Zakaria Knunetsi, Manuscript 4831 (Matenadaran, Yerevan), 1575.

[25]Evdokimov, *Art of the Icon*, 335-44, esp. 341.

answer more explicitly.[26] In many instances, an open right hand emerges from the top of the composition, actively giving (usually the dove of) the Holy Spirit to the church (fig. 2.5). The visual context from which this hand emerges often combines both architectural and botanical allusions to new Jerusalem and/or new creation. In many images, the source of this giving is explicitly depicted as the risen, ascended Christ.[27] In many Eastern Orthodox images, this giving is more overtly cast into eschatological dimension by depicting the fountainhead of the Pentecost event as the prepared throne (see Mt 22:1-14; 24:36-51), representing the throne awaiting Christ's eschatological reconciliation of all things.[28] Insofar as Acts 2 leaves the question of "From where?" underdetermined, these various images go further than the Rabbula Pentecost in offering diverse visual-theological elaborations on the ontological and temporal structure of the Spirit's outpouring.

Conclusion

Christian speech about the Holy Spirit's activity in the world is highly spatial, and thus it (often implicitly and never fully intentionally) is embedded in and reliant on larger spatial conceptualizations that vary across cultural-historical situations. The creation of and critical engagement with visual-spatial images of Pentecost thus constitute a vital domain for understanding this language, both critically and constructively. In some respects, images become highly problematic on this count, insofar as their reception converts spatial language into overly concrete (and hermeneutically flattened) forms—whereby a descending dove, for example, simplistically symbolizes "Holy Spirit" with no deeper reflection on the sheer weirdness and exegetical audacity of such imagery. In other respects, it is precisely the underlying weirdness and audacity, and spatial plurality, of

[26]For this modest/apophatic approach, see folio 32v of Manuscript Français 916 (Bibliothèque nationale de France, Paris), 1474; Giotto's *Pentecost*, Scrovegni Chapel (Padua, Italy), 1304–1306.

[27]See folio 6v of Armenian Gospel Book, Manuscript 2744 (Matenadaran Museum, Yerevan), 1305.

[28]The prepared throne (known in Greek traditions as the ἑτοιμασία) appears in several Syriac lectionaries, including folio 158r of Manuscript SOP-348 (Syrian Orthodox Patriarchate, Damascus), ca. 1221. For a Byzantine example, see folio 301r of Manuscript Graeca 510 (Bibliothèque nationale de France, Paris), 879-83. For an Armenian example, see folio 379r of T'oros Roslin Gospel Book, Manuscript 539 (Walters Art Museum, Baltimore), 1262.

such images that proves to be both theologically generative and appropriately humble in relation to its subject—resisting, for example, a reduction of the church's language of ascent and descent to merely creaturely coordinates. Indeed, this chapter argues that the images discussed above are not concerned with visualizing the text or the events narrated in those texts. Rather, the kinds of visual reasoning at work in these images are capable of engendering (1) heightened sensitivity to the visuality of the biblical texts, (2) intertextual readings across the biblical canon, and (3) a critical testing and constructive reworking of the implicit visual-spatial understandings operating in readers' imaginations.

As such, this chapter offers multiple angles for rethinking what visual theology and visual exegesis might offer to pneumatology, which has tended to ignore the history of Christian art as a vital stream of historical theology. In turn, this inquiry thus also provides angles for rethinking what pneumatology (and visual theology generally) might offer to art history, which as a discipline has significantly underinterpreted the theological sources and implications of the images it studies. In that sense, this chapter seeks both to retrieve the history of art as a domain of constructive theological reasoning and thus also to retheologize art history.

3

THE ILLUMINATING SPIRIT

SEEING THE TRINITY IN BASIL OF CAESAREA AND OLAFUR ELIASSON'S *BEAUTY*

Christina Carnes Ananias

Olafur Eliasson's (b. 1967) *Beauty* confounds the expectations of museumgoers in many ways.[1] It is uncommon, for instance, to encounter a veil of mist in an art museum, such that one's skin becomes dewy and one's hair begins to curl. It is also uncommon to encounter an ordinary rubber garden hose, a water spigot, and an exposed spotlight in the prestigious and dignified halls of the museum. Perhaps most surprising, though, is the presence of an actual rainbow, hovering in the middle of Eliasson's darkened room. The darkness of the room—the lack of any standard museum illumination, save a single bright spotlight trained on the mist—establishes this space as set apart from the museum or gallery. This is an environment that heightens one's awareness of what one is seeing and how one is seeing it. One can view this miracle—this indoor rainbow—because of the light.

In Eliasson's work, light becomes a central character, fundamental to the work as a material but also as the means of one's experience of the work. Upon colliding with the minuscule water droplets, the light breaks open, producing the rainbow's spectrum of colors, which reflect and

[1] Olafur Eliasson, *Beauty*, 1993, Spotlight, water, nozzles, wood, hose, and pump, Various installation spaces, https://olafureliasson.net/artwork/beauty-1993/.

refract into the eyes of the viewers. In recognizing the simple mechanics of illumination that enables the present rainbow, viewers might be reminded that it is "impossible to separate light from the image."[2]

These latter words are not from Eliasson's artist statement but from Basil of Caesarea's (330–379) fourth-century treatise on the third person of the Trinity, *On the Holy Spirit*. Basil's pneumatological vision in this text asserted a crucial influence on the language for the Spirit in the Niceno-Constantinopolitan creed of 381, and the text remains a foundational work for understanding the doctrine of the Holy Spirit today.[3] In this treatise, Basil is at pains to insist on the coequality of the Holy Spirit with the Father and the Son. At the climactic point of his argument, he reaches for an artistic metaphor to demonstrate his point: the Son is bound to the Father as a portrait to its subject. That portrait is only seen, known, and experienced through the effects of light. In a similar way, Basil contends, the Holy Spirit illumines the minds of the faithful to perceive the image of the invisible God (Col 1:15).

Basil's modern readers might find themselves unconvinced by this metaphor, however, because of the unique art-viewing practices developed in the last two centuries. In our contemporary context, informed primarily by the viewing practices in fine-art museums, light is subordinated to the art object and the depicted archetype. Such an approach would certainly undermine Basil's argument for the coequality of the light (Spirit), image (Son), and archetype (Father). As a leading contemporary artist working in the "light and space" tradition, Eliasson's works challenge the assumed subordination of light in the practice of art viewing. *Beauty's* pneumatological contribution, I will argue, is in clearing away the uniquely modern assumptions that might obscure the finer points of Basil's metaphor, reorienting Basil's readers to more clearly

[2]Basil, *On the Holy Spirit*, trans. Stephen M. Hildebrand, Popular Patristics Series (Yonkers, NY: St. Vladimir's Seminary Press, 2011), 26.63, p. 103.

[3]Stephen M. Hildebrand, "Introduction," in Basil, *On the Holy Spirit*, 21. "The Creed of Constantinople is a lasting reminder of Basil's service to the Christian faith, for in it one can readily recognize his concern to establish the genuine equality of Father, Son, and Spirit, along with their eternal distinction one from another. . . . The clause on the Holy Spirit asserts the divinity of the Holy Spirit, against the Spirit-fighters, just in the language that Basil would."

perceive the illuminating invitation of the Spirit of Jesus, the image of the invisible God.

In what follows, I introduce Basil's pneumatological masterwork, *On the Holy Spirit*, by way of a synecdochal reading of his metaphor of the king's portrait. Then I suggest ways in which modern theological interpreters might challenge this metaphor's pneumatological strength due to what I contend are modern assumptions about the visual economy of artworks. Then, drawing on the art-historical and philosophical grounding of the artwork, I draw Eliasson's *Beauty* into conversation with Basil's metaphor in the hope that this pairing will restore an aesthetic framework more closely akin to that of Basil's era and thereby enrich a modern interpretation of his pneumatology. By recasting Basil's assumed visual economy through this pairing with a contemporary artwork (rather than, say, a historical description of ancient optics or visual cultures), I hope to attune Basil's readers to his visual economy phenomenologically rather than analytically, as well as to demonstrate the potential theological possibilities for contemporary artworks.

Basil's Metaphor of the King's Portrait in *On the Holy Spirit*

In the second section of Basil's *On the Holy Spirit*, the theologian is at pains to counter the charge of tritheism from the *pneumatomachoi* (or "Spirit-fighters"). While Christians confess the "particularizing of the persons," Basil's contention is that these particular three are coequal in nature, that the three are one.[4] To explain just how this is so, Basil reaches for an artistic metaphor used by his heroes before him:

> It is said that there is a king and the image of the king, but not two kings, for the power is not divided, and the glory is not portioned out. As the power that rules over us and the authority is one, so also one, not many, is the doxology from us. On account of this, the honor of the image passes over to the archetype. Therefore, the image is the prototype by way of imitation in the case of the king and his image; the Son is this by nature. And

[4]Basil, *On the Holy Spirit* 18.45, p. 80.

> just as in the arts there is a likeness according to form, so with the divine and incomposite nature, the unity is in the communion of the Godhead.[5]

The portrait of the king and the king himself share a common identity, power, and glory and therefore can be understood as one, even while they are distinct. In the ancient world, images of the ruler were ubiquitous and powerful, a "significant aspect of everyday life in the first four centuries of the Common Era."[6] They operated as mediatory devices for signaling the authority and presence of the ruler. As Robin Jensen explains, the emperor's image was a "vital presence" that operated with a kind of living agency in the empire: "It witnessed official acts, presided over judicial hearings, enforced laws, guaranteed oaths, dispensed clemency, and accepted gifts and sacrifices."[7] Even after Constantine commanded the sacrifices to imperial images to cease, the ritual of affording honor to the image remained ingrained in the cultural habitus, such that the practice (formerly understood as idolatry) could now serve a metaphorical function as Basil employs it. The Son, as image (Col 1:15), is united to the Father as the image of the emperor is united to the king, its archetype.

In the next section, Basil returns to this metaphor of a portrait to demonstrate the inseparability of the Spirit from the Father and Son.

> When through his [the Spirit's] illuminating power we fix our eyes on the beauty of the image of the unseen God, and through the image are led up to the more than beautiful vision of the archetype, his Spirit of knowledge is somehow inseparably present. He supplies to those who love to see the truth the power to see the image in himself. . . . As it is written, "in his light we will see light," that is, in the illumination of the Spirit, "the true light that enlightens every man coming into the world" (Jn 1:9) And so, he shows in himself the glory of the only-begotten and furnishes to true worshippers the knowledge of God in himself.[8]

---

[5]Basil, *On the Holy Spirit* 18.45; cf. Athanasius, *Third Discourse Against the Arians* 3.23.5.

[6]Robin Margaret Jensen, *Face to Face: Portraits of the Divine in Early Christianity* (Minneapolis: Fortress, 2005), 52.

[7]Jensen, *Face to Face*, 52.

[8]Basil, *On the Holy Spirit* 18.47, p. 82.

The Spirit is the "illuminating power" that actualizes and enables knowledge of God in God's worshipers, and so is essentially tethered to what is known and seen. In the same way that light is integral to a viewer seeing the king in his portrait, God's Spirit is integral in a worshiper's encounter with God in Jesus Christ. The light is so basic to the portrait's purpose that it is in fact constituent of the portrait.

It is important to note that Basil is in fact arguing an ontological point in his treatise—he is defending and expanding a Nicene trinitarian coequality of the Father, Son, and Holy Spirit.[9] Basil does not demur from arguing for unity within the immanent Trinity. However, within this key metaphor and throughout his text, trinitarian personal unity is accessed and understood only through God's self-revelation within the economy. The Spirit is related to the Son as that which illumines the image, and the Son is the image that makes present the archetype. Accordingly, the created, human *viewer* of the portrait is an essential character in the metaphor. And the primary site for that self-revelation is in worship: the honor given (by worshipers) to the image is passed over to the prototype; the doxology offered to the king through the image is one; and true worshipers see the beauty of the image of the unseen God by the illuminating power of the Spirit. For Basil, the persons are made manifest in their relationship to one another *in and through* their relationship of self-revelation to the worshiper.[10]

[9]In *On the Holy Spirit*, Basil uses the language of *coequality* to describe the relationship between the Spirit and the other persons of the Trinity, refraining almost entirely from *homoousios* or *consubstantiality*. In Basil's post-Nicaea and pre-Constantinople milieu, *homoousios* carried significant complexities, as thinkers from all sides of the theological spectrum—from those who Basil would have considered modalists to tritheists—used the term to defend their claims about the Son's relationship to the Father. While we cannot know with certainty why Basil avoids the term here, we can note this theological baggage that the term carried, as well as observe that the term was *not* used strategically by Basil's primary opponents in *On the Holy Spirit*, the *pneumatomachoi*. For more about how Basil carried forward and advanced pneumatological language in the post-Nicaea period, see Lewis Ayers, *Nicaea and Its Legacy* (Oxford: Oxford University Press, 2004), 187-222.

[10]What virtues or habits must a worshiper possess to receive this self-disclosure of God? Basil, most likely drawing from Jesus' words to his disciples in Jn 15, references this dynamic in the course of his argument. Interestingly, he uses the terms of the visual-artistic metaphor to explain: "The carnal man, who does not have a mind trained to contemplate, but who allows it to be buried completely in the mind of the flesh, as if in filth, is unable *to look up at the spiritual light of truth*. And so the world, that is, a life enslaved to the passions of the flesh, does not receive the grace of the Spirit, *as a weak eye does not receive the light of a sun-beam*" (*On the Holy Spirit* 22.53, pp. 91-92).

Basil's artistic metaphor set in the economy discloses a rich circuit of interdependent relationships constitutive of the Trinity's ontological unity, personal distinction, and self-communication. Cast as the illuminating power, the Spirit takes on a presence that is deeply embedded in communication. To state the obvious principle behind the metaphor: light is an essential aspect of art's self-communication. Without illumination of some sort, the emperor's portrait, the icon of Christ, or the family picture on one's mantle cannot be accessed by a viewer.[11] Basil puts it thus:

> Therefore, in worship the Holy Spirit is inseparable from the Father and the Son, for if you are outside of him, you will not worship at all while if you are in him, you will in no way separate him from God—at least not more than you will remove light from the objects of sight. For it is impossible to see the Image of the invisible God, except in the illumination of the Spirit, and it is impossible for him who fixes his eyes on the image to separate the light from the image. The cause of seeing must be seen together with the things seen. And so, first we behold the radiance of the glory of God through the illumination of the Spirit, and then, we are led up through the character of him of whom he is the character and identical seal.[12]

Basil was ahead of his time in discerning the science of optics in this metaphor.[13] The cause of seeing—light—truly cannot be separated from things seen for at least two reasons. For one, the eye takes in optical information by receiving light rays that have reflected off the surface of the objects seen. And two, without a surface against which to reflect and

---

While there is not sufficient space to extend this discussion to include the virtues of a strong eye here, I could imagine how an engagement with the environmentally conscious works of Olafur Eliasson might clarify Basil on this point.

[11]The metaphor has limitations, in that Christians confess the self-standing of the immanent Trinity apart from the economy in the principle of divine freedom. However, the metaphor reminds Basil's readers that Christians can only begin epistemologically from where they are positioned—within the economy.

[12]Basil, *On the Holy Spirit* 26.63, p. 103.

[13]The theologian most likely understood vision in terms of one of the ancient theories of optics: Plato's extramission, which proposed that the eye emitted a ray that took hold of observed objects; or Aristotle's intromission, which argued that the eye received an object's emitted rays. Throughout Western history, each theory has had influential proponents. In *From Sight to Light*, A. Mark Smith argues that Johannes Kepler was the first to discover the importance of light for retinal imaging. See Smith, *From Sight to Light: The Passage from Ancient to Modern Optics* (Chicago: University of Chicago Press, 2015).

bounce back, light cannot be seen.[14] Just as a portrait would not be a successful representation without an archetype, a portrait would not be a successful image without the illuminating power of light. The image, archetype, and light are therefore inseparable and mutually constitutive.

Moreover, as light, the Spirit is hypostatically particularized as that which is made known in its making known the objects of sight. The Spirit is therefore understood as the reflected light that discloses the image of the invisible God to the worshiper in the economy. The hypostasis of the Spirit is particularized as that person of the Trinity that makes the image visible. The Spirit illumines the Son as the image of the Father. This, of course, accords with the scriptural testimony of the Spirit as the revealing principle within the economy. The Spirit enables and activates the conception of the Son in Mary (Lk 1:35), the Spirit publicly anoints Christ (Mt 3:16), the Spirit enables the preaching of the Son at Pentecost (Acts 2:4), the Spirit knits together the visible body of Christ (1 Cor 12), and the Spirit makes Christ present in the sacramental life of God's church.

Contemporary Christian thinkers might balk at Basil's use of light as a metaphor for the Spirit, suggesting that it falls prey to various pneumatological dangers. As a mere support mechanism for the image, these critics may claim, light as a metaphor for the Spirit suggests a personhood that is less substantial, less weighty, less real than the image and its archetype. Critics could further claim that light is not an essential aspect of the artwork and therefore would not be an appropriate metaphor for defending the coequality of the Spirit with the Father and the Son. Moreover, because light falls indiscriminately on any number of illumined objects, one might argue that the analogy fails to adequately describe the fundamental connection between the Spirit and its particular object of illumination—the second person of the Trinity, the image of God.

---

[14]This simplified physiological description of the science of optics has been forcefully challenged by cultural critic Jonathan Crary in his book *Techniques of the Observer: On Vision and Modernity in the Nineteenth Century* (Cambridge, MA: MIT Press, 1992). He argues that various philosophical, institutional, and scientific forces converged in the nineteenth century to represent vision as a neutral, empirical phenomenon. His argument would easily align with my thesis here—that Basil assumes an economy of the artwork that is more participatory, communal, and affective than modern art viewers are prone to assume.

Concerns multiply when the metaphor is considered as a description of the Spirit's work toward humanity in the divine economy. Is the Spirit merely a mechanism for the transfer of divine insight, as light enables the transfer of visual information? Does the Spirit reveal God to the individual perceiver *alone*, as the individual's eyes take in the light reflected from the painted portrait? And, crucially, is encountering the image through the illumination of the Spirit adequately analogized by a momentary experience of a static deposit of visual data? Is the image illumined a mere object for one's visual consumption?

While there are certainly limitations to any attempt to analogize the triune life of God, this kind of protestation over the visual analogy stems largely from the uniquely modern assumptions of the contemporary art experience. Basil and his contemporaries would have approached the viewing of a public image such as the emperor's portrait in the metaphor with much different expectations and conventions than we have for viewing artworks today. Nicholas Wolterstorff has compellingly addressed the contemporary situation of art viewing as it differs from that of earlier eras, and Robin Jensen has thoroughly surveyed the early Christian approach to imaging in multiple places.[15] Rather than rehearsing their arguments and descriptions in an attempt to refute these potential criticisms, the rest of this essay will seek to extend and expand Basil's metaphor in conversation with a contemporary artwork that addresses these key issues. Through engagement with Olafur Eliasson's *Beauty*, twenty-first-century readers and art viewers might better appreciate Basil's visual analogy and therefore come to greater clarity about his unique contribution to pneumatology in *On the Holy Spirit*.

[15]See Nicholas Wolterstorff, *Art in Action: Toward a Christian Aesthetic* (Grand Rapids, MI: Eerdmans, 1980), 19-61; Jensen, *Face to Face*, esp. 51-59; see also Wolterstorff, *Art Rethought: The Social Practices of Art* (Oxford: Oxford University Press, 2015), especially part one, "The Grand Narrative of Art in the Modern World"; Robin Jensen, *Understanding Early Christian Art* (New York: Routledge, 2000); Mark D. Ellison and Robin Jensen, eds., *The Routledge Handbook of Early Christian Art* (New York: Routledge, 2018).

Beauty and Basil

Beauty is an early and paradigmatic example of the work of Scandinavian artist Olafur Eliasson. Originally produced in a Copenhagen warehouse in 1993, the artwork employs multiple themes that now form the center of Eliasson's practice: immersive environments, natural and ordinary elements, and, most importantly for our purposes, the focused control of light. The work consists in rudimentary construction materials, including a perforated hose placed close to the ceiling that yields a gentle curtain of mist that divides the darkened room. From a corner of the space, a prismatic spotlight blazes forth its light, trained onto the veil of water. The effect of this particular arrangement of ordinary materials produces the extraordinary: a domesticated rainbow.

Commentators who write on Eliasson's work often remark on his juxtaposition of ordinary and extraordinary. An encounter with an Eliasson piece often produces wonder, awe, and self-reflection, but the artist never seeks to hide the utilitarian means of this experience's production. In an Eliasson piece, the sublime is courted by the mundane. Like Basil, Eliasson wants to draw his viewer's attention to the light as a critical material component of the artwork. While a pneumatological parallel is not Eliasson's stated aim, the art-historical significance of such a move should help highlight and clear away modern assumptions that might occlude the best interpretation of Basil's metaphor.

Recall that for Basil, the Holy Spirit's relationship to the other persons of the Trinity is like the relationship of light to a portrait of an emperor. The Holy Spirit illumines the second person of the Trinity as the image of the archetype, the Father. To contemporary readers, however, the metaphor might not serve Basil's intended purpose (to defend the coequality of the Spirit with the Son and Father), because contemporary Westerners have come to understand light as a subordinate consideration when viewing artwork.[16] As an artist working within the traditions of light and space as well as minimalism, however, Eliasson is motivated to dispel this assumption about light in his work.

---

[16]Wolterstorff, *Art Rethought*.

Light's substance. *Beauty* references and reflects key insights from the light and space art movement. Light and space art, made by artists such as James Turrell (b. 1943) and Robert Irwin (1928–2023), originated in the 1960s in Southern California. This artwork is characterized by the manipulation of perceptual phenomena and the creation of immersive, experiential sites to the end of creating an evocative and ethereal encounter for the viewer.[17] For example, a quintessential Turrell piece, *Skyspace: The Way of Color,* consists in an aperture cut into the ceiling of a dome-like structure in which the viewer shelters.[18] Twice a day, once at dawn and once at dusk, the enclosure is lit with precisely colored hues, choreographed to contrast and accentuate the slowly changing blues of the natural sky.

Light and space art carries forth the avant-garde tradition of critiquing what had become traditional or academic modes of art creation and appreciation. While light and space have long been essential aspects of artistic creation, they had been mostly relegated to operate within the confines of the canvas or frame. These midcentury avant-garde artists brought these elements outside the enclosure of the frame and into the space of the beholder, challenging what had become a reified model of art consumption. For instance, Caspar David Friedrich conveys a monk's encounter with the sublime in his emblematic nineteenth-century Romantic painting *Monk by the Sea* by using light and shadow to depict the overwhelming magnitude and fearsome beauty of the natural world on the painting's canvas. Turrell and Eliasson, however, bring the evocative power of light and shadow out of the frame-space and into the real-time space of the contemporary beholder, hoping to provoke an encounter for the beholder similar to that of Friedrich's monk. These works seek to "renew the experience of vision by disrupting normative exhibition conventions."[19] In this way, the critical distance between the viewer and

---

[17]An important retrospective exhibit of key works from the movement was organized by the Los Angeles County Museum of Art in 2021. See Carol S. Eliel, ed., *Light Space Surface: Art from Southern California* (Los Angeles: DelMonico Books/Los Angeles County Museum of Art, 2021).

[18]James Turrell, *Skyspace: The Way of Color,* 2009, stone, concrete, stainless steel, and LED lighting, 228 × 652", Crystal Bridges Museum of American Art, Bentonville, Arkansas.

[19]Klaus Biesenbach and Roxana Marcoci, "Toward the Sun: Olafur Eliasson's Protocinematic Vision," in *Take Your Time: Olafur Eliasson*, ed. Madeleine Grynsztejn (New York: Thames & Hudson, 2007), 186.

the artwork is effectively removed, plunging the beholder into the world of the artwork and its component parts.

Both Turrell and Eliasson are courting a situation much closer to that of Basil's in the fourth century. For Basil (and, for that matter, for most humans in history), the relationship between light and sight was a much more tangible and pressing reality than it is for us today. In the modern West, light is somewhat easy to come by—more often than not, the flip of a switch can illumine vast expanses of space. Illuminating the emperor's image in an indoor public forum would have been a much more expensive and unreliable undertaking in Basil's time. Light sources would need to be procured and maintained, and architecture would be negotiated and reconciled, just as they are in the contemporary light and space artworks. In contrast to the early modern object-oriented approach to artwork, Turrell and Eliasson, like Basil, regard light as an essential and constitutive substance of the artwork. The self-proclaimed "sculptor of light," Turrell requires that "LED light" is in the work's materials list, where one might expect to find oil, stone, or enamel.[20] In Eliasson's *Beauty*, light is similarly regarded as a fundamental medium for the artwork's creation. The materials list for this project reveals this, as "spotlight" is the first item listed among "water, nozzles, wood, hose, and pump."[21]

In *Beauty* and other similar artworks, Eliasson takes this emphasis on light farther than Turrell by intentionally exposing the apparatuses of the artwork's creation. For "space and light, as Eliasson's work amply demonstrate, are no mere abstractions. They are deeply material things."[22] These ordinary materials, found in any local hardware store, are the opposite of the pristine, delicate, and untouchable oils, canvas, and tempera that one expects to encounter in a museum. The components of this artwork, the light most especially, might be better described as equipment: familiar and utilitarian materials that are tangible and subsistent. The tangible and

[20]Beth Harris and Steven Zucker, "James Turrell, *Skyspace, the Way of Color*," *Smarthistory*, September 25, 2018, https://smarthistory.org/james-turrell-skyspace-the-way-of-color-2/.

[21]Olafur Eliasson, "Beauty, 1993," https://olafureliasson.net/artwork/beauty-1993/.

[22]Pamela M. Lee, "Your Light and Space," in Grynsztejn, *Take Your Time*, 35.

conspicuous presence of the spotlight in *Beauty* reframes contemporary art-viewers' expectations in a number of ways.

First, the spotlight itself forms a sort of sculptural presence within the space, reminding viewers that light has a material and weighty presence. It is a nonnegotiable component in the world of the artwork, not just in name but in presence. Second, the conspicuity of the spotlight activates the possibility of the spotlight's *absence* in the viewer's mind, reminding her that without light, there would be no possibility of engaging the artwork. Further, this is not an ambient or unspecified light source but a *spot*light, purposely trained on the veil of mist to reveal the rainbow to the spectator. In this way, the viewer is brought to a higher sense of the inseparability of the light, water, and rainbow: their unchangeable and specific relation. The light is present to reveal the rainbow in the water; the water is present such that the refracted light might manifest the rainbow; the rainbow is present through the simultaneous operations of the water and light. Finally, the play between these constitutive and conspicuous parts establishes a dynamic, living, and active work. The reciprocity between spotlight and water creates a circuit of interdependence and relationship that generates a living and somewhat unpredictable phenomenon.

After viewing *Beauty*, a contemporary reader of Basil's metaphor in *On the Holy Spirit* might find her perspective more attuned to its pneumatological subtleties. Light is not merely an important support for the portrait of the king; it is essential and constitutive of the work. As such, light can be understood as coequal with the portrait and archetype, just as Basil argues that the Spirit is coequal with the image (the Son) and the archetype (the Father). Moreover, after considering *Beauty*, the materiality of the light source Basil is referencing might be newly appreciated. The light from the candle or the oil lamp, or the sunshine from the window, is not merely an ethereal aftereffect but a material product that pressures and activates a response from other materials. The light in Basil's metaphor is just as *substantial* as the image and the archetype, which, Basil contends, analogizes the way in which the Spirit is coequal in substance to the image and the archetype. Further, after viewing *Beauty*, Basil's readers might more easily imagine the intentionality with which the light illumines the image of the king. The candle or lamp would be brought to the image *for* the portrait's illumination. It is a light specifically intended *for* illuminating the image, just as Eliasson's spotlight is *for* illuminating the rainbow. Thusly, Basil's metaphor might remind us that the Spirit (as light) is *for* illuminating the image (the Son) of the archetype (the Father). This light is the light of Christ, the Son of God.

Finally, a reader who has viewed *Beauty* might be more likely to sense the intensely dynamic relationality between Basil's light, image, and archetype. The light, water, and rainbow of Eliasson's installation are mutually constitutive, deeply interdependent, and constantly in flux. As the light is reflected and refracted off the surface of a portrait that re-presents a living person, so the Spirit, image, and archetype are interdependent and dynamic. To hazard an extension of Basil's metaphor, however, I would argue that the presence of *Beauty's* rainbow is more active, more living, than the presence of the king in his portrait. *Beauty's* spotlight illumines not a static image gathering dust and smudges of candle smoke (like the candlelight that illumines Basil's image of the king might); instead, this light illumines a *living* water, bringing forth a dancing, vibrant image that shines with the color of its source. Through Eliasson's *Beauty*, then, the Spirit as light can be better understood relationally as the living presence who reflects and refracts through the living water, calling forth the ever-renewing, wonderous, colorful life of God. Such an analogy might simultaneously resist tritheism and the underpersonalization of the Spirit by characterizing the Spirit (as light) as utterly other-centered and *kenotic* in an ever-renewing *perichoretic* way.

The spiritual-visual economy. Another set of questions that Basil's readers might raise challenge the adequacy of the economic dimension of the metaphor. Is the experience of viewing the illumined portrait of the emperor an adequate analogy for the Christian's experience of viewing the Spirit-illumined image of God? Here again, Eliasson's *Beauty* and the art-historical ground on which it stands is helpful for clearing away modern assumptions from which this objection might develop. In addition to the light and space movement just discussed, Eliasson was also influenced by the American minimalism of the 1960s. This movement reduced the displayed art object to its most basic forms in an attempt to dramatically reorient and expand art viewing, with the goal of bringing more attention to the experience itself.[23] Robert Morris, a pioneering minimalist artist, wrote that the art object itself is "but one of the terms in the newer aesthetic. . . . The better new work takes relationship out of the work [the object in the frame] and makes them a function of space, light, and the viewer's field of vision."[24] The relationships that matter in an artwork, in other words, are not those among color, shape, and line on a canvas but those among the viewer, the environment, and the object.

This approach, heavily indebted to conceptual art, happenings, and dada, brought new emphasis to the relationships implied in perception. Morris's work *Untitled* from 1965, for instance, is composed of four structural cubes, resembling pedestals, made from reflective mirrored glass. In perceiving this piece, one inevitably observes oneself observing (and *others* observing), bringing greater awareness to the ways in which the work and the work's environment create a renewed perspective in the viewer(s). This is art that demands and interrogates the viewer's participation in the artwork, a concept that challenged the more traditional approach to art appreciation that had become conventional: those who view a minimalist work cannot stand over, above, or apart from the art but are confronted with their participation in the perception of the work. As Madeleine Grynsztejn points out, this phenomenological approach to artwork greatly inspired the development of Eliasson's practice:

> [Eliasson] recognized that Minimalism had brought to a head the shift in avant-garde practice from a focus on the object—on its autonomous, internal and formal compositional makeup—to a concern with the subject, or with a primary engagement of the spectator. . . . Minimalist objects sought to blur the relationship between the viewer and the viewed, making

---

[23]See Michael's Fried's extremely critical commentary on minimalism (what he calls "literalism") in his highly influential essay, "Art and Objecthood," in *Art and Objecthood: Essays and Reviews* (Chicago: University of Chicago Press, 1998), 148-72.

[24]Robert Morris, "Notes on Sculpture Pt. 2," in *Continuous Project Altered Daily: The Writings of Robert Morris* (Cambridge, MA: MIT Press, 1993), 15.

> both more permeable to the space at large; thus the work came to fruition in a reciprocal and mutual interaction between object and spectator.[25]

In *Beauty,* the invitation and challenge to participate is central—and is enabled and activated by the light.

Beauty carries forward the legacy of minimalism in that the work is not an object to be visually consumed or critically analyzed but a *presence* to engage. Time and again Eliasson insists in his writings that his works are meant to create an ecstatic experience for the viewer. The viewer is put in situations where she can "see herself seeing" as she is caught up into the reflection and refraction of the installation's illumination.[26] This is perhaps most elegantly achieved in *Beauty*, as the bouncing rainbow beckons viewers to come dance through its mist. Museums and galleries that have hosted *Beauty* testify to the work's gentle pull toward playfulness, as guests jump, walk, and dance in and through the rainbow's misty veil.[27] One critic describes the effect as the "the pleasure of presence."[28]

This presence is a shared pleasure, as Eliasson prefers his works to be presented in public spaces that are radically inclusive and accessible.[29] "Because people do not stand in front of *Beauty* as if before a picture, but rather *inside* it, actively engaged, the work posits the very act of looking as a social experience."[30] Because the rainbow changes dramatically from

---

[25]Madeleine Grynsztejn, "Attention Universe: The Work of Olafur Eliasson," in *Olafur Eliasson*, ed. Madeleine Grynsztejn, Daniel Birnbaum, and Michael Speaks (London: Phaidon, 2002), 44.

[26]"Perceiving yourself perceiving," says Robert Irwin in his interview with Olfaur Eliasson, to which Eliasson responds, "Or 'Seeing yourself seeing'—I probably took that from you!" See Olafur Eliasson and Robert Irwin, "Take Your Time: A Conversation," in Grynsztejn, *Take Your Time*, 55. See also Olfaur Eliasson, *Projects 73: Olafur Eliasson; Seeing Yourself Sensing*, exhibition brochure (New York: Museum of Modern Art, 2001), n.p.

[27]See, for instance, this effect captured on video in "'Beauty' 1993–2020," Studio Olafur Eliasson, April 7, 2020, https://vimeo.com/404947237.

[28]Madeleine Grynsztejn, "Attention Universe," in Grynsztejn, Birnbaum, and Speaks, *Olafur Eliasson*, 47.

[29]"A central aspect of his [Eliasson's] oeuvre is its social dimension. The work is fundamentally activated by the perception and participation of oneself *and* others, by 'the very apprehension of other people and their movements . . . [amid] the optical [and physical] texture of the work.' Sharing our sinfular impressions in this way, we come into a 'being-in-common' or 'being-with,' as opposed to a 'being-in-solitude'—into a community of sorts . . . defined by . . . a copresence in a 'constructed situation' designed (in part) to generate provisional but compelling social bonds." Madeleine Grynsztejn, "Your Entanglements: Olafur Eliasson, The Museum, and Consumer Culture," in Grynsztejn, *Take Your Time*, 19.

[30]Biesenbach and Marcoci, "Toward the Sun," 186.

moment to moment and inch to inch, participants' differing viewpoints multiply the perception of the work. The shared space of the art environment means that the work can almost never be viewed without necessarily viewing another viewer viewing it. Participation in the perception is always participation in *shared* perception for *Beauty*. Most centrally, Eliasson's stated hope for his work is nothing less than the transformation of one's perceptions, which might kindle agency and motivate action outside the museum.[31] To encounter *Beauty*'s light is to encounter a communal, transforming, and motivating presence.

The kind of participatory viewing to which *Beauty* calls the beholder echoes (albeit in a distinctly avant-garde key) the situation of the imagined viewer of Basil's image of the king. The situation of viewing an image of the king would always have been a public situation, in a shared (and perhaps crowded!) space. Beholding the portrait was not an enlightened experience of aesthetic contemplation, wherein the image could be judged from a critical distance, but was intentionally participatory. Viewing the image of the king, with one's fellow citizens, identified the viewer as subject and archetype as authority, eliciting a "doxology."[32] The illumined portrait of the king called forth a response from the viewer, inevitably connecting that viewer to the larger world of the kingdom.

After considering Eliasson's *Beauty*, the economic dimensions of Basil's metaphor might bear more pneumatological fruit. First, a reader who participates in the art-world of Eliasson's *Beauty* might be convinced that the implied visual economy of Basil's image of the king is far from disinterested contemplation of an object. The illumined image commands a response, a doxology from the viewer, that appropriately analogizes the effect of the Spirit's illumination of image of God. In just one of many examples of this dynamic from Scripture, John the Baptist is compelled to preach after the Spirit's revelation of Jesus as the Son of God: "And John testified, 'I saw the Spirit descending from heaven like a dove, and it

---

[31]"I . . . regard museums . . . as spaces where one steps even deeper into society, from where one can scrutinize society." Olafur Eliasson, "Vibrations," in *Olafur Eliasson: Your Engagement Has Consequences; On the Relativity of Your Reality*, ed. Caroline Eggel and Studio Olafur Eliasson (Baden, Switzerland: Lars Müller, 2006), 72.

[32]Basil, *On the Holy Spirit* 18.45, p. 80.

remained on him.' . . . And I myself have seen and have testified that this is the Son of God" (Jn 1:32, 34 NRSV). The Spirit's illumination of God in Christ magnetically motivates a response of praise, thanksgiving, and participatory action.

Moreover, concerns about the artistic metaphor implying an autonomous or solely individual experience of the Spirit might be mitigated after consideration of *Beauty.* For the artwork radically accentuates the necessarily public nature of most art viewing, reminding Basil's readers of the most likely *public* and thereby *communal* viewing of the king's portrait. The Spirit, in the metaphor, is therefore always already illuming an image for a people together—and particular people who are allegiant to this king. As the Spirit fell on that early *gathering* of Christ's followers at the first Christian Pentecost (Acts 2:1-13), more often than not, the Spirit's continued illumination of Christ as the Son of God is experienced by a gathered people: the church.

Finally, after experiencing Eliasson's beckoning rainbow, Basil's words about the transforming power of the Spirit's illumination might ring even more clearly. In a particularly apt passage, Basil is building on Paul's words in 2 Corinthians 3 to compare the Spirit-inspired reading of the law to Moses' beholding of God. Through Spirit-inspired contemplation, the glory of the Trinity is manifest in God's people:

> Therefore, he who strips off the letter in his reading of the Law turns to the Lord—the Lord here is called the Spirit—and becomes similar to Moses whose face was glorified by God's epiphany. For, *as those things that are near brilliant colors are themselves colored because of the rays of light that flow around them, so he who clearly fixes his eyes on the Spirit is somehow transformed by the Spirit's glory into something brighter as his heart is illuminated by the truth of the Spirit, as if by a light.*[33]

Spirit-led contemplation economically reveals the triune glory through sharing that glory with the contemplator. By God's "light, we see light" (Ps 36:9). In Eliasson's piece, it is the character of *Beauty*'s light itself that elicits this response in its viewers. The viewer finds herself cloaked in

[33]Basil, *On the Holy Spirit* 21.52, p. 90.

darkness in *Beauty*'s black box until she responds to the invitation to be illumined by the colorful light of the rainbow. One's face and features are only perceived with clarity when brought into the light of the rainbow. Those who find themselves colored with the flowing bands of light in *Beauty* parallel those who find themselves transformed by the Spirit's illumination of God's image into God's redeemed *imago*.

Beauty as a supplemental metaphor for the triune life has its obvious limitations. Most obviously, the components of the artwork are not *hypostases*. The irreducibility of divine hypostatic identity only finds analogue in the hypostatic identity of the human—the *imago Dei*—and the community of God's people, the church. However, the other-directed reflecting and refracting relationships found in the artwork can nonetheless provide an additional facet of reflection for trinitarian theology, especially as it finds expression pneumatologically. In shifting the entry point to the visual economy of wonder, both Basil and *Beauty* avoid tritheism while simultaneously renewing a commitment to the living, active, subsistent presence of the Spirit as coequal to Father and Son. Grynsztejn reminds Eliasson's admirers of the power of such an encounter: "For Eliasson, wonder is an ethical imperative; it is the quality of experience that prompts us toward an intensive engagement with the world, that continually reawakens us to a fresh consideration of the everyday and the lives we choose to live in it."[34] *Beauty*'s gift, I contend, is in reawakening Christians to the illuminating invitation of the Spirit of Jesus, the image of the invisible God.

---

[34]Grynsztejn, "Your Entanglements," 27.

4

THE SPIRIT OF SHALOM

CONTEMPORARY NATIVE ART AND THE QUESTION OF KINCENTRICITY

Erin Shaw and Taylor Worley

In fall 2023, the National Gallery of Art in Washington, DC, played host to a truly remarkable exhibition of contemporary art titled *The Land Carries Our Ancestors*. For this momentous collection, curator, and artist Jaune Quick-to-See Smith (citizen of the Confederated Salish and Kootenai Nation) brought together works by an intergenerational group of nearly fifty living Native artists from across the United States. While Native art and craft are regularly displayed in American museums, this exhibition was remarkable for its focus on living artists and the diverse forms of artistic practice that make up contemporary Native art. On its surface, the exhibition both invites associations with traditional Native motifs and forms and at the same time disrupts those associations, defying easy categorization.

Much like groundbreaking Native artists such as Robert Houle, Bonnie Devine, or Brian Jungen, these artists often blended familiar motifs with thoroughly modern sensibilities, and what was showcased here was the way that such efforts are moving in directions that Native art and contemporary art have not seen before. Despite the range of methods and materials—including weaving, beadwork, sculpture, painting, printmaking, drawing, photography, performance, and video—the organizers say, "These works share a worldview informed by thousands of years of reverence, study, and concern for the land."[1] In its own decidedly poignant and exultant way, *The Land Carries Our Ancestors* thus echoes a diverse chorus of voices repeating, "We're still here." At the same time, the exhibition demonstrates how open the possibilities for contemporary Native art remain today.

Yet, while promising developments such as *The Land Carries Our Ancestors* offer a great deal of hope, the current reception of contemporary art by Native Americans reveals significant challenges. We name just three here. First, contemporary art by Native Americans is not getting the attention it deserves and yet represents one of the most socially and culturally significant art movements today. As demonstrated again and again by the voices of curators and critics, the works of contemporary Native artists reflect consistently the kind of remembrance, lament, and ache for healing that American society so desperately needs. Second, as critic and curator heather ahtone (Choctaw/Chickasaw Nation) points out, the critical methodologies of modernist art history are incomplete and ill-equipped for a true assessment of Native American art. For instance, ahtone highlights the ways in which tribal creation stories can supply the guiding framework of theory for understanding Native art, but modernism rejects outright such forms of religiosity.[2] Third, while a theology of human origins in contemporary Native art could inspire renewed approaches to art today, such possibilities are limited by an unfortunate dividing line between creation accounts. Indeed, prominent voices such as Robin Wall Kimmerer, author of the bestselling *Braiding Sweetgrass*, put tribal creation stories in opposition to the Christian Scriptures because the latter have played such a pivotal role in the legacy of colonialization.[3]

---

[1]This statement comes from the description on the exhibition webpage: "The Land Carries Our Ancestors: Contemporary Art by Native Americans," National Gallery of Art, accessed August 20, 2024, www.nga.gov/exhibitions/2023/ancestors-contemporary-art-native-americans.html.

[2]heather ahtone, "Indigenous Art as a Beacon of Survival," in *Art for a New Understanding: Native Voices, 1950s to Now*, by Mindy N. Besaw, Candice Hopkins, Manuela Well-Off-Man, heather ahtone, and Norman Akers (Fayetteville: University of Arkansas Press, 2018), 23.

[3]The opposition surfaces in each of the essays published in the catalogue for *The Land Carries Our Ancestors*. See Jaune Quick-to-See Smith, Joy Harjo, heather ahtone, and Shana Bushyhead Condill, *The Land Carries Our Ancestors: Contemporary Art by Native Americans* (Washington, DC:

These challenges deserve significant attention, but our focus here will be on exploring key concepts within Native perspectives on art that represents a promising path for theological dialogue. We believe that significant harmony exists between the concept of kincentricity in Native art and theological understandings of the Holy Spirit by Native American followers of Jesus. Moreover, we contend that such dialogue would prove uniquely illuminating to the Spirit's role in uniting the past of God's creation with the future of a fully renewed, kincentric creation.

Critical voices on contemporary Native art have often employed the generative concept of kincentricity, and it plays a key role in understanding Native art's aesthetic integrity.[4] As a new term from the field of biological ecology, *kincentricity* has functioned more recently as a way to describe the kinship worldview reflected broadly among Indigenous communities.[5] While some may see such notions as a beautiful but abstract ideal, or a rather impersonal force operating in the world, dialogue with theological voices that share an Indigenous perspective could lead to a better appreciation and expansion of the deep wisdom of kincentricity. How might these ways of thinking and seeing the world mutually benefit each other? What can Native American testimony about the Holy Spirit offer to notions of kincentricity? And how might kincentricity expand or enlarge traditionally Western Christian understandings of the Holy Spirit?

National Gallery of Art, 2023). For greater context, see Robin Wall Kimmerer, *Braiding Sweetgrass: Indigenous Wisdom, Scientific Knowledge and the Teachings of Plants* (Minneapolis: Milkweed Editions, 2013), 7; Kaitlin B. Curtice, *Native: Identity, Belonging, and Rediscovering God* (Grand Rapids, MI: Brazos, 2020), 20-23.

[4]Besaw et al., *Art for a New Understanding*, 18-27; Jill Ahlberg Yohe, Teri Greeves, and Kaywin Feldman, *Hearts of Our People: Native Women Artists*, ed. Laura Silver (Minneapolis: Minneapolis Institute of Art with University of Washington Press, 2019). See also Kathleen E. Ash-Milby, ed., *Off the Map: Landscape in the Native Imagination* (Washington, DC: NMAI Editions, 2007); Sherry Farrell Racette, Candice Hopkins, Steve Loft, Lee-Ann Martin, and Jenny Western, *Close Encounters: The Next 500 Years* (Winnipeg: Plug In Editions, 2011); and Jeffrey Gibson, ed., *An Indigenous Present* (New York: BIG NDN, 2023).

[5]Enrique Salmón, "Kincentric Ecology: Indigenous Perceptions of the Human-Nature Relationship," *Ecological Applications* 10, no. 5 (2000): 1327-32; Deniss J. Martinez, Clare E. B. Cannon, Alex McInturff, Peter S. Alagona, and David N. Pellow, "Back to the Future: Indigenous Relationality, Kincentricity and the North American Model of Wildlife Management," *Environmental Science & Policy* 140 (2023): 202-7; Donald Trent Jacobs and Darcia Narváez, eds., *Restoring the Kinship Worldview: Indigenous Voices Introduce 28 Precepts for Rebalancing Life on Planet Earth* (Huichin, unceded Ohlone land aka Berkeley, California: North Atlantic Books, 2022).

In what follows, we explore such possibilities by first examining notions of kincentricity in conversation with the biblical notion of shalom. At the center of this exploration stands the living witness of one Native artist, Erin Shaw, and the embodiment of both Chickasaw heritage and Jesus' call to discipleship in her artistic practice. Because her art brings together these enduring threads of identity, Erin's testimony is set apart in the text and presented as a first-person report here. In doing so, we seek to weave together Erin's testimony with multiple witnesses of Native American experience on the role and work of the Holy Spirit as related to kincentricity. By drawing together these stories, we hope to show forth a harmonious path for Spirit theology and kincentricity.

Kincentricity and Shalom

What is kincentricity? Simply put, it is "the Indigenous concept of interconnectivity and relationships."[6] In her essay, "Sky as Place, Land as Body, Landscape as Spiritual Compass," ahtone writes, "Kincentricity describes the Indigenous perspective of the interdependency that exists between Indigenous people with animate and inanimate life forms and forces, including the clouds, rain, animals, plants, and earth."[7] As a concept, its scope and relevance for Native art cannot be overstated. It is vital, ahtone contends, for understanding what is happening with Indigenous art. Such vitality is aptly demonstrated in the decision by the organizers of the 2019 exhibition *Hearts of Our People: Native Women Artists* to make ahtone's use of kincentricity a guiding theme for the exhibition. They write, "In Native understandings of art, there is a relationship between all things and a recognition of reciprocity at all levels of being. Thus, Native American people have a dynamic relationship with art. . . . In this worldview, art is not static; it is alive. And it continues to interact with its community and loved ones over time."[8]

---

[6]Ahlberg Yohe, Greeves, and Feldman, *Hearts of Our People*, 20.

[7]heather ahtone, "Sky as Place, Land as Body, Landscape as Spiritual Compass," in Quick-to-See Smith et al., *Land Carries Our Ancestors*, 17.

[8]Ahlberg Yohe, Greeves, and Feldman, *Hearts of Our People*, 22.

This dynamism is further evidenced in the artist testimonials published in the catalog for *The Land Carries Our Ancestors*. For example, painter and sculptor Jeffrey Gibson (Mississippi Band of Choctaw Indians/Cherokee Nation), who became the first Indigenous artist to represent the United States at the Venice Biennale, describes his practice in terms of kincentricity:

> Indigenous kinship philosophies have provided the conceptual and philosophical framework for my work. These perspectives acknowledge the elements of our natural environments as our equal ancestors, living relatives, and extensions of our own minds and bodies. When we damage or treat the land without regard for its own sustainable well-being, we are in turn hurting and damaging ourselves and disregarding our own well-being, safety, and health.[9]

Similarly, Rose B. Simpson (Pueblo of Santa Clara, New Mexico) describes how the comprehensive scope of a kincentric worldview is actualized in her practice:

> My life-work is an investigation into what aesthetic tools I can create to heal the damages I have experienced as a human being of our postcolonial (postapocalyptic) era—objectification, stereotyping, and the disempowering detachment of our creative selves through the ease of modern technology. These tools are figurative and interactive sculptures that function in the psychological, emotional, social, cultural, spiritual, intellectual, and physical realms. They exist to witness, and they erode our objectifications. They remind us of the animate truth in all things—from our family of natural world beings to the consciousness in material. They reflect the movement of generations, the very verb of existence itself. The intention

[9]Quick-to-See Smith et al., *Land Carries Our Ancestors*, 72. Gibson offers a similar explanation of kincentricity's importance when introducing the artists included in his recent edited collection *An Indigenous Present*: "The land as material, as concept, as kin, as body and place, is central to many of the artworks in this book. We all have distinct creation stories, but a unifying theme is that we are born of the land, and all our relations are shared with the cosmos. This perspective, unique to the Indigenous and Native art world, is at the core of how we make objects that have the potential to negotiate space for ourselves, our communities, our spiritual practices, our collective past, and our future. This has always been the case with Indigenous creatives. We share a consciousness that prioritizes community over the individual and aims to create a better world than the one we have been born into" (48).

> of these tools is to cure, therefore, my hope is that they become hard-working utilitarian concepts.[10]

Such examples reflect an understanding of kincentricity as extending through space and time. Reflecting on Indigenous landscape art, ahtone explains, "We have understood through our genesis stories that we survive because the earth survives. We are connected to the moment of genesis through a continuum of creation. We are as close to the past as we are to the future. Our gratitude for this connection provides a path for our continued efforts to prepare for the future—and to understand the land is not ours to exhaust."[11] In these voices and so many others, then, kincentricity points to a theology of the utmost connectedness; such forms of thought are as needed as they are appealing. From our perspective as authors of this essay, kincentricity represents a particularly generative concept for the ongoing, still-incomplete efforts of contextualizing the Christian faith in the North American context and fostering a mutually beneficial exchange with Native theologies of the Holy Spirit.

Like these advocates for a kincentric worldview, Native American followers of Jesus also have to deal with the mostly disenchanted worldview of the modern West, which often places the so-called spiritual at odds with the physical world. As Terry and Jeanine LeBlanc (Mi'kmaq-Acadian) explain, many Christians today operate from a misguided starting point (i.e., the tree of the knowledge of good and evil in Gen 3 rather than the tree of life). They describe the effects of this disconnect thusly: "It is difficult to be holistically relational when what you see and describe in the creation around you is viewed largely or only through a tainted lens. Today that lens is often simultaneously individually egocentric and collectively ethnocentric—the challenge of the 'I' and the 'we.'"[12]

In its stead, they offer the Indigenous perspective as a potential theological corrective. In their words, "In parallel with the biblical narrative,

---

[10]Quick-to-See Smith et al., *Land Carries Our Ancestors*, 120.

[11]ahtone, "Sky as Place," 17-18.

[12]Terry LeBlanc and Jeanine LeBlanc, "Liberation: Self and Community in Relationship," in *Evangelical Theologies of Liberation and Justice*, ed. Mae Elise Cannon and Andrea Smith (Downers Grove, IL: IVP Academic, 2019), 185.

Indigenous creation stories make clear that human beings were intended for right relationship with their Creator and other spiritual powers, right relationship with one another, and right relationship and relatedness to the rest of creation, of which they are part."[13] Similarly, Martin Brokenleg (Rosebud Sioux) writes, "Indigenous people live in a world that is not separated into conceptual departments. We do not live in a world in which the spirit world is differentiated from the physical world. We do not have a dualism of the physical and spiritual."[14]

Echoing this perspective, Native theologian Randy Woodley acknowledges, "Traditionally, our Native Americans understand all creation to have spirit, soul, or life-force—what some would call panentheism."[15] However, as one of the most prominent voices on this topic, Woodley relates his understanding of the kincentric worldview of Indigenous peoples directly to the biblical concept of *shalom* (the Hebrew word for "peace"), and he encapsulates this understanding in what he calls "the harmony way."[16] In the biblical sense of the term, *shalom* describes a comprehensive, just, and flourishing picture of peace, and this picture connects almost seamlessly with the universal scope and ethical force of how the term *kincentricity* functions today. For instance, Woodley emphasizes, "Shalom is communal, holistic, and tangible. There is no private or partial shalom. The whole community must have shalom or no one has shalom."[17] Consider how Woodley arrived at this insight:

> As a result of the colonial enterprise, most indigenous communities are quite broken and fragmented. In one sense, we are like the "canary in the coal mine" for the Euro-western colonial experiment. Native Americans,

[13]LeBlanc and LeBlanc, "Liberation," 189-90.

[14]Martin Brokenleg, "Church—Wocekiye Okolakiciye: A Lakota Experience of the Church," in *Coming Full Circle: Constructing Native Christian Theology*, ed. Steve Charleston and Elaine A. Robinson (Minneapolis: Fortress, 2015), 147. See also Daniel R. Wildcat, "Just Creation: Enhancing Life in a World Full of Relatives," in *Buffalo Shout, Salmon Cry: Conversations on Creation, Land Justice, and Life Together*, ed. Steve Heinrichs (Waterloo, ON: Herald, 2013), 295-309.

[15]Randy Woodley, *Indigenous Theology and the Western Worldview: A Decolonized Approach to Christian Doctrine* (Grand Rapids, MI: Baker Academic, 2022), 65.

[16]Randy S. Woodley, "The Harmony Way: Integrating Indigenous Values Within Native North American Theology and Mission" (PhD diss., Asbury Theological Seminary, 2010).

[17]Randy Woodley, *Shalom and the Community of Creation: An Indigenous Vision* (Grand Rapids, MI: Eerdmans, 2012), 21. See also Randy Woodley, *Becoming Rooted* (Minneapolis: Fortress, 2022).

> like all of humanity, are in desperate need of living out a concept of healing and wholeness that includes a real partnership with creation. When I first studied shalom and the Native American Harmony Way, I wondered if these two concepts working in tandem could serve the purpose of restoration among our indigenous peoples. Later, I came to realize that the two constructs are essentially one and that all humanity has the same desperate need of healing, because God has designed us all to live in a world of shalom.[18]

In the same way, then, that notions of *kincentricity* invite our imaginations to picture a just and balanced connectedness throughout all of creation, so also the biblical concept of *shalom* suggests that the world began in a state of harmony and that all of creation longs for its restoration to harmony. In other words, just as the kincentric artworks of contemporary Native artists help to provoke a different story of the world's origins, the testimonies of Native American Christians also implore us to heed another story about creation's destiny in shalom. Contemporary artist Erin Shaw (Chickasaw) is one such voice, and what follows is a personal account of her experience as Native artist and follower of Jesus, which highlights particularly well the themes of this chapter.

INHABITING A KINCENTRIC PRACTICE: ERIN SHAW'S ARTWORK

In Chickasaw belief, the material is always connected to the spiritual. Creation is a doorway, always speaking. Knowing this has made all the difference for me as an artist, and at this point I couldn't step away from this way of seeing the world if I wanted to. I feel Creator's presence everywhere. There is no distinction between the material and spiritual worlds. The world we live in is connected on an intimate level, and I believe, as my ancestors did before me and have continued to teach me, that we are moving about in a sacred geography. I receive the miracle of life that is written into my DNA a hundred times a day. In my backyard, a pecan falls on my head as I am lying in the hammock, and I am reminded of the stories my ancestors told of how pecans sustained them. I am reminded of the times on my grandmother's

[18]Woodley, *Shalom and the Community*, 20.

farm where I gathered up pecans for her. I have a conversation with a stranger, and I notice the way their eyes light up over something and think I know that same delight. I am completely swept up into the miracle that I am living within dozens of times a day. I sincerely believe our lives can be lived in a sort of technicolor miraculousness just by spending time in creation. When we give it our attention, it does its work in us, reminding us how interconnected we are and of the true miracle of life. Creation is shouting to us. We just have to avail ourselves of it. The world is generous, inexplicably so. I feel Creator's presence everywhere because it is everywhere. When I am far from this understanding, all I need to do is fill my lungs with air and be reminded.

This idea that everything is interconnected demands some sort of expression in the work I do. I was born loving God and have followed Jesus my whole life. So that interconnectedness was some of the earliest truth of who I was, but because of my experience with the church and perhaps even more the legacy of colonization, I learned to separate, categorize, divide, label, and judge. Even in my early work, I was stuck in exploring the idea of duality. But now I want to create connection. It's always been about this for me, and I am just looking at it from a different angle today. I sometimes see myself imaginatively traveling

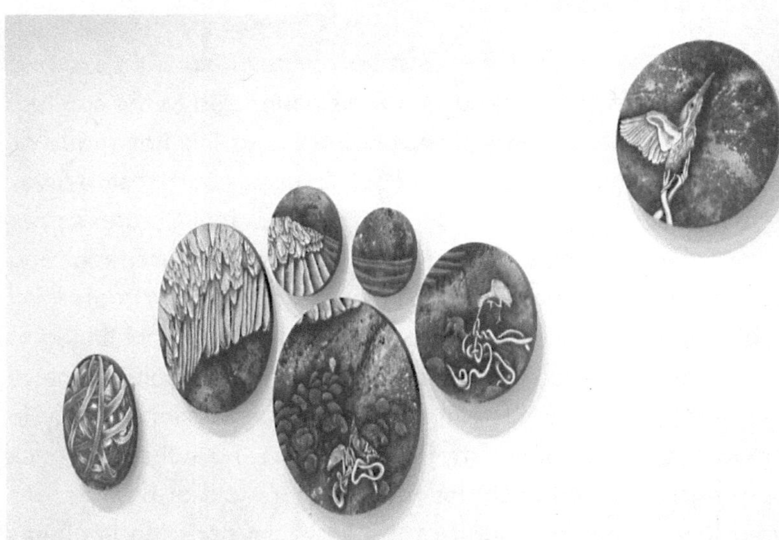

Figure 4.1. Beneath the Ancient Sea, acrylic on canvas, 2018

back to ancient times, gathering up stories and bringing them into my current context. Our ancient stories are vital, but it is not enough to merely retell these stories. We must actively participate with our stories and allow them to evolve, even as we do. This element of my work is vital as I investigate what it means to be a Chickasaw today and what it will mean for generations to come. Recently, my work has explored that interconnectedness more directly with the 2017 work Beneath the Ancient Sea.

In 2012, I made my first trip to the Chickasaw Homelands, located around Tupelo, Mississippi. We call it this because it is the original land from which my ancestors were removed and sent to what is now Oklahoma. This place has a different sense of home to me, and in my time there I have always felt a mysterious connection to my ancestors through the physicality of a place. On a tour with an anthropologist, we visited an area where the ground was covered with marine shells. As far as you could see—where there should have been grass or dirt—there were only shells. I didn't understand what I was seeing. The anthropologist explained that we were standing on what was once the floor of an ancient, shallow sea. The physicality of that place opened me to something mysterious, spiritual, and outside a linear understanding of time. I took a shell home with me and couldn't stop thinking about it. One day in the studio, I felt as if this story just came to me. I've come to think of it as a creation story, a dream about how certain birds came to be. I believe this story came to me, and yet it is not something you would read in a book or hear from an elder. I wondered whether it was okay for me to create something like this, and then talking about it with a dear friend, she told me, "If it is a story you tell, it is a Chickasaw story."

Beneath the Ancient Sea is made up of seven round panels, ranging in size from a four-foot circle to a twelve-inch circle (fig. 4.1). Beginning on the far left, the first circle is a tightly wound ball of thread. The thread has become a central visual element in my work. The thread has always represented my inner knowing, the way out and sometimes the way in. It's what connects me to the world around me, and many times it acts as the beginning of a story I am about to tell. The ball of thread contains what is hidden and what becomes seen as it unfurls. In the top panels, you see a large wing outstretched. The story told within the panels happens underneath the protection of this wing. The center panels are filled with shells, just like what I saw on my trip to the homelands. Across the surface of the shells, there are birds pulling threads from underneath the shells. I imagined these threads coming from deep within the earth. In Chickasaw cosmology, the world is layered. I saw the threads coming from deep within the earth, the unseen places. The birds are seen weaving these strands together, and in the final top panel, you see a kingfisher emerging. It is a snippet of a creation story, of how the kingfisher came to be.

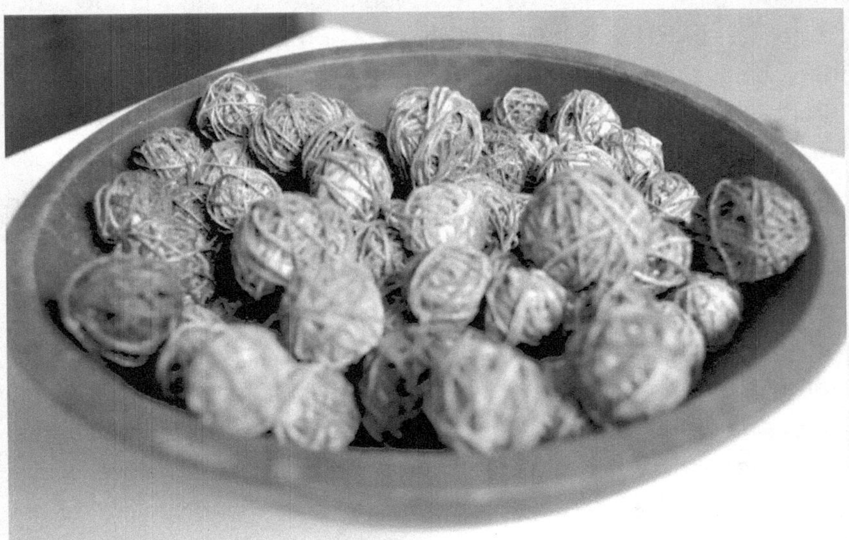

Figure 4.2. All My Sorrows, wound string and paper, 2020

The ball of thread has become a vital element in my work, a visual motif that I have returned to over and over. In some ways it articulates visually that connection between the material and the spiritual. It has a curious origin story of its own in my practice. I began by laying down string in wet canvas at some point. I never liked painting on a white canvas, and it was just something I started to do with no real understanding of why. These background images started to look like some sort of cartography to me, like a satellite image of a person's lived experience. When the paint would dry, I would pull up the string and wind it up. There were bundles and bundles of this string in my studio.

I walked past them regularly, not able to bring myself to throw them away. They kind of looked like little nests to me. During this time, I was experiencing a lot of loss in my personal life. It was painful and hard to understand. I felt like God was continually asking me to hold the pain in my hands and let it teach me what it would.

One day I walked into the studio and decided to make something out of the string. I really don't even know what I was doing, but I began to take these little scraps of paper and write one-word or one-phrase prayers on them. I took these prayers and wound the string tightly around each prayer. I was thinking about how most of our life is lived in this internal space of thoughts, emotions, and prayers and that most of that goes unseen by others. Yet, those prayers and longings and hopes amount to so much in so many mysterious ways. I made hundreds of these tightly wound little balls of string, as a physical or material emblem of an unspoken prayer. In this way, they continue to represent prayer and the relationship between what is seen and unseen. In this creative act, I was holding the pain in my hands, and it was teaching me. In just the same way that God asked me to hold the pain, God also asked me to open up my hands and let it go. As I let the pain go, all of these beautiful things began to be made manifest in my life and work. So, I began to depict those balls of strings over and over in my painting, and it has become a central part of my personal iconography ever since.

Creator's presence with my own work has gifted me with a new intuition. In so many ways, it feels like this is the basis for my practice. I had a trusted voice in graduate school observe how incredibly intuitive I am within my life. That intuition is probably the strongest gift I have, a connection to the inner reality of God in me. I don't know why, but I have always been in dialogue with this inner knowing and often feel like I am stumbling through life, being led but not understanding. This adviser remarked there was a serious demarcation in the way I lived my life from that space and the way I embodied my art practice. The advice was simple: make room for your intuition in your art practice. So simple, but it made a huge difference for me.

Getting in touch with that intuition and allowing it space within my creative practice has proven to be vital to my work as a visual storyteller. Because of our histories and the remarkable loss that exists within our communities, it can often feel difficult to find information, stories, data, research, and so on. I come to this place often within my research, and it is always a reminder of the pain and loss. One thing I have come to realize is that the closest, most accessible and reliable information or research I have access to is inside me. I have been Chickasaw every day of my life, and any story I tell is a Chickasaw story. My intuition has made room for the stories I carry inside me. Some of those stories are in the process of being written; some of them are ancient. So, my work is very much the manifestation of my belief that I am caught up in this terribly interconnected, holistic weaving together of every time and place, person and plant, animal and thing that has ever lived. Perhaps this is what I am being brought home to, that we are all connected. But I don't believe the colonizers understood this. They didn't understand that when they brought harm to those they encountered in North America, they were also bringing harm to themselves. And so maybe this recognition is the greatest of gifts that American Indian lifeways could offer the North American church.

Harmony with the Creator's Spirit

As we see in the example of Erin's art practice, the intentional collaboration between a thoroughly Indigenous view of the world (kincentricity) and a remarkable Christian hope (shalom) brings freedom, balance, and belonging for the artist, as well as new forms of creativity in expression and storytelling through artwork. Such generative collaborations, it seems, could be multiplied by a greater commitment to unite the past of God's creation with the future of a fully renewed creation, and the Holy Spirit remains indispensable for making this enriching connection. We wish in the following section to elucidate the relationship of kincentricity to the Holy Spirit, more specifically to the Spirit of shalom.

Creation and the Spirit of shalom. The Holy Spirit plays an integral role in establishing the kincentric origins of creation. For instance, Woodley's harmony way is so named for the ontological harmony within the trinitarian community of God's own self and the metaphysically nondualistic nature of the world God has made. As he explains, "While Native

North Americans do have room in their worldview for Trinity, and sometimes even with direct historic evidence of a trinitarian understanding of God, this understanding has been overlooked because of categorical differences."[19] In particular, Woodley points to the presence of explicitly trinitarian frameworks in multiple Native American traditions.[20] Thus, from reflection on precontact notions of Trinity, Woodley seeks to build a picture of God that is more representative of the Indigenous worldview: "In the trinitarian model, God is community, which may also reflect the divine sense of community in all creation; in other words, community is innate to, and created by, the community of the Creator."[21] But, crucially, Woodley highlights the Holy Spirit when looking for ways that Western theology and Indigenous theology might complement each other here: "Perhaps there's a lot of commonality between our understandings of Spirit, or Holy Spirit."[22] Woodley suggests the following as a possible connection between the two:

> I understand the Trinity as a Community of Creator. I don't just talk about Trinity because the creeds say *Trinity*. I think about starting with creation

[19]Randy Woodley, "Beyond 'Homoiousios' and 'Homoousios,'" in *The Trinity Among the Nations: The Doctrine of God in the Majority World*, ed. Gene L. Green, Stephen T. Pardue, and Khiok-Khng Yeo (Grand Rapids, MI: Eerdmans, 2015), 45.

[20]For instance, striking similarities emerge from the following examples: Cherokee tradition tells of a divine group of three with the names *Uhahetaqua*, *Atanati*, and *Usquahala*, who are also called "Creators," "Masters of Life," and "Givers of Breath" (Woodley, "Beyond 'Homoiousios' and 'Homoousios,'" 47, 49). Chickasaw tradition, as reported by John Wesley, no less, involves a divine group of three: "We believe there are two with him [One that lives in the clear sky], three in all" (48). Saponi tradition includes what Woodley describes as a "Creator within a communal theistic structure" (49). Cree tradition involves what Woodley describes as the "worship of a Supreme being, yet with three manifestations of power, including Manitou, Thunderbird, and Bear" (49-50). Similarly, Rosemary McCombs Maxey explains, "In the Muscogee (Creek) language, the name of the creator-spirit deity is *Hesaketvmese*, that is 'Breath-Holder.' Other meanings include Creator (earth), Sustainer (air), Redeemer (water), Intervener (unexpected events), Lover, Intimate Confidant, and Fun-Loving Friend (gentle breezes and small whirlwinds). The deity is accessible and present throughout the entire cosmos." Such insights lead her to reflect, "Indigenous peoples call for the recognition of the Breath Holder who through the act of creation permeates all life forms. . . . All of creation is sacred." Maxey, "Who Can Sit at the Lord's Table? The Experience of Indigenous Peoples," in *Native and Christian: Indigenous Voices on Religious Identity in the United States and Canada*, ed. James Treat (New York: Routledge, 1996), 45.

[21]Woodley, "Beyond 'Homoiousios' and 'Homoousios,'" 53.

[22]Woodley, *Indigenous Theology and the Western Worldview*, 77-78. He continues, "But when the comparison becomes positional, versus a relational, trinitarian view, then I think there is trouble reconciling the two."

> and asking, What are God's fingerprints on all of creation? . . . So, I'm starting on the earth and I'm going back and understanding shalom as Jesus's mission. And so then, for me, the Trinity—if we want to use the terms *Father, Son, Holy Spirit,* that's fine—are perfect shalom and live in perfect harmony preferring and deferring to one another.[23]

Thus, Woodley emphasizes the Spirit's relationship to creation, which began with the Spirit's work to give birth to the world and initiate shalom: "From God's purview there is an interconnectedness of all God has made. All things are designed and created beautifully by their Creator." The relationship reached its salvific climax with the embodiment of shalom in the life and ministry of Jesus: "Jesus lived out a shalom life, pleasing to God, being led by the Holy Spirit and in communion with God." Jesus operated with a "creation-centered" worldview and invited his followers to participate in his life of making shalom. So, Woodley also emphasizes, "There is no place we can go where Jesus is not *already* present and active."[24] At this point, we can presume that the unity of divine presence that is so fundamental to his theological outlook means that the Spirit is also present in every place. We might speculate that Woodley would permit that it is through the agency of the Holy Spirit that Jesus is also able to be present in every place. Such a holistic picture of divine presence thus anticipates a holistic restoration of creation.

---

[23]Woodley, *Indigenous Theology and the Western Worldview*, 86-87. Such a reconciliatory picture is confirmed by Steven Charleston (Choctaw) in *The Four Vision Quests of Jesus*. In the final vision quest of the cross, Jesus' death, as Charleston explains, "restored the most essential aspect of creation: kinship." Charleston elaborates: "In the person of Jesus, all of humanity is drawn together. The sacred balance is perfected. What has been out of balance in our relationships in the past now has a chance of returning to a holy equilibrium." Steven Charleston, *The Four Vision Quests of Jesus* (New York: Morehouse, 2015), 158, 155. Such restored harmony, then, is maintained by the connection between creation and Spirit, for as George Tinker (Osage) explains, "We will discover that respect for creation can become the spiritual and theological basis for justice and peace just as it is the spiritual and theological basis for God's reconciling act in Christ Jesus and the ongoing life of sanctification in the Holy Spirit." George E. Tinker, *American Indian Liberation: A Theology of Sovereignty* (Maryknoll, NY: Orbis Books, 2008), 39.

[24]Woodley, *Shalom and the Community*, 41-42, 32, 47, 108. Woodley begins his ten-point enumeration of the values within the harmony way in this way: (1) "The earth and everything on it is sacred. '*Respect everyone. Everything is sacred*,'" and ends with (10) "Natural connectedness to all creation . . . '*We are all related*.'" See also Woodley, *Indigenous Theology and the Western Worldview*, 92-94.

New creation and the Spirit of shalom. While there is much in Native Christian reflection to commend a connection between creation and the Holy Spirit, it appears that there is less in terms of new creation. Thus, those working from Western theological paradigms will likely be surprised to find that it is immensely difficult to discern a discrete theology of the Spirit from Indigenous theological sources. Along with the sheer diversity of Native Christian perspectives, there are multiple names and descriptions of the Spirit's role that do not conform to the traditional scripts found in Western paradigms. In other words, it seems that Indigenous understandings of the Spirit operate in a more embedded and implicit way than Western theology might expect. Admittedly, the fabric of Indigenous belief and practice is woven so tightly that the strength of Native reliance on the Spirit becomes almost invisible to Western eyes.[25] This condition is no doubt due to the priority given in these exchanges to the account of origins and the character of creation. Indigenous theologies, in fact, impart a picture of the Spirit supporting an intricate web of placemaking beliefs and practices aimed at a restored harmony between Creator, community, and land.

Therefore, we must listen carefully to the hope and dreams that these Native Christian voices raise in anticipation of what the Spirit will do. Perhaps there is no better voice among them than Episcopal priest and theologian Steven Charleston (Choctaw), as reflected in his 2023 collection of prayers and meditations *Spirit Wheel.* In part two of the

[25]Take, for instance, the way that the Spirit is characterized in the recent set of devotional publications from Steven Charleston (Choctaw), a ministry leader who describes himself as a "listener" to "the Spirit's messages." He approaches the matter of identifying the Spirit obliquely and without prioritizing precise theological definition. In his own words, he states up front: "The Spirit I refer to can represent the Holy Spirit of Christians, the Great Spirit of traditional Native American wisdom, or the Buddha-nature in all living beings. For some, the Spirit may signify the underlying force that binds all life together, like the Tao. It can be understood as God or Allah by Jews and Muslims. It can embody Brahman for Hindus. It can be the collective human spirit for humanists." He sets forth this approach as someone who has also served as the Episcopal bishop of Alaska, president and dean of the Episcopal Divinity School, and professor at Luther Seminary. And yet, he shares his rationale for doing so: "I intentionally leave the interpretation open because my messages are not dogmatic—that is, they do not demand conformity to any one system of belief." Steven Charleston, *Ladder to the Light: An Indigenous Elder's Meditations on Hope and Courage* (Minneapolis: Broadleaf Books, 2021), 5, 10. See also Steven Charleston, *Spirit Wheel: Meditations from an Indigenous Elder* (Minneapolis: Broadleaf Books, 2023), 10.

collection "Kinship with Creation," Charleston acknowledges the power of kinship when he prays:

> In the great family of Spirit
>
> The spirals of kinship
>
> Weave us all into relationship
>
> Mutual, caring, connected.
>
> Since all that Spirit does is done in love
>
> All that Spirit created was created in love.
>
> There are no orphans left standing alone
>
> For all are embraced by the compassion
>
> Of a common Creator.[26]

Not surprisingly, these words name so well the hopeful consolation that so many are seeking. On the same theme, with a meditation titled "Come Stand Here," Charleston again anticipates a time in which kinship will characterize all of creation once more, praying:

> All of you who are frightened and confused,
>
> Come stand here.
>
> Here on the high ground of reason
>
> Here on the rock of faith unshaken
>
> Here where you can see tomorrow
>
> . . .
>
> Come stand here, in freedom and love
>
> And together we will build the sanctuary
>
> For which so many have longed and so many have prayed.[27]

---

[26]Charleston, *Spirit Wheel*, 90.
[27]Charleston, *Spirit Wheel*, 122-23.

The sense of anticipation for what the Spirit alone can do is certainly palpable, if not exactly spelled out. Along these lines, we can perhaps see the witness of Native Christian thinkers as sympathetic to accounts of the Holy Spirit as the "perfecting Spirit" or the "Spirit of new creation," drawn from the insights of fourth-century Christian bishop Basil of Caesarea.[28] Pneumatological contributions in this vein, then, emphasize the Spirit's work of leading the mission of God to its fullest completion in shalom. For instance, in *God the Peacemaker: How Atonement Brings Shalom,* Graham Cole singles out the Spirit's unique role: "In this view, the Holy Spirit for example uses our evangelism, witness, apology, shalom-making and mercy-showing (the list is not exhaustive but is indicative) to bring to fruition the divine plan."[29] Drawing from the same well, Steven Guthrie offers a similar affirmation but includes a decidedly aesthetic dimension: "It is right to speak of the new creation and the eschatological work of the Spirit as 'beautifying' if by this beauty we mean the perfection of *integritas* [suggesting wholeness and completeness]. The work of the Holy Spirit is to perfect the creation by bringing it to completion, making humanity and each created thing what it most truly and fully is."[30] In these words, we find an ache of hopefulness that is deeply resonant with the Indigenous value of kincentricity.

Like in the experience of Erin's art practice, the testimony of numerous Native American leaders and theologians affirms the role of kincentricity in the Creator's world. It parallels how Native American

---

[28]Basil writes: "Through Him [the Holy Spirit] hearts are lifted up, the infirm are held by the hand, and those who progress are brought to perfection. He shines upon those who are cleansed from every spot, and makes them spiritual men through fellowship with Himself. When a sunbeam falls on a transparent substance, the substance itself becomes brilliant, and radiates light from itself. So too Spirit-bearing souls, illumined by Him, finally become spiritual themselves, and their grace is sent forth to others. From this comes knowledge of the future, understanding of mysteries, apprehension of hidden things, distribution of wonderful gifts, heavenly citizenship, a place in the choir of angels, endless joy in the presence of God, becoming like God, and, the highest of all desires, becoming God. These are only a few of the many things we have been taught concerning the greatness, dignity, and working of the Holy Spirit, and we have learned them from the Spirit's own words." Basil, *On the Holy Spirit*, trans. David Anderson (Crestwood, NY: St Vladimir's Seminary Press, 1980), 44.

[29]Graham A. Cole, *God the Peacemaker: How Atonement Brings Shalom* (Downers Grove, IL: InterVarsity Press, 2009), 216.

[30]Steven R. Guthrie, *Creator Spirit: The Holy Spirit and the Art of Becoming Human* (Grand Rapids, MI: Baker Academic, 2011), 200.

followers of Jesus understand the world as made and redeemed by the Creator. In other words, kincentricity as a concept speaks to both the design and the destiny of our world. At the same time, their testimony to the role of the Holy Spirit in the Creator's redemptive mission can invest the idea of kincentricity with a fuller sense of empowerment, agency, and—most importantly—a *telos* or an end. In this way, kincentricity is safeguarded from being seen as an impersonal force or merely an abstract ideal and instead is given a personal name, the name of God's Spirit—the Spirit of shalom.

Conclusion: Works of the Spirit

Many challenges remain and threaten the possibilities of a mutually beneficial dialogue around important concepts such as kincentricity. It does not seem that things are moving in a healthy or reconciliatory direction, and the implications for all followers of Jesus on North American land remain serious. In recent days, such challenges are emerging from unfortunate cases of Christian leaders attempting to force Indigenous followers of Jesus to choose between their faith and their culture.[31] In reflecting on a Christian school's threat to expel his daughter over her participation in one of her people's traditional ceremonies, Chester Colelay (White Mountain Apache) expresses his inability to choose between his Christian faith and his Native heritage this way:

> We tell our stories to our kids. We want them to feel it, see it, live it, and be part of it. . . . When the Spirit gets to you, you can either be at the river, on top of the mountain, praying in front of your house, inside a church, it could be at a Sunrise ceremony. Wherever the spirit catches you is where you belong. That's where God is at. God is not just in church. God is everywhere.[32]

---

[31]Nicolle Okoren, "They Took Part in Apache Ceremonies. Their Schools Expelled Them for Satanic Activities," *The Guardian*, June 24, 2024, www.theguardian.com/us-news/ng-interactive/2024/jun/24/apache-students-school-reservation. See also Deepa Bharath, "Apache Christ Icon Controversy Sparks Debate over Indigenous Catholic Faith Practices," Associated Press, July 27, 2024, https://apnews.com/article/new-mexico-apache-christ-painting-catholic-controversy-5e8c0331dabb1a80b36b08c7327601f1.

[32]Quoted in Okoren, "They Took Part."

In the face of such challenges, we have to ask ourselves, Why? Why does the North American church resist the Indigenous contextualization of the gospel? In doing so, does it resist the work of the Holy Spirit? Such warnings cannot be fully explicated here, but in closing, we offer the following cautionary thoughts and questions.

If we listen to Indigenous elders, a deeply troubling picture of the church emerges, one that should elicit deep conviction. For instance, in his 1916 autobiography *From the Deep Woods to Civilization,* Charles Alexander Eastman (Ohiyesa) recounts the process of indoctrination and assimilation into Anglo-American life at the age of fifteen, his advanced education at Dartmouth College and Boston University, and his service as physician at the Pine Ridge Agency, where he witnessed the events that culminated in the Wounded Knee massacre of 1890.[33] Under the heading "The Soul of the White Man," Eastman offers his time-worn reflections on the curious character of American Christianity:

> From the time I first accepted the Christ ideal it has grown upon me steadily, but I also see more and more plainly our modern divergence from that ideal. I confess I have wondered much that Christianity is not practised by the very people who vouch for that wonderful conception of exemplary living. It appears that they are anxious to pass on their religion to all races of men, but keep very little of it themselves. I have not yet seen the meek inherit the earth, or the peacemakers receive high honor.[34]

Many years after Eastman, another Indigenous intellectual echoed that critique with stinging words of his own. In his widely influential volume *God Is Red,* activist, historian, and theologian of Native religion Vine Deloria Jr. writes, "American Christianity in particular appears to be a willing captive of American culture."[35] Such indictments are not easily escaped, especially as the evidence against the American church seems to be mounting. In particular, the words of Eastman and Deloria show us once more that in many ways Christianity's ability to be contextualized at

[33]Charles A. Eastman, *From the Deep Woods to Civilization: Chapters in the Autobiography of an Indian* (Lincoln: University of Nebraska Press, 1977).

[34]Eastman, *From the Deep Woods*, 193-94.

[35]Vine Deloria Jr., *God Is Red: A Native View of Religion*, 3rd ed. (Golden, CO: Fulcrum, 2003), 219.

various times and in diverse places is its great strength. At the same time, however, it can be a weakness, if through encounters with new peoples and cultures Christians choose to hold too tightly to their own cultural expressions and resist any adaptations. Such moments serve to calcify the living faith and limit its reach. For this reason, it is all the more important to appreciate the embodied witness of artists such as Erin who remain unashamedly Native and unashamedly following Jesus, because it is in these very spaces of artistic creativity that we see the reconciling efforts of the Spirit at work to give us glimpses of God's new creation.

According to Erin, if you ask Native folks what they believe, they will show you what they do. Belief and action are intertwined. Echoing a typically Orthodox or Jewish mindset, belief for Native believers is not something you hold in your mind—belief is how you live your life; it's what you do. Jesus himself says, in Matthew 7:16, "You will know them by their fruit." As we have seen thus far, in the testimony of Native leaders such as Randy Woodley and with Erin's *Beneath the Ancient Sea,* Indigenous followers of Jesus seek to bear the fruits of harmony and unity because they believe that the Creator longs for all of creation to live out its connectedness in Jesus. Such are the works of the Spirit that these sisters and brothers labor for. By the same token, then, we must wonder whether the North American church also seeks these fruits of connection. How long must we wait for the North American church to remember what our Lord prayed on our behalf in John 17:20-21: "I pray that all who walk with me will be joined together as one, in the same way that you, Father, are in me and I am in you—that they may be one in us"?[36]

[36]Terry Wildman, *First Nations Version: An Indigenous Translation of the New Testament* (Downers Grove, IL: InterVarsity Press, 2021), 201.

5

THE SPIRIT AS BREATH

POETIC IMAGINATION AND THE WORD-BEARING BREATH

Devon Abts and Joelle A. Hathaway

"ERIC GARNER WAS LUMBERING along a sidewalk on Staten Island on a July day when an unmarked police car pulled up." These words form the opening sentence of a June 13, 2015, article published in *the New York Times* titled, "Beyond the Chokehold: The Path to Eric Garner's Death." The article offers an in-depth exploration of events leading up to the brutal murder of an unarmed Black man at the hands of police officers in the New York borough of Staten Island eleven months prior.[1] At the time of publication, readers would have been familiar with the story of Garner's homicide: the entire incident had been captured on film, and footage had been widely circulated on social media and news networks. Viewers around the world had watched in horror as a police officer attempting to arrest the forty-three-year-old placed him in an illegal chokehold and crushed his head into the sidewalk as Garner gasped, "I can't breathe" eleven times before losing consciousness. Paramedics were slow to arrive and failed to act swiftly at the scene; meanwhile, the officers made no meaningful effort to resuscitate or aid Garner as he lay dying on the ground.

Garner's final moments were marked by unspeakable violence and utter dehumanization; yet the media conversation that unfolded in the

[1] Al Baker, J. David Goodman, and Benjamin Mueller, "Beyond the Chokehold: The Path to Eric Garner's Death," *New York Times*, June 13, 2015, www.nytimes.com/2015/06/14/nyregion/eric-garner-police-chokehold-staten-island.html.

wake of his murder was far from sympathetic. Indeed, a 2019 study of the media's response to this event concluded that "the true cause of Garner's death was subverted by a dominant, false narrative," which served to further dehumanize a victim of police brutality while simultaneously minimizing the culpability of the officers responsible for his death. The medical examiner's report listed Garner's cause of death in unambiguous terms: "homicide." Underlying health issues were listed as "contributing conditions," but these did not directly cause his death. However, according to the study, "stigmatizing and coded language" permeated the national discourse in the wake of Garner's murder, "reducing him to his conditions of obesity and asthma, blaming those conditions, and thus Garner himself, for his own death." Many in the media also relied on racially charged stereotypes to present Garner as an absentee father and criminal whose record of arrests and refusal to submit to police harassment "made him a criminal, complicit in his own death." Even his grieving family was stigmatized, presented in the media as "unworthy poor" who sought to capitalize on Garner's death at the expense of New York City taxpayers.[2]

In view of all this, the opening description in the *New York Times* article—of Garner as a "lumbering" figure, drifting "along a sidewalk" in the middle of the day, seemingly without purpose—can be read as the coded language of stigma and stereotype. At the very least, the tone is demeaning and degrading. At worst, this description reinforces a toxic and misleading portrait of those who are poor, Black, and/or disabled as a menace to the social order and thus deserving (at least on some level) to be harassed by police, perhaps even deserving to be denied access to breath.

Written the same year as the *New York Times* article, Ross Gay's poem "A Small Needful Fact" offers an alternative vision of Garner's life that reframes the narrative to restore dignity that has been lost. This astonishing poem packs immense insight and pathos into fifteen short lines,

[2]Lydia P. Ogden, Anjali J. Fulambarker, and Christina Haggerty, "Race and Disability in Media Coverage of the Police Homicide of Eric Garner," *Journal of Social Work Education* 56, no. 4 (October 2019): 654-56.

flowing in a single sentence from the title. Written in this way, the poem extends an invitation to read it in full with one breath; yet to do so will necessarily leave a reader breathless. Either way, in parsing the poem line by line, we will see how Gay's lyric forces the reader to slow down and pay attention to the particularities of breath as the vitalizing energy of poetic form. This in turn will lay the foundation for a theological reflection on the Spirit as giver of breath—and, crucially, the way human speech participates in the creative action of Word and Spirit.

"A Small Needful Fact": Reimagining Garner and Relationality

Instead of presenting Garner as a dehumanized object whose entire identity is bound up with his violent and degrading death, Gay invites his reader to encounter him in a different light:

> A Small Needful Fact
>
> Is that Eric Garner worked
>
> for some time for the Parks and Rec.
>
> Horticultural Department, which means,
>
> perhaps, that with his very large hands,
>
> perhaps, in all likelihood,
>
> he put gently into the earth
>
> some plants which, most likely,
>
> some of them, in all likelihood,
>
> continue to grow, continue
>
> to do what such plants do, like house
>
> and feed small and necessary creatures,
>
> like being pleasant to touch and smell,
>
> like converting sunlight

into food, like making it easier

for us to breathe.[3]

We may start with the poem's title: "A Small Needful Fact" announces the scope and significance of Gay's intended theme. The poem, he tells us, is concerned with a single, minute detail that nevertheless carries the full weight of an untold truth; as "fact," this detail is concerned with dispelling falsehoods. The choice of *needful* over *necessary* may be more than rhythmic, for *needful* conveys a sense not only of necessity but also of an as-yet-unmet need. There is a side of Garner's story that has yet to be told, that needs to be communicated as an alternative to the disingenuous and cynical account that has come to dominate the public sphere.

Moving into the main body of the poem, we immediately notice that the first line continues seamlessly from the title: the entire poem is composed as a single sentence. The expected space between title and opening line has been eliminated, forcing the reader to carry on reading without pausing for a full breath. The "small needful fact" signaled in the title is in its simplest sense "that Eric Garner *worked*." The subtle pause indicated by the break after *worked* creates a space where readers are invited to breathe in the final word of the line and recognize it as a subversive counternarrative to the portrait of Garner as an unemployed miscreant who spent his entire life selling illegal cigarettes to earn an illicit income. The poet reminds us that "for some time" Garner held a position in a highly respected branch of local government dedicated to cultivating and sustaining life for the benefit of a community.

Having plainly stated the "small needful fact" that inspires his poem, Gay next proceeds to a series of more speculative thoughts based on the revelation that Garner "worked / for some time for the Parks and Rec. / Horticultural Department." It is worth noting the way that lines 4-8 enact what poet Geoffrey Hill describes as "return[s] upon the self," staging a performance of self-questioning that prevents the poet's narrative from completely settling.[4] Unlike the media narrative, which deals in the

---

[3]Ross Gay, "A Small Needful Fact," in *The Quarry: A Social Justice Poetry Database*, 2015, www.splitthisrock.org/poetry-database/poem/a-small-needful-fact.

[4]Geoffrey Hill, "Redeeming the Time," in *The Collected Critical Writings of Geoffrey Hill* (London: Oxford University Press, 2009), 88-108.

reductive language of stereotypes, Gay's poem opens up new imaginative possibilities for the reader. When the poem is recited out loud, these turns and returns act on the reader's breath in sophisticated and provocative ways. Interjections of "perhaps," "in all likelihood," and "most likely," along with qualifiers such as "*some* time" and "*some* plants," press the language of Gay's proposed alternative narrative to the breaking point, thereby forcing the reader to slow down and attend with great care. The poem literally opens a breathing space even as the space to breathe between words is nearly obliterated.

As an avid gardener himself, Gay is compelled by the image of Garner as one who was responsible for handling and caring for plants. Here again, the poet's imagery is deeply subversive. Garner's "large hands"—which became a dog whistle in mainstream discourse, conjuring images of an enormous figure whose very presence posed an imminent threat to the officers who sought to arrest him—are transformed into an emblem of tending and of tenderness. Gay imagines Garner's putting his big hands "gently into the earth" in order to nestle plants into a space where they might root and grow.

Line 9 marks a pivot for the poem as the focus shifts from constructing an alternative story for Garner to considering how we, as readers, might still—perhaps, in all likelihood—share a connection with him through the plants that "continue to grow" after his brutal end. In asking us to imagine some of the plants Garner may have handled, as well as the possibility that some may even have endured beyond his own lifespan, the poet invites us to imagine his legacy in new, life-giving terms. Such a shift requires a new rhythm, and thus the self-stultifying returns of the first half of the poem are abandoned in favor of a more fluid cadence.

A new narrative reveals new connections, which come into sharp focus in the latter half of the poem as Gay shifts focus from rewriting the story of Garner's death to meditating directly on the life-giving legacy of his horticultural work. Gay thus imagines the plants Garner may have cultivated as existing in a vital ecosystem, providing food and shelter for "small and necessary creatures"—beings we can easily fail to notice, yet who share the same air we breathe and on whom we depend for our continued survival.

One cannot help but remember, too, that Garner himself was a father to six children, including a three-month-old infant, at the time of his death.

But of course, plants do more than provide for the physical needs of creatures. They also make our world more beautiful by "being pleasant to touch and smell." Theologically minded readers may recognize in this line something of the gratuity of divine bestowal in the more-than-functional beauty of created things. There is also a touch of the miraculous in the reminder that plants are capable of "converting sunlight" into nutrients.

Of course, these are all traits of plants, but the underlying implication of these lines is that Garner himself played a small but necessary (perhaps even "needful") part in an ecology where each created being is called on to protect and preserve the inherent sanctity of all life forms. Hence, the poem ends by transfiguring the final words Garner uttered in the moments before his death. Rather than a suffocating victim crying out for breath, Garner is powerfully reimagined as a nurturer who made it "easier / for us to breathe." In this line, Gay reminds his reader that Garner not only nurtured life for the "small and necessary creatures" that human beings so often overlook; he also played a part in bestowing life to all humanity—perhaps, in all likelihood, even those who would so callously rob Garner of his own breath.

The final seven lines of the poem form a catalog, propelled on the breath by repetitions of the word *like* at the start of each item in the list of things plants "do." Crucially, the structure of these lines is such that each *like* conditions the verb *continue*, so that readers are invited to imagine the plants Garner laid in the earth as *continuing* to house small and necessary creatures, *continuing* to be pleasant to touch and smell, and so on. These lines therefore underscore the poignant loss to humanity in the wake of Garner's murder, while simultaneously speaking to the hope of connection even after death by way of his horticultural work.

When the reader arrives at the final word—*breathe*—she is invited to inhale deeply and, in so doing, to participate in a new and invigorating ecology of breath. Since the entire poem is written as a single sentence, the reader is carried forward by a propulsion of breath that grows in energy as the poem unfolds: from the breathless transition between title and opening line, through the interpolated imaginings in the first half of the poem, to the smoother cadences in the final lines. It is only upon reaching this climactic line that momentum breaks and the reader is able to fully take stock of various changes to her own breathing patterns. The poem thereby enacts the imaginative transformation it seeks to instantiate within the reader, and it does so formally at the level of breath.

There is a deep theological poignancy in the poet's gift to his reader, which in turn is made possible by the gifts that Eric Garner himself bestowed on the world. No longer a disempowered victim of police brutality, Garner becomes a literal *steward of breath* whose work as a horticulturalist continues to bear on the world in vitalizing ways. Moreover, what begins as a point of inspiration for the poet opens new imaginative possibilities for the reader. In what follows, we will consider how this aspiration to renew our breath, when pursued in the power of the Spirit, produces an occasion for cooperation with the Word in form and substance.

The Holy Spirit as Breath and Breath Giver

The second half of "A Small Needful Fact" invites us to consider the connections between our breath and Garner's. This poem is not intentionally religious, and yet it is thoroughly theological: to talk about breath and life is always to talk about the action of the Holy Spirit. For Christians, the breath we breathe is our physical breath and is at the very same time the breath of life breathed into us by the life-giving Spirit of Christ sent from the Father. Acknowledging the Spirit as the giver and sustainer of breath has serious implications for Christian anthropology and Christian ethics in an age when the phrase "I can't breathe" has become a rallying cry for those who have been denied access to the Spirit's gift through the violence of systemic racism.

Numerous theologians and biblical scholars in recent years have highlighted how in the Scriptures *rûaḥ* (Hebrew), as well as its translations *pneuma* (Greek) and *spiritus* (Latin), can be variously translated as "breath," "wind," "spirit," and "Spirit." Old Testament scholar Jack Levison notes that *rûaḥ* occurs 378 times in Hebrew and 11 times in Aramaic in the Jewish Scriptures. While mere numbers should not be equated with importance, the overwhelming proportion of *rûaḥ* to other theologically significant scriptural themes should cause us to take notice. Compare these 389 occurrences with the frequency of other key words: *blessing* (71 times), *Sabbath* (111 times), *glory* (200 times), *Torah* or *teaching* (223 times), *shalom* or *peace* (237 times), and *covenant* (287 times).[5]

Nearly a third of these 389 occurrences likely refer to the wind, such as Psalm 1:4, where the wicked are like chaff that the wind drives away.[6] Yet in the world of the Scriptures, where the entire creation is sustained by and subject to God, we should not be so quick to separate these various meanings. Indeed, many texts in both the First and Second Testaments turn on the generous ambiguity of *rûaḥ* and *pneuma*, of the movement or agency of God's Spirit-Breath-Wind in God's creation and on behalf of God's people. English, for example, is not able to hold the full weight of the rich of associations of *rûaḥ* and *pneuma*, or to easily exhibit the play on words in texts such as John 3:5-8:

> Very truly, I tell you, no one can enter the kingdom of God without being born of water and Spirit [*pneuma*]. What is born of flesh is flesh, and what is born of the Spirit [*pneuma*] is spirit [*pneuma*]. Do not be astonished that I say to you, "You must be born from above." The wind [*pneuma*] blows where it chooses, and you hear the sound of it, but you do not know where it comes from or where it goes. So it is with everyone who is born of the Spirit [*pneuma*]. (NRSV)

In this text like gives birth to like, *pneuma* gives birth to *pneuma*. Yet this is a *pneuma* on the move, invisible yet active, powerful yet mysterious. The various senses of *pneuma* resonate with one another here, the divine Spirit, the human spirit or the spiritual renewal of the person, and the wildness and uncontainable power of the wind. Even the sense of breath is implied, for breath is necessary from the moment of birth. New life in Christ includes a fresh bestowal or breath of the Spirit.

This harks back, of course, to the earthling's initial bestowal of breath-Spirit in Genesis 2:7, "Then the Lord God formed *ʾādām* from *ʾădāmâ*,

---

[5]Jack Levison, *A Boundless God: The Spirit According to the Old Testament* (Grand Rapids, MI: Baker Academic, 2020), 1.

[6]Levison, *Boundless God*, 19.

and breathed into his nostrils the breath of life; and the *ʾādām* became a living being." The arithmetic, Norman Wirzba reminds us, is not body + soul = human being, as if the body were an envelope for the spirit.[7] It is instead dust + *rûaḥ* of life = a living being or living soul.[8] Echoing the *rûaḥ* "hovering" or "sweeping" over the primordial deep in Genesis 1:2, the actions of the Spirit-Breath-Wind of God again bring forth life.

In the Scriptures, therefore, there is no tidy or definitive way to determine whether the language is referring to divine Spirit, divine breath, or divine wind, or natural wind, human spirit, or human breath. Indeed, as in John 3:5-8, the biblical authors often trade on this ambiguity in their artful employment of the term and encourage us to hear the multiple relational resonances, even if readers are fairly sure which reading is intended. The Spirit-Breath-Wind of God brings both life and new life, bodily breath and a transformed spirit.

These multiple senses of *rûaḥ* and *pneuma* remind us that "the spirit of salvation is the spirit of creation, the *spiritus sanctificans* is the *spiritus vivificans*."[9] There is only one Spirit: the Spirit of Christ from the Father, who gives breath to our mortal bodies, is the same Spirit who is bringing new life "from above." The one in whom the whole creation is being renewed and restored is the one in whom it was created at the beginning and by whom it is sustained now. The Holy Spirit is both "the Lord, the giver of life" and the giver of *new* life.

This joint identification of giver of life and giver of new life—that the Spirit is not only the *spiritus sanctificans* but also and always the *spiritus vivificans*—implies for theologian and preacher Luke Powery that *rûaḥ-pneuma* is radically democratized. "Breath, Spirit," he writes, "is God's grand equalizer." *Everyone* who breathes is Spirit-Breathed. His account of the Spirit-Breath of God emphasizes what he calls a "natural

[7]Or a "sleeve," as the sci-fi show *Altered Carbon* dramatizes, where bodies are interchangeable and clone-able receptacles into which a "stack" containing the true "person"—a person's memories, personality, skills, and perhaps soul—is inserted or removed as needed, allowing for a warped and tragic vision of eternal life.

[8]As he often puts it in classes at Duke Divinity School.

[9]Jack Levison, *Inspired: The Holy Spirit and the Mind of Faith* (Grand Rapids, MI: Eerdmans, 2013), 193.

pneumatology."[10] Because breath is part of our common humanity, it joins us to one another and the rest of the created world. As Gay's poem intimates, humans cannot live without plants making it possible for us to breathe. Powery explains the significance of natural pneumatology:

> Breathing is a shared experience of the Spirit as we give and receive God's breath from one another and from all of creation. Acknowledging this gift of breath, the gift of the Spirit, the gift that is the Spirit, fosters a counterpoint to racial hierarchies, because breath cannot be racialized, nor can it be segregated for the privileged and powerful. . . . In the Spirit, all can say, "We can breathe."[11]

Not only that, but this democratizing of the Spirit is a recognition that "all flesh is in-spirited" flesh and thus, in receiving gifts of life and breath, "all are called to be stewards of breath."[12] The Spirit-Breath binds us to others, both in terms of connection and in terms of responsibility. We are connected, one to another, inasmuch as we each receive and transmit breath as divine bestowal; we are responsible, one to another, for ensuring that this bestowal is not impeded by creaturely violence. The democratization enacted by the Spirit makes ethical demands, particularly in a world where persons of color cry, literally and metaphorically, "I can't breathe."

In his last words, Eric Garner testified to the depths of horror that result from our failure to act as caretakers of divine breath. Yet as Gay reminds us in "A Small Needful Fact," there is more to Garner's story than the narrative of his violent death. In ruminating on the possibility that he dedicated some part of his life to "making it easier / for us to breathe," Gay reimagines Garner as an exemplary steward of breath in a sacred ecology, bestowing life from one form to another—miraculously, even after his own breath has been cruelly taken away.

Additionally, the book of Acts reminds us at Pentecost that the Spirit is in the business of transfiguring and enabling speech. Indeed, as Powery notes, breath is also crucial to human life in that it carries words and

[10]Luke Powery, *Becoming Human: The Holy Spirit and the Rhetoric of Race* (Louisville, KY: Westminster John Knox, 2022), 55-56.

[11]Powery, *Becoming Human*, 56.

[12]Powery, *Becoming Human*, 56-57.

enables communication. The Spirit-Breath of God bestows not only breath but words, speech, prophecy. *Rûaḥ-pneuma* is Word-bearing Breath. The Spirit of creation and salvation is also the Spirit of communication, the Spirit of truth. Highlighting the story of Pentecost, Powery notes that there is both inspired speech and inspired understanding.[13] The Spirit-Wind-Breath of God falls on those gathered, and there is a unique event of Spirit-led communication, an event that bore witness to the reality of the person and work of Jesus Christ.

Similar to the way in which some early church fathers saw in Psalm 33:6 a reflection of the cocreative agency of Christ and the Holy Spirit as sent by the Father[14]—"By the *word* of the Lord the heavens were made, and all their host by the *breath* of his mouth" (NRSV)—in Pentecost we have a collaborative vision of Spirit-breath and word-Word, of human speech inspired by divine *pneuma* and the Word carried forth on human *pneuma*. Drawing on this word-breath dynamic of creative speech, theologian Elizabeth Dodd argues that human speech, then, provides "an alternative model of participation in the Spirit as a partnership between breath and word in creative action."[15] Her vision attempts to connect the work of Christ and Spirit even more intimately than metaphors that present their agency in creation as a partnership, such as the "two hands of the Father."[16] The collaborative dynamics of Word and Breath highlight the deep interdependence of Spirit and Son. Both breath and pause in breath give form and thus meaning to words and sentences, without which there would be no communication.[17]

Human speech, as a creative partnership of breath and word, is a way to participate in the creative action of Spirit and Word. Not only *what* we say but *how* we say it. Poetry and poetic language intensifies the meaning of ordinary speech, calling forth additional layers of resonance. As we

---

[13]Powery, *Becoming Human*, 58.

[14]See, for example, Paul M. Blowers, *Drama of the Divine Economy: Creator and Creation in Early Christian Theology and Piety* (Oxford: Oxford University Press, 2012), 116-17, 294.

[15]Elizabeth Dodd, "Spoke Word and Spirit's Breath: A Theopoetics of Performance Poetry," *Literature & Theology* 33, no. 3 (September 2019): 294.

[16]For example, theologian Colin Gunton, following Irenaeus.

[17]See, for instance, Dodd's discussion of the "form" or "substance" of words ("Spoke Word and Spirit's Breath," 295).

have observed in "A Small Needful Fact," Gay's poem bestows life at the level of breath, from the verbal disruptions—"perhaps," "in all likelihood"—that force the reader to pause and take an extra breath, to the rhythmic catalog of horticultural descriptors, to the exhale of relief that comes in the final word, *breathe*. The construction of the poem summons the reader to attend more closely to their breath and so invites them to a foretaste of what it might look like to realign their breathing to a new narrative of prophetic witness that begins by honoring the particularities of Garner's life and work. This is not to suggest that the poem is sufficient in itself to effect a complete imaginative transformation in the reader; rather, both in form and in content, Gay's poem presents a "small, needful fact" as a summons to turn from idle indifference and, to put the point Christianly, to breathe in the Spirit of truth.

Indeed, these connections should be unsurprising to Christians because the connection between poetry and prophecy, poetry and prayer, poetry and praise is all over the Scriptures. A full 30 percent of the Scriptures come to us in poetic form.[18] God did not tell God's Word without poetry: the inspiring Spirit of God inspires and collaborates with the human imagination to bring forth poetic revelations of the truth of God. This same inspired collection of texts, Christians claim, is then read again and again in Christian worship and personal study. It is expounded in sermons and testimony. It is imagined in hymnody and prayer. The *rûaḥ-pneuma* continually bears the *logos* to God's people.

Dodd's argument and Gay's example push this connection between Spirit-Breath and Word beyond the Scriptures, or even beyond Christian speech, to gesture toward further ways in which our poetic modes of speaking and writing offer potential ways of breathing with the Spirit, including one that is potentially prophetic.

Poetic Imagination and the Bestowal of Life

As breathing is the process of inhaling and expelling air, it can be tempting to think of one's breath as something purely ephemeral, insubstantial,

[18]W. David O. Taylor, *Glimpses of the New Creation: Worship and the Formative Power of the Arts* (Grand Rapids, MI: Eerdmans, 2019), 136.

even disembodied. Through its subtle rhythmic manipulations, "A Small Needful Fact" summons the reader to deeper awareness of their breath as bodily. From the breathless transition between the poem's title and its first three lines, to the multiple interjections of "perhaps" and "in all likelihood" that force pauses in breath, to the smooth cadences propelling the poetic catalog in its latter half—the entire poem is calculated to draw the reader's attention to the sheer physicality of one's own breath. One does not necessarily need any theological lens to appreciate this particular poetic achievement; however, a pneumatological interpretation does offer several distinctive insights.

Spirit-empowered speech can be prophetic speech. Theologian Willie Jennings suggests that prophetic utterance is intimately bound up with bodily experience: "To allow the Spirit to give voice through our bodies to depths of the human life that God has created. To allow the Spirit to give voice through our bodies to the depths of the divine life God has joined to our lives." The Spirit as Breath acts in and through our bodies to enable prophetic witness in the form of truthful speech and action. As Jennings further notes, this account of the prophetic has specific implications for the artist: "Everything pivots on denial or truth telling, on revelation or concealment. We need artistic practice so bound to prophetic practice that by its very nature it not only makes visible the operations of death but also points toward life."[19]

Jennings's description of prophetic artistic practice could have been written to describe "A Small Needful Fact." As we have seen, Gay's poem is fundamentally concerned with truth telling, both in the narrow sense of dispelling media falsehoods and in the broader sense of rewriting the narrative to restore Eric Garner's essential human dignity. The mere mention of the name Eric Garner necessarily calls up a mass of violent images and stories, particularly the video of his death and repeated gasping, "I can't breathe." Yet Gay's poem refocuses the reader's attention away from this infamous tragic event and instead centers the reader's attention on the small needful fact that "Eric Garner worked / for some time

[19]Willie James Jennings, "Embodying the Artistic Spirit and the Prophetic Arts," *Literature & Theology* 30, no. 3 (September 2016): 257, 259.

at the Parks and Rec. / Horticultural Department." Refusing to conform the words of his poem to the racially coded narratives surrounding Garner's death, Gay instead offers a glimpse of something vital, a deeper truth. Garner may have died breathless in the chokehold of racial injustice, but he also participated in the work of nurturing our communal breath. Read pneumatologically, Gay's poem invites us to consider how Garner cooperates with the Spirit and giver of life in and through his care for plants.

Dare we call "A Small Needful Fact" a prophetic poem? We think we should. As an imagination-bearing and imagination-forming collection of words and images, this poem invites its readers into a deeper truth about our connection to the world, to one another, and even to Eric Garner. It is a poem that is extraordinary both technically and in its challenge to prevailing racialized narratives.

Part of the Spirit's sanctifying work must be to sanctify our imaginations, not merely our beliefs or our actions. We need poems, poems like Gay's, that participate in this sanctifying process. Read pneumatologically, "A Small Needful Fact" calls for not only a review of the facts surrounding Garner's death but a wider and deeper recognition of our "natural pneumatology," of the intimate and interdependent connection we have with others through *rûaḥ-pneuma*, both natural breath and the Spirit of Life. This is a call for the conversion of our whole imagination. Offering a new aesthetics of tenderness and care that resists the coded language of our racialized social imagination, it invites us to recognize that the same Spirit who gifted Eric Garner with breath sustains the plants that were once—perhaps—nurtured by his hands. It reminds us that these same plants are—in all likelihood—continuing to grow and helping us to breathe.

And it summons us to creative cooperation with the Spirit working through the poem to transform and sanctify the reader's imagination. It summons us to become stewards of breath, ones "making it easier / for us"—*all* of us—"to breathe."

6

THE SPIRIT AS BREADTH

BLK HALOS AND SPACIOUS PLACES

Phil Allen Jr. and Justin Ariel Bailey

You have not given me into the hands of the enemy
but have set my feet in a spacious place.

Psalm 31:8

"I can't breathe!" is an utterance-turned-anthem for the Black Lives Matter movement. It also symbolizes the primal cry for Black life in White spaces, evoking horrific images of lynching: Emmett Till, Nate Allen, and thousands of breathless Black bodies hanging as "strange fruit" from southern trees.[1] Christians often speak of the Holy Spirit as God's "breath," and scholars such as Angela Parker connect this naming of the Spirit to the struggle for Black breath, asking, "If God breathes, why can't I?"[2]

If the Spirit is God's breath, this essay takes up a theme that is related but distinct. We argue that the Spirit also brings about *breadth*; indeed,

---

[1]The lesser-known story of the murder of Nate Allen in Georgetown, South Carolina, just eighteen months prior to Emmett Till's murder is told in Phil Allen Jr., *Open Wounds: A Story of Racial Tragedy, Trauma, and Redemption* (Minneapolis: Fortress, 2021). The song "Strange Fruit," originally a poem, was written by Abel Meerepol and performed by Billie Holliday. The song, released in 1939, was Meerepol's response to racism in general and of lynching Black bodies in particular.

[2]See Angela Parker, *If God Breathes, Why Can't I? Black Lives Matter and Biblical Authority* (Grand Rapids, MI: Eerdmans, 2021), 16.

the struggle to breathe is connected to a denial of the space to do so. We argue in this chapter that the Holy Spirit is the Space Maker, moving within and against the chaos to create "a spacious place." We follow the biblical narrative in developing this in two ways, in both habitable and sanctifying spaces, in opposition to contemporary myths of space that occlude the biblical vision and deny the breadth that the Spirit intends for creation. Indeed, the literal denial of space for Black bodies through practices such as redlining, and the psychological constricting of space through racist rhetoric, calls to mind the way that Blackness has had to survive in conditions of suffocation rather than spaciousness. We argue that the Spirit, as Space Maker, invites Christians to seek and foster liberative spaces where the Spirit continues to move against the chaos.

Serving as a case study for our thesis is *Blk Halos*, a performance and mixed-media installation, presented in January 2023 following the Martin Luther King Jr. holiday and in his honor. For several months following the performance, *Blk Halos* continued to serve as an installation space featuring curator Dea Jenkins's textile art. The full project, we suggest, instantiated the theme of spaciousness, both as a physical space for artistic collaboration and as an imaginative space to nourish practices of liberation toward King's vision of the "beloved community."[3] *Blk Halos* demonstrated, we again suggest, the power of the arts to manifest a space for the Spirit's work, where participants were invited to dwell together in joy and lament, discern God's liberative work among them, and join the Holy Spirit in making space for others to breathe and be sanctified.

To make this case, we first examine the biblical foundation for a theology of the Holy Spirit as *breadth*. Attending in particular to the work of the Spirit in establishing both habitable and sanctifying spaces, we contrast this scriptural account with the suffocating myths in modernity of space as merely there for our exploitation and commodification. In the second half, we then explore how the *Blk Halos* performance challenged

[3]King frames his concept of "beloved community" in familial language by describing a reconciled and redeemed multiethnic "household" that expands into and forms a broader community, a global neighborhood. This community is intent on resisting the divisions of ideology and worldview that so divides the people. See excerpt of *Where Do We Go From Here?* in *A Testament of Hope: The Essential Writings and Speeches of Martin Luther King, Jr.* (New York: HarperOne, 1986), 617-33.

such constricting accounts and instead sought to foster spaces where all would be drawn into the work of the Spirit as giver of breadth. In doing so, we hope to prompt further reflection about the distinct ways the arts can both be inspired by and make manifest the spacious and sanctifying work of the Holy Spirit.

Spirit as *Breadth*: The Spirit of God Creates Space

In God's good world, living creatures are given room to *breathe*, which signifies the experience of both safety and freedom. Helen Schüngel-Straumann points out the lexical connection in Semitic languages between the roots *rwḥ* ("spirit, breath") and *rḥb* ("space, breadth"): "*Ruach* creates space. It sets in motion. It leads out of narrow places into wide vistas, thus conferring life."[4] Thus, while we might sing of welcoming the Spirit, ("Holy Spirit, you are welcome here"), the Spirit as breadth welcomes *us* into the wide-open spaces of God's hospitality. This theme is developed over the narrative of Scripture in terms of both ordinary, habitable space (a safe place where life can unfold amid contestation) and holy, sanctifying space (where God dwells, deals with evil, and heals creation).

We can see the theme of habitable space from the opening scene of Genesis in which the Spirit/wind/breath of God (*rûaḥ ʾĕlōhîm*) moves over the watery chaos, and God speaks to create space. Commentators note the symmetry between days 1-3, during which God *forms* spaces (day and night, sky and sea, dry land and vegetation), and days 4-6, during which God *fills* the spaces (with sun and moon, birds and fish, animals and humans).[5] Throughout the Hebrew Scriptures, habitable space (dry land) is often paired with the image of chaos (the sea). Yahweh is the one who "made the sea and the dry land" (Jon 1:9; see Ps 95:5).[6] Like "heaven

---

[4]Helen Schüngel-Straumann, "Ruah," in *Feministische Theologie: Perspektiven zur Orientierung*, ed. Maria Kassel (Stuttgart: Kreuz-Verl, 1988), 61. Cited in Jürgen Moltmann, *The Spirit of Life: A Universal Affirmation (Minneapolis: Fortress, 2001),* 43. We note another semantic connection in cognate language, Arabic, where the greeting *marḥaban* ("welcome!") is derived from the verb *rahuba* ("to be wide, spacious, and broad").

[5]See, for example, Meredith G. Kline, "Space and Time in the Genesis Cosmogony," *Perspectives on Science and Christian Faith* 48, no. 1 (April 1996): 2-15.

[6]Unless otherwise noted, Bible quotations in this chapter follow the NIV.

and earth," "sea and dry land" function as a merism, indicating the universal scope of Yahweh's creativity. The pair is also meant to evoke the dynamic, saving action of Yahweh in the exodus, in making the dry land to emerge in the midst of the sea so that God's people could pass through safely: "the Lord drove the sea back with a strong east wind [*rûaḥ*] and turned it into dry land" (Ex 14:21). The spirit/wind/breath drives back the sea and brings forth dry land, echoing back to the creation narrative, in which God makes dry land to appear out of the chaotic waters (Gen 1:9).

The point is that Yahweh is both Creator (who made the sea and the dry land) and liberator, who brought Israel out of slavery, making a way through the sea, on the way to the wide and spacious place that is the Promised Land. In both cases, God's Spirit/wind/breath is active in making space. As Jürgen Moltmann notes, "According to Israel's seminal experience, experience of God means experiencing liberation from slavery in the Exodus, and experiencing the promised land into which it entered: 'Now the Lord has made room for us, and we shall be fruitful in the land' (Gen. 26:22)."[7] Freedom *from* oppression now gives birth to freedom *for* flourishing. Relief prepares the way for roominess, with the Spirit making space.

The biblical motif of habitable space is connected to the concrete promise of land (Gen 12:1) where God's people can dwell securely (Lev 26:5), with hope of fruitfulness ("a land flowing with milk and honey," Ex 3:17; cf. Deut 8:7-8) and without fear of further oppression (Deut 12:10). The Promised Land, like Eden, is a place of abundance and delight, where "everyone will sit under their own vine and under their own fig tree, and no one will make them afraid" (Mic 4:4).

Not only does the Spirit make space; to encounter God's Spirit is an experience of spaciousness. The tangible security of habitable land is connected to the psychological security of freedom from distress, so that the psalmist can say, "You have not given me into the hands of the enemy but have set my feet in a spacious place" (Ps 31:8; see also 2 Sam 22:20; Ps 18:19; 118:5). As Moltmann notes, "To experience *ruach* is to experience what is

[7]Moltmann, *Spirit of Life*, 277.

divine not only as a person, and not merely as a force, but also as a space—as the space of freedom in which the living being can unfold."[8] As Paul puts it, "where the Spirit of the Lord is, there is liberty" (2 Cor 3:17 KJV).

This brings us to our second theme, sanctifying space. Habitable spaces can become holy places through the divine presence that sets them apart for a purpose.[9] The Promised Land generally and the temple specifically function in this way; they are sanctifying spaces where God dwells among Israel as covenantal partner and Lord. The peace of dwelling safely (Ps 4:8) is joined to the purpose of dwelling in and with God (Ps 90:1; 91:9). If habitable spaces signify the removal of barriers that prevent ordinary flourishing (e.g., the absence of oppressive forces), sanctifying spaces focus flourishing in a particular direction, toward the *telos* of justice and joy in the Holy Spirit (Rom 14:17).

Carrying this forward, Christians speak of God's Spirit in spatial language, experiencing life in the Spirit (*en pneumati;* note the NIV's translation "in the realm of the Spirit," Rom 8:9). So writes Basil of Caesarea: "Although paradoxical, it is nevertheless true that Scripture frequently speaks of the Spirit in terms of place—a place in which people are made holy. . . . The Spirit is indeed the dwelling-place of the saints, and the saint is a suitable abode for the Spirit, since he has supplied God with a house, and is called a temple of God."[10] By God's Spirit, believers become both corporately and individually the place where God dwells, and by God's Spirit they themselves are sanctified, made into holy places (Eph 2:21).

This second theme elevates ordinary life without leaving it behind, allowing it to be sanctified and healed as believers are united to Christ by God's Spirit. We note Jesus' prayer that this sanctifying work will not occur by removing his disciples from the world but by preserving them within it "from the evil one" (Jn 17:15-17). Similarly, inhabiting the Spirit's

---

[8]Moltmann, *Spirit of Life*, 43.

[9]Within the literature one frequently finds rhetorical distinctions between *space* and *place*, and Craft notes that what one writer signifies by one, another writer might signify by the other. Thus, in this essay we use *space* and *place* to refer to the same reality, differentiated by adjectives such as *habitable* and *holy*. Jennifer Allen Craft, *Placemaking and the Arts: Cultivating the Christian Life* (Downers Grove, IL: IVP Academic, 2018), 9-10.

[10]Basil the Great, *On the Holy Spirit* 62.

sanctifying space does not exempt God's people from cultural and historical contingencies (such as the violence of the Roman Empire). Sanctifying space is co-located in the midst of it, as God's people resist the world's idols (1 Jn 2:15), seek God's justice (Mic 6:8; Mt 6:33), and form communities that testify to God's kingdom (Rom 12:9-21). For although this Spirited space is intangible, it is always embodied concretely in flesh-and-blood practices of liberation, celebration, and just peacemaking that have tangible effects in ordinary life (Lk 4:18-19).

Opposing Contemporary Myths of Space

The biblical theme of the Spirit as Space Maker has profound resonance amid the cramped conditions of modernity. But it also signifies a prophetic challenge to the diseased conception of space that fuels those conditions. The biblical account described above is a protest against the modern conception of space as empty and undefined, ripe for commodification and colonization.[11] When the biblical vision of the Spirit's breadth is lost, rival conceptions of space begin to intrude, where space is reconfigured without reference to the life it is meant to nourish.

Among the dominant cultures of modernity, disenchantment—the loss of a sacred structure in which human action is embedded—has led to a new conception of space, a blank canvas on which to impose one's will.[12] As philosopher Charles Taylor writes: "In this purposeless universe, we decide what goals to pursue. . . . We are alone in the universe, and this is frightening; but it can also be exhilarating."[13] The felt exhilaration of this undefined freedom can be seen in songs and stories about America that celebrate the myth of vast, untamed spaces for its inhabitants to master. William Dyrness shows how this formative story of open and expansive space remains lodged deep in the national psyche: prime real estate is

[11]As Brueggemann writes, it is "a protest against the unpromising pursuit of space. It is a declaration that our humanness cannot be found in . . . undefined freedom." Walter Brueggemann, *The Land: Places as Gift, Promise, and Challenge in Biblical Faith* (Minneapolis, Fortress, 1989), 4. Brueggemann distinguishes space from place but clearly has the modern conception of space as the object of his critique.

[12]Charles Taylor, *The Ethics of Authenticity* (Cambridge, MA: Harvard University Press, 1991), 4-5.

[13]Charles Taylor, *A Secular Age* (Cambridge, MA: Harvard University Press, 2007), 367.

located near major freeways, and towns are organized not around a central square but along "Main Street"; the ideal of freedom and prosperity often includes space (a yard!).[14] Americans think of themselves as people on the move, manifesting a pioneering, entrepreneurial spirit, with a willingness to explore.

But this conception of space has also produced a willingness by the powerful to *exploit*, to colonize and commodify the space, harming ecosystems and displacing inhabitants. In this revision, the Spirit's freedom, which has a sanctifying and liberative purpose, is replaced by a will to power. Joining is replaced by domination, connection by conquest. In America, claiming the space meant the exploitation of Indigenous peoples and enslaved Africans. Divine image bearers were denied breadth—space to flourish—and their vulnerable bodies became a blank space for victors to inscribe false narratives justifying their subjugation.[15] More recent practices of racial segregation such as *redlining*—in which African Americans are literally denied real estate or the financial services to obtain it—testify to the way that contemporary myths of space continue to exert themselves in opposition to the space-making Spirit.

The modern myth of space is manifestly untrue. Despite the promise of unfettered empty space, modern people feel trapped in Max Weber's "iron cage," at the mercy of more powerful forces.[16] The suffocating sense in which human agency is colonized and constricted continues to fall more heavily on some than others, but even those who are insulated from the worst forms of violence often feel isolated and lonely, creatively cramped and psychologically paralyzed. The first step to recovering the Spirit's breadth is to diagnose the imaginative diseases that have infected

---

[14]William Dyrness, *How Does America Hear the Gospel?* (Grand Rapids, MI: Eerdmans, 1990), 44.

[15]Tragically, this tendency has often been abetted by theological justification. As Willie James Jennings writes, "It is as though Christianity, wherever it went in the modern colonies, inverted its sense of hospitality. It claimed to be the host, the owner of the spaces it entered, and demanded native peoples enter its cultural logics, its ways of being in the world, and its conceptualities." Jennings, *The Christian Imagination: Theology and the Origins of Race* (New Haven, CT: Yale University Press, 2011), 58.

[16]This refers to the sense that in the modern world our options are constrained by impersonal, institutional mechanisms that dictate our lives, especially the market and the state. Taylor, *Ethics of Authenticity*, 8.

our sense of space. Here artists can help us in naming our cramped conditions, offering prophetic resistance, and imagining alternative forms of life. If this is the case, then artists may also offer something more, a new kind of spaciousness in the Spirit, manifest in the artistic projects such as *Blk Halos*, to which we now turn.

Blk Halos: The Artist as Space Maker

Dea Jenkins, founder and curator of *Blk Halos*, designed the installation as a space for artistic resistance and liturgical performance. The entire room, an open space with black walls adorned by textile creations—the oldest known medium of art—became a shared pulpit for artists, hosting poetic and prophetic performers who offered their gifts back to God in a symphony of word, song, and dance.[17] Taken together, the various art forms—textile, poetry, and song—told a common story, reimagining Blackness in its fullness, honoring its dignity amid a society in which it is persistently debased. Each artist embodied a freedom to speak, crying out in both exasperation and affirmation.

During the performance, the audience was invited to pause, reflect, and react, representing the larger invitation to join in lament, joy, and heightened social consciousness. As both performance and installation, *Blk Halos* facilitated fresh ways of seeing and entering into Blackness. To use the language from earlier, it provided a habitable space for catching collective breath and a sanctifying space in which God's Spirit could work within and through artistic offerings. The multifaceted nature of the performance makes it difficult to systematize the aesthetic impact, much less the Spirit's mysterious agency among the participants. Yet we can identify two mutually reinforcing aspects in which the artist seeks to join the Spirit's work: dwelling together and fostering liberative space.

[17]It is worth noting that the presence of dancer Ayanna Bullock, Jenkins's friend and mentor, played a significant role in the installation. During the performance, a still shot of Bullock, captured mid-dance, was projected onto the wall as if an angelic figure whose memory and presence superintended and participated in the event. While paying homage, Jenkins invited her friend into the space as well as introduced the audience to someone who left an indelible mark on her and *Blk Halos*. Though no halo was explicitly visible, her influence on Jenkins was enough to mark her sacredness, her memory, her light.

Habitable Space: Dwelling Together

As a participatory performance, *Blk Halos* sought to instantiate the "breadth-making" work of the Spirit by making a space for artists and audience to dwell together in collective inspiration. This connects the aim of the artist to the biblical theme of *habitable space*. The almost all-Black cast was given space to breathe (be present), to take in the life-giving Spirit and to exhale and breathe on (inspire) the audience for reflection and action. In sharing this space, the audience was invited to breathe in or inhale imagination, creativity, and a prophetic vision for a more just and equitable society. In this vision, the performance of *Blk Halos* would only be as powerful as the response of the audience as they returned to their respective spaces with what they received. Their response as witnesses to the performance is a kind of exhalation—a breathing out—into new spaces, a participation in the continued *breadth* work of the Spirit. It is in fact the work of the Spirit because *Blk Halos* is a demonstration of the Spirit's work of "creating [new spaces], reconciling [estranged people groups], and redeeming [humanity]."[18]

The curated space where the artists sought to join the Spirit was not an exclusive space. Part of reimagining Blackness is to not see Black skin, Black culture, and Black people as "other" but as another—another of the *same* kind. In other words, Blackness is to be shared, to be intimately engaged, to dwell with something (or *someone*) in a familial way. *Blk Halos* disarms the practice of otherness and inspires a move toward beloved community—a community embodying justice, equity, and solidarity—that does not rely on the ideology of White supremacy. Instead, it confronts these divisive and dehumanizing ideas with an alternative vision. As curator, Jenkins set the precedent by presenting with her natural hair as one who herself is free from European beauty standards, reminiscent of a queen's crown perfectly fitted on the pinnacle of her brown skin. Her gait signified an ease of body and spirit that conveyed to all in attendance that the space itself and the performance was one of hospitality.

---

[18]Samuel Kelton Roberts, *African American Christian Ethics* (Cleveland: Pilgrim, 2001), 112.

The audience was invited not only to gaze at her hair and skin as if viewing a painting but also to feel the emotions in her face, expressions of woundedness and a triggered nervous system from the repetition of hearing and repeating the lyrics in real time. This required them to be present in their own bodies and to take inventory of what their individual and collective nervous system communicated as they took in the lyrics. It was an invitation to lament and celebrate all that is Blackness—Black hair, Black skin, Black creativity, Black intellect, and Black drama. Dwelling together meant grappling with the allusions to a reimagined Blackness, and receiving the divine blessing on Blackness, conveyed in the title *Blk Halos*.

As the performance continued, poetry played a central role, serving as extended lyrics to Jenkins's songs. The poems were written and performed in a free-flowing style, in sync with the jazz-like improvisation of the music that scored the event. Its performance was a liberating witness in the sense that the poet prophesied over Blackness (bodies, culture, etc.), affirming its inherent value and sacredness by narrating its suffering and, more importantly, its resiliency. The poetry and dialogue between two African American men were displays of "the freedom to speak for themselves" in ways that are self-defining rather than a perpetuation of narratives imposed on them to which they themselves "would not have created or ascribed."[19] The poet did not uplift Blackness by means of diminishing Whiteness or any other ethnic identity. Instead, he confronted and presented structures and systems of oppression and othering and invited all to join in their dismantling. Here is one example:

I keep bumping up against the red line

Drawn on a map to entrap

Black and brown bodies restricting them to that side of the tracks

To protect the whites from the blacks

Their children their families and their properties

[19]Willie James Jennings, *Acts: A Theological Commentary on the Bible* (Louisville, KY: Westminster John Knox, 2017), 87.

But that red line had more freedom than us . . .

One day that red line will disintegrate into nothingness

Smeared away by the amplification of my voice

And the red line makers will be left without a choice

'Cause *I'll be* at the table . . .

And those outside that red line reinforcing its ideals

Legitimizing its existence

Will come to eat on this side of the line

Except my line is one of invitation not imprisonment

So folks will know they've reached a new space

But in the meantime

I'll be sure to ricochet into spaces consciously prohibited from welcoming me[20]

This excerpt from the poem "The Red Line" highlights the legacy of *de jure* discriminatory redlining practices that continues to segregate (*de facto)* White communities from communities of color, especially African Americans. Yet, the poem casts a vision of a day when that red line and its practices have ended aided by prophetic voices, including his own, that bring about a new reality, a beloved community. Such a reality is itself enacted in the poem's performance as the entrapping red lines invoked in the first stanza gradually take on new meaning and are transformed into the lines of the poem, inviting and imagining new spaces free from imprisoning narratives.

As the poem was recited, a dancer, Mietta McLaurin, matched the poet's words with her movements. She moved to the rhythm and emotions of the poet. Her body's movements added a visual texture to the words. The dance performance on the surface appeared to be a solo act. But it was a dance between mediums of art and social realities, between

[20]Phil Allen, "The Red Line."

words and body, between injustice and protest, between oppression and resilience, and between aesthetics and activism. The hope was that the choreography of this performance would evoke in the audience a desire to participate with words and body as activists of protest against injustice, demonstrating resilience in the face of oppression (even if they have managed to evade the oppression). The dance also aimed to orient the audience toward God, bringing not only their thoughts but also their bodies, presenting their whole selves in holy posture before and movement with God.

Sanctifying Space: Fostering Liberative Space

The installation thus suggests that in order to join the Spirit, colonized space must give way to liberative space, and colonized imaginations must give way to liberated imaginations. Here we can connect the aim of the artist to the biblical theme of sanctifying space. Jenkins opened the performance with these lines:

> *Their skin is so ugly. (That's a lie.)*
>
> *Black hair is too kinky. (That's a lie.)*
>
> *Black people are so dirty. (That's a lie.)*
>
> *Black bodies mean nothing. (That's a lie.)*

The pace of the delivery invited the audience to pause—to breathe—and to reflect on the force of the words. By naming these false narratives, Jenkins directed the audience's attention outward at her and inward to detect within themselves any lingering traces of the deceptions they had heard. The performance was intended to confront lies about Blackness and to counteract them with an affirmation of the aesthetic and rhythmic beauty of Blackness. It sought to honor and reclaim its sacredness from centuries of dehumanizing mistreatment that degraded its presence and attempted to strip away the humanity it clothes.

Accentuating the holiness of Blackness is essential in contesting the dishonoring narrative around Black bodies. *Blk Halos* was a demonstration of an artist's capacity to create a decolonized space from a historically marginalized perspective. The performance spoke truth to power while inviting "others" to commit to join in solidaric community to not only see Blackness differently but to also honor its dignity, sacredness, and instincts and resilience to advocate for justice and liberation.

Thus, as a kind of sanctifying space, a liberative space is one that disentangles people from the bondage of self-interest and orients them toward God, justice, and sharing space in beloved community. As a demonstration of fostering liberative space, *Blk Halos* also existed within a liberated space. It was not arranged to preserve colonized space; rather, the performance sought to demonstrate the spontaneity as common to African/African American worship and culture—whether dance, song, music, or words [e.g., poetry and preaching]—born from experiences of suffering, resiliency, and victory.[21] Similarly, the performance sought to liberate those present from the restraints of the sacred/secular divide, reflecting the African/African American tradition that holistically integrates all of life. As Peter Paris notes, "There is no evidence that either the [enslaved African in the US] or their African forebears ever believed in the modern Western distinction between sacred and profane. Rather, both presupposed a sacred cosmos. . . . Hence they viewed everything as sacred in some respect and saw nothing as totally profane."[22] *Blk Halos* sought to participate in the Spirit's creation of *breadth* by removing this sacred/secular border, welcoming refugees and border crossers from either side (in the social sense) to an immersive cultural experience.

To facilitate this experience, the musicians provided the soundtrack to create another layer of drama in particular scenes. The music served as a temporary symphony in the midst of a social cacophony of sounds: shrieks of pain versus deafening silence (both also heard in the *Blk Halos* performance). As a universal language, the music offered rhythm for healthier communal breathing. Its cadence had the capacity to arrest

---

[21]Will Coleman, *Tribal Talk: Black Theology, Hermeneutics, and African/African American Ways of "Telling the Story"* (University Park: Pennsylvania State University Press, 2000), 118.

[22]Peter J. Paris, *The Spirituality of African Peoples: The Search for a Common Moral Discourse (Minneapolis: Fortress, 1994)*, 33-34.

anxiety, soothe nervous systems, and relax constricted bodies. As the musicians and vocalist (Jenkins) breathed together and gave birth to a song, it served as a demonstration for the audience of what it looks like to breathe freely together in an intimate yet spacious community.

This collaboration of music, lyrics, and community meant more than a context for metaphorically breathing together. It connected the performers to participants to history, especially the tradition of Negro spirituals, in which the lyrics served as secret language that assisted enslaved Africans fleeing to freedom.[23] The music in *Blk Halos* was thus both cryptically and explicitly instructive. However, the instructions were directed toward the oppressing elements and figures of society, for when agents of oppression are liberated, all of society will be as well: "Point blank, don't shoot! / Open the register of our dreams. / And out spills the change." The music evoked memories of struggle, activism, and resistance to oppression for African Americans.

Like Negro spirituals, the lyrics in the *Blk Halos* performance "were born as a response to the labor pains of cruel treatment."[24] Through its songs, *Blk Halos* similarly sought to "transform the canonized [biblical] narrative into one suited for their present situation of bondage."[25] Ultimately, *Blk Halos* drew from the Scriptures to create a narrative suited for the present-day battle against anti-Black racism. In doing so, bodily art forms—words, music, and movement—combined with the practices of hospitality and prophetic confrontation to break participants out of mental prisons, fostering commonness and community across traditional borders.

Conclusion: Breadth to Breathe

Throughout this essay we have noted the parallels between the work of the Spirit as Space Maker and the aims of the artist. *Blk Halos* sought to curate a habitable and sanctifying space to encounter God's liberating

[23]Robert Darden, *People Get Ready! A New History of Black Gospel Music* (New York: Continuum, 2004), 16.
[24]Coleman, *Tribal Talk*, 128.
[25]Coleman, *Tribal Talk*, 128.

Spirit. While respecting the mystery of the Spirit's work, we want to suggest a synchronization present in *Blk Halos* between human and divine agency similar to the description given by theologian Willie Jennings regarding the church in Acts: "The voice of the Spirit and the voices of the disciples are together but not confused. The agency of the one does not negate the action of the other."[26] Similarly, as artists seek to follow the Spirit's initiative, an installation and performance like *Blk Halos* can not only signify but also become a site of the Spirit's action.

In a world of oppressive ideologies that divides and dismembers society, artistic projects such as *Blk Halos* participate in the mission of God on earth to re-member humans. In a world of rigid restrictions, *Blk Halos* unharnesses creativity and imagination toward a beloved community, the kingdom vision of peace, justice, and joy in the Holy Spirit (Rom 14:17). In a world of explicit anti-Black racism, including its implicit acceptance, it affirms the dignity and humanity of those of the African diaspora while inviting non-Black brothers and sisters to breathe out this vision for community together. *Blk Halos*, whether in the activity of the performance or in the stillness of the installation, oriented the audience and its performers toward a telos of a more just and joyful society, welcoming the work of the space-making Spirit who offers breadth for collective breath: African Americans may exhale (through art forms) while others might inhale (through attentive gaze). As the Spirit moves amid the chaos, artists and audiences join in, dwelling together and discerning the Spirit's work to make a spacious place.

[26]Jennings, *Acts*, 133.

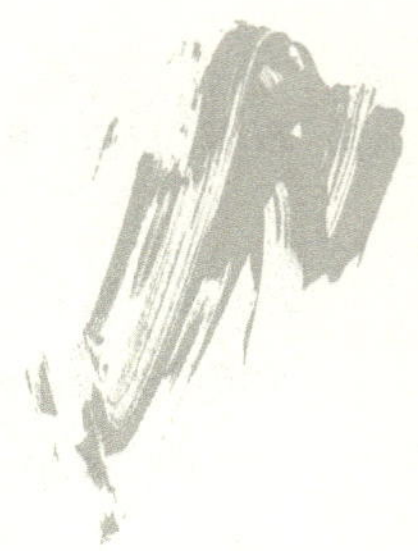

7

THE OVERSHADOWING SPIRIT

MARY, INCARNATION, AND UNEXPECTED MUTUALITY IN OLIVIER MESSIAEN'S *VINGT REGARDS SUR L'ENFANT-JÉSUS*

Chelle Stearns

In the first chapter of Luke's Gospel, a young woman of little social standing or power named Mary is visited by the angel Gabriel. The angel tells her that God has found favor with her and that she should not be afraid. Gabriel proclaims that God will work a great marvel in her and she will bear a son. When Mary wonders how this could happen since she is a virgin, she is told that "the Holy Spirit" (*Pneuma Hagion*) will "come upon her" (*epeleusetai epi se*) and "the power of the Most High" (*dynamis Hypsistou*) will "overshadow" (*episkiasei*) her so that she can bear this child into the physical world of human bodies, betrothals, barnyards, and donkeys (Lk 1:35). With this work of the overshadowing Holy Spirit over the womb of Mary, the world shifts and the invisible God becomes visible.

The overshadowing action of the Spirit is not a proper name in this passage, and yet this term names the agency and relationship the Spirit has with Mary—and through Mary with all of creation. Mary is an intriguing pneumatological focal point because she, in a significant moment in God's work in the world, is overshadowed with God's glory so that she might conceive in her womb and give birth to the Son of God. Though the word *overshadowing* has the connotation of one being overpowered or even diminished, in this story Mary is instead empowered and lifted up. She is not manipulated or coerced but given agency and voice as she is first asked for her consent to participate in this story. Something unfolds for Mary as she says yes to God's work that is not a power over her but a joining with her will and her body.

This chapter will consider this overshadowing Spirit and how it speaks to God's drawing near to humanity and mediating God's own glory and presence through particular places, persons, and bodies. That is, the Spirit brings forth and reveals the presence of God within space and time, but does so precisely by enabling a mutual-indwelling wherein God's presence is made manifest in our very bodies; in turn, we are invited to participate in the eternal giving and receiving love of the triune God. To help in our exploration of the overshadowing Spirit, I turn to French composer Olivier Messiaen's (1908–1992) work for solo piano, *Vingt Regards sur l'Enfant-Jésus* (*Twenty Contemplations of the Infant Jesus*). In stark contrast to what one might expect for a composition on the nativity, *Vingt Regards* readily evokes cosmic imagery on a grand scale—stars and galaxies rather than shepherds and placid donkeys. Nonetheless, the work unfolds as a continual interplay between descending and ascending themes, a clear effort to reflect through music the miraculous joining of the infinite with the finite, the ineffable with the material, and the divine with the human in Christ's incarnation.

But crucially, Messiaen reserves a pivotal role for Mary in his meditations on the infant Jesus, and focusing on Mary's presence in *Vingt Regards* reveals the significance of the overshadowing Spirit at play in the incarnation of the Christ child. The Spirit is implicitly present throughout the *Vingt Regards*, but it is in the movements featuring Mary that the overshadowing Spirit is most unambiguously at work in the story. Ultimately, what Messiaen's composition helps us to understand (or, more precisely, hear in a new way) is that the Spirit, within the story of Mary, enables and honors the capacity of human flesh and material existence to participate in and with God in an unexpected mutuality. Thus, not only is Mary exalted rather than diminished or eclipsed in partnership with the Spirit, but perhaps even our associations with the word *overshadow* can be transformed as we encounter this music and are prompted to revisit wider resonances of the overshadowing spirit in the biblical framework.[1] For the overshadowing Spirit facilitates presence and incarnation (Christ's participation in humanity) and our participation in Christ. Like Mary, we are enabled through the work of the overshadowing Spirit to become a dwelling place for God as our bodies, too, become temples of the Holy Spirit (1 Cor 6:19).

In what follows, I first examine further scriptural allusions to and resonances with the Spirit's overshadowing work. Together, these point to an integral relatedness between God's self-revealing, healing presence through the overshadowing Spirit, Mary's womb, and the birth of the church as those baptized in Christ. I then explore not only the cosmic implications of God's indwelling of Mary's womb through Messiaen's *Vingt Regards* but the way his composition can ultimately deepen our appreciation of the overshadowing Spirit's partnering work within Mary's body to instantiate God's new kingdom. I conclude with some reflections on why this matters for the church today.

The Overshadowing Spirit

"Overshadowing" (*episkiazō*) is not just a biblical term but also an evocative theological concept that gives shape to implicit and explicit theologies of the Spirit's mediation and agency. Liturgical, sacramental, aesthetic, and visual theologies are rife with allusions to the overshadowing Spirit, sometimes merging images of the Spirit hovering (over the waters at creation), descending (as a dove), and covering (as a cloud) persons, events, and structures. Both literal and more allusive images of the overshadowing Spirit name how the transcendent God engages the immanent creation, allowing the invisible God to become visible.

The Greek terms for "overshadowing" (*episkiazō*) occur in five places in the New Testament (six if we count Heb 9:5, *kataskiazō*), with four of those referring to the agency of the Spirit in the annunciation and the

[1]For one example of this kind of empowering vision of the overshadowing Spirit, see Jerusha Matsen Neal, *The Overshadowed Preacher: Mary, the Spirit, and the Labor of Proclamation* (Grand Rapids, MI: Eerdmans, 2020).

transfiguration. An additional passage is found in the Septuagint in Exodus 40, when the cloud of God's glory covers and fills the tabernacle.[2] In these passages, God's presence comes to dwell among humanity, for the purpose of worship (Ex 40:34-38 LXX), the conception of Jesus in the womb of Mary (Lk 1:35), and the revelation of Jesus' divine identity in the three synoptic accounts of the transfiguration (Mt 17:5; Mk 9:7; Lk 9:34-35). In addition, in Acts 5:15 we see the effects of the Spirit dwelling within Peter and the other disciples (Acts 2) as miraculous events began to happen around them (Acts 5:12). In response to this, people position sick loved ones in such a way that Peter's shadow might overshadow (*episkiazō*) them as he walks past, hoping that they might be healed. The overshadowing of the Spirit, then, initiates not only God's presence in these narratives but new realities and abilities that have both temporal and eternal ramifications. When the overshadowing Spirit appears in biblical narratives, God's glory is revealed and God's reconciling purposes begin to unfold. Moreover, within the context of other references to overshadowing, we see that the Spirit's movement in the annunciation is adamantly not one of imposition or dominion over against Mary but rather speaks of God's self-revealing presence, an indwelling that brings healing to those who are enfolded by the glorious shadow.

The theological meaning of the Spirit's overshadowing also leads to other biblical narratives even though other metaphors and images are employed, such as the parallel theophanies between the baptism of Jesus and the transfiguration. At Christ's baptism, "the Holy Spirit descended on him in bodily form like a dove. And a voice came from heaven: 'You are my Son, whom I love; with you I am well pleased'" (Lk 3:22). In the story of the transfiguration, the term *overshadowing* is used to similar purpose as the image of the descending dove: "a cloud came and overshadowed [*episkiazen*] them, and they were terrified as they entered the cloud. Then from the cloud came a voice that said, 'This is my Son, my Chosen; listen to him!'" (Lk 9:34-35 NRSV). The key difference is that in the baptismal story, the Father speaks directly to Jesus when the Spirit descends on him,

[2]Veli-Matti Kärkkäinen, *Pneumatology: The Holy Spirit in Ecumenical, International, and Contextual Perspective* (Grand Rapids, MI: Baker Academic, 2002), 25.

revealing an eternal, loving relationship between the Father and the Son. In the transfiguration narrative, the Spirit overshadows the disciples so they might hear the message from the Father about the Son, that God has come as Jesus to befriend humanity. Again, the overshadowing Spirit seems to mediate God's self-revelation to humanity.

This image of the Spirit descending as a dove also has a rich history in icons and paintings of the annunciation, so much so that most observers would not question the ubiquitous presence of the dove descending on the Virgin, even though it is absent in the biblical story. This visual tradition draws a parallel between the annunciation and Jesus' baptism, and recognizes the similarity between the overshadowing Spirit and the Spirit descending as a dove. This overlap of images most likely occurred early in Christian history because in the early church the womb of Mary was associated and sometimes equated with Jesus' baptism, baptismal fonts, and the rite of baptism. As Robin Jensen maintains, the womb of Mary became the birthplace not only of Jesus but also of the church.[3]

In this way, the annunciation, the baptism of Jesus, and the baptism of believers are all connected by the work of the Holy Spirit overshadowing the womb of Mary. As Leo the Great once preached in a nativity sermon, "The same Holy Spirit fills the font as filled the Virgin."[4] In this theology, Christ enters the parallel waters of Mary's womb and the waters of the Jordan River to prepare the way for the baptism of future Christ followers. The waters bear witness to Jesus' conception and his baptism even as the waters are consecrated by the body of Christ (womb and baptism) in preparation for the birth of the church. Jensen points out that early baptismal fonts were fashioned in the shape of a womb and were simultaneously considered "a watery tomb and watery womb."[5] Believers then and now are baptized into the death of Christ and birthed into their new life in Christ. The implication is that the overshadowing Spirit over Mary's womb also overshadows the new believer as they are born into new life.

---

[3]Robin Jensen, *Baptismal Imagery in Early Christianity: Ritual, Visual, and Theological Dimensions* (Grand Rapids, MI: Baker Academic, 2012), 56-58.

[4]Leo I, *Sermon* 24.3, trans. Robin Jensen, quoted in Jensen, *Baptismal Imagery in Early Christianity*, 56.

[5]Jensen, *Baptismal Imagery in Early Christianity*, 3.

It might seem strange to consider the womb of Mary as a location for theological inquiry, but the overshadowing Spirit had no such qualms, nor did early Christian theologians. Eugene Rogers goes so far to claim that those who are offended by the contemplation of Mary's womb as a fulcrum of God's history with humanity verge on heresy and expose their "inner Nestorius." As he argues, "Distaste before the womb is not just pathology, it is heresy. . . . If God did not avoid the womb, neither may Christian thought and liturgy."[6] At the heart of Rogers's claim is how the overshadowing Spirit chooses to work with and alongside physicality rather than against it, such as in the virginal womb of Mary. His conclusion is that God both "befriends" and "likes" to work *with* or *alongside* human bodies (*para physin*) because God loves creation.[7] In Mary we have an example of how God befriends bodies. Rogers continues, "In the womb of Mary, the Spirit takes the lost cause of human flesh to be her own cause, her own resting place; the place of wastage to be the site of winning, the flesh unseated to become the throne of grace."[8] Thus, through the womb of Mary, the Spirit works *with* the flesh to uphold the redemptive purposes of God, and the earthly, vulnerable, and creaturely reality of the conception, gestation, and birth of Jesus mirrors the believer's initiation into the household of God.

This idea of Mary's womb as a key pivot point of God's interaction and involvement with humanity and creation makes sense of Irenaeus's claim that Mary is the second "Eve."[9] Frances Young notes that Irenaeus "draws a parallel between the virgin earth from which Adam was formed and the virgin from whom the Lord was born, 'recapitulating this man,' so as to 'demonstrate the likeness of embodiment [*sarkōsis*] to Adam.'"[10] Thus,

---

[6]Eugene Rogers, *After the Spirit: A Constructive Pneumatology from Resources Outside the Modern West* (Grand Rapids, MI: Eerdmans, 2005), 112.

[7]"It can only be that God chooses this way because God likes it; chooses because God desires and loves and befriends human bodies. God the Spirit does not have disgust at the physical: she has *philia* for it; she takes up a place alongside (*para*) and in solidarity with it; she loves and befriends it; at creation she hovered over and at the resurrection will consummate it" (Rogers, *After the Spirit*, 103-4).

[8]Rogers, *After the Spirit*, 101. He is commenting on a hymn by Romanos the Melodist.

[9]"That a virgin, become an advocate for a virgin, might undo and destroy the virginal disobedience by virginal obedience." Irenaeus, *On the Apostolic Preaching* 33, trans. John Behr, *St Irenaeus of Lyons: On the Apostolic Preaching* (Crestwood, NY: St Vladimir's Seminary Press, 1997).

[10]Frances Young, *God's Presence, Current Issues in Theology* (Cambridge: Cambridge University Press, 2014), 205.

through Mary's womb and nature as the second Eve, Christ can become the second Adam on behalf of all of humanity. Irenaeus puts it this way: "As the protoplast Adam had his substance of the virgin earth . . . so the Word himself, recapitulating Adam in himself, duly received from Mary, still a virgin, the birth of that nature in which Adam was recapitulated."[11] The overshadowing Spirit makes this exchange between Mary and Jesus not only possible but efficacious for all humanity, just as Jesus makes the great exchange between his divine nature and human nature effective for all.

A theology of the overshadowing Spirit demonstrates how God honors and befriends human bodies in the working out of redemption. Mary is a central example of how God does this because through the womb of Mary, the overshadowing Spirit manifests God's physical presence. Mary's womb, then, enables the Word to become flesh, granting to Jesus a human body and human nature so that he can recapitulate Adam for the sake of humanity. Mary can be thought of as birthing the church, the first human in the new covenant to be overshadowed by and filled with the Spirit. She is baptized by the Spirit just as the church throughout the ages will be baptized into the death of Christ and the Spirit of Christ's resurrection. Mary's womb, then, is the location of the overshadowing Spirit's initiation of the new creation, the consummation of God's reconciling work with all of creation.

Olivier Messiaen: Vingt Regards sur l'Enfant-Jésus

In *Vingt Regards sur l'Enfant-Jésus* (*Twenty Contemplations of the Infant Jesus*), Olivier Messiaen emblazes the glory of the incarnation in sound and deepens our theological contemplation of Jesus' vulnerability as an infant. For Messiaen, this small child reshapes the cosmos, and Messiaen seeks to capture this reality in his masterpiece. Moreover, through a complex series of musical movements departing from and returning to a central theme, he weaves the mother of Jesus into this work, contemplating how Mary makes a home and cares for the Son of God within

[11] Irenaeus, *Against Heresies* 21.10; as quoted in Young, *God's Presence.*

finite time. The eternal one through whom all things were made is now dependent on his earthly mother first for his physical existence and then, when a vulnerable infant, for his shelter, sustenance, and safety. Messiaen's music enables the listener to linger in the mystery of the infant Jesus and to not only wonder at the cosmos-shifting-reality of this event but also to sit with Mary as she contemplates the child growing in her womb. In doing so, I suggest, Messiaen's music can help listeners hear afresh, in perhaps ways that we could not otherwise, the overshadowing Spirit's invitation to dwell in God as God dwells in us.

Olivier Messiaen (1908–1992) was a French Catholic composer who is considered one of the great innovators of contemporary European music for his creations of unique forms of harmonic and tonal grammar and syntax. In his compositions, he rarely creates hummable melodies or expected music forms. Instead, his works manifest divine glory in sometimes dizzying rhythmic exploits, spiritual vision through the brilliance of chordal clusters, and joy using alien-sounding instruments (the *ondes martenot*) and birdsong (his *Turangalîla-Symphonie* could be the soundtrack for a science fiction movie). His impact on new musical language is undeniable, but what makes him significant in this context is the purposefulness of his thinking theologically *through* music. In his compositions, music thinks theologically in novel ways, helping us to reimagine what has become too familiar or staid within our thinking.[12]

1. Regard du Père ("Contemplation of the Father")
2. Regard de l'étoile ("Contemplation of the Star")
3. L'échange ("The Exchange")
4. Regard de la Vierge ("Contemplation of the Virgin")
5. Regard du Fils sur le Fils ("Contemplation of the Son upon the Son")
6. Par Lui tout a été fait ("Through Him Everything was Made")
7. Regard de la Croix ("Contemplation of the Cross")

[12]See Jeremy Begbie, "Through Music: Sound Mix," in *Beholding the Glory: Incarnation Through the Arts*, ed. Jeremy Begbie (Downers Grove, IL: InterVarsity Press, 2000), 139.

8. Regard des hauteurs ("Contemplation of the Heights")
9. Regard du temps ("Contemplation of Time")
10. Regard de l'Esprit de joie ("Contemplation of the Joyful Spirit")
11. Première communion de la Vierge ("The Virgin's First Communion")
12. La parole toute-puissante ("The All-Powerful Word")
13. Noël ("Christmas")
14. Regard des Anges ("Contemplation of the Angels")
15. Le baiser de l'Enfant-Jésus ("The Kiss of the Infant Jesus")
16. Regard des prophètes, des bergers et des Mages ("Contemplation of the Prophets, the Shepherds and the Magi")
17. Regard du silence ("Contemplation of silence")
18. Regard de l'Onction terrible ("Contemplation of the awesome Anointing")
19. Je dors, mais mon cœur veille ("I sleep, but my heart keeps watch")
20. Regard de l'Eglise d'amour ("Contemplation of the Church of Love")

Figure 7.1. Movements of *Vingt Regards sur l'Enfant-Jésus* by Olivier Messiaen

One such example is how Messiaen reinterprets the nativity and the incarnation in his *Vingt Regards sur l'Enfant-Jésus* for solo piano (fig. 7.1). Here Messiaen circumvents the typical telling of the nativity by meditating on the cosmos-shifting impact of the incarnation of the second person of the Trinity and the redemptive purposes of God in and through the created order. Instead of emphasizing typical nativity images such as shepherds, magi, lowing cattle, or quiet manger scenes, Messiaen offers swirling galaxies, discordant and sparkling stars, the somewhat chaotic beginnings of creation, beautiful yet uneasy lullabies, and the sound of love in the eternal church. He also features theologically important characters such as the cross, the star, the great exchange between God and humanity, and the Spirit of joy. Ultimately, Messiaen's *Vingt Regards* is a contemplation of the mystery of the incarnation and of the relationship between eternity and finitude that is embodied in Jesus. As Paul Griffiths argues, "It is the capturing of the eternal within the temporal that provides the work with its overriding challenge."[13] Throughout the twenty contemplations or movements, the work of the overshadowing Spirit joins together the divine and the created, the finite and the infinite, the eternal God working with, not against, what is material and finite. This intermixing of time and eternity connects to Messiaen's conviction that this child's participation in humanity enables humanity in turn to become children of God.

The exchange between divinity and humanity in Christ is a central and recurring theme in Messiaen's compositions and writings, and it can be summed up by second-century theologian Irenaeus's maxim, "He became what we are so that we might become what he is."[14] Most likely, as Stephen Schloesser notes, Messiaen borrows this concept from theologian Dom Columba Marmion, OSB. Marmion had an enduring influence on the theological content of Messiaen's compositions, especially through sounding out the doctrine of adoption or exchange. As Marmion maintains, "'In exchange for the humanity that He has taken to Himself, the Incarnate Word permits us to share in his divinity, He makes us participants in His divine nature: And thus is accomplished the most wonderful exchange we could ever celebrate.'"[15]

Schloesser argues that this is evident in the fifth and central movement of Messiaen's earlier work for organ, *The Nativity*, titled "The Children of God." He points out that *The Nativity* is chiastically organized (like a Greek letter *chi*, so every movement moves toward or out of the central movement, emphasizing the centrality of humanity's adoption as children of God; Jn 1:12-13; Gal 4:6). This doctrine returns in his later work on the nativity in *Vingt Regards* in the third movement, "The Exchange." As Griffiths suggests, the musical themes in this movement exemplify this exchange, with some phrases sounding eternity entering finite time by descending musical gestures, and others through ascending lines

---

[13]Paul Griffiths, *Olivier Messiaen and the Music of Time* (London: Faber & Faber, 1985), 114.

[14]Irenaeus, *Against Heresies* 5, preface: "Following the only true and steadfast Teacher, the Word of God, our Lord Jesus Christ, who did, through His transcendent love, become what we are, that He might bring us to be even what He is Himself." Trans. Alexander Roberts and William Rambaut in *Ante-Nicene Fathers*, ed. Alexander Roberts, James Donaldson, and A. Cleveland Coxe, vol. 1 (Buffalo, NY: Christian Literature, 1885), www.newadvent.org/fathers/0103500.htm.

[15]Dom Columba Marmion, as quoted in Stephen Schloesser, *Visions of Amen: The Early Life and Music of Olivier Messiaen* (Grand Rapids, MI: Eerdmans, 2014), 236.

demonstrating something of how Christ raises humanity, enabling us to participate in his divine nature.[16] The motif of crossing over (or more technically the "star + cross" motif, fig. 7.2) repeats throughout the movement, and one can almost feel the joining together of divine and human. Messiaen sounds out how Christ became a child of humanity, the Word becoming flesh, so that we might become children of God.

While Messiaen's Christology is quite explicit in his doctrinal explorations in *Vingt Regards*, it is in and through Mary that his implicit pneumatology can be delineated; for Messiaen, that is, it is the Spirit's *exchange* with Mary that sets this cosmic upheaval in motion. In movement four, "The Contemplation of the Virgin" (the first of the Marian movements), Messiaen attempts to capture her innocence and purity as she meditates on the annunciation. The beginning musical phrases descend in a repeating pattern throughout the movement, as if the Holy Spirit were descending and overshadowing this young woman as she contemplates Gabriel's words: "Do not be afraid, Mary, for you have found favor with God. And now, you will conceive in your womb and bear a son, and you will name him Jesus" (Lk 1:30-31 NRSV). She contemplates the work of the overshadowing Spirit and the possibility of such a child in her womb. She is only at the beginning of this story and wonders what it would mean for her to say yes and be filled with God's glory. Mary, a humble young woman of little standing, "becomes the Ark of the New Covenant between God and man," as Marmion argues.[17] She is a precursor to all those who will be found in Christ and will also become temples of the Holy Spirit and members with Christ (1 Cor 6:15, 19), becoming the body of Christ as the church.

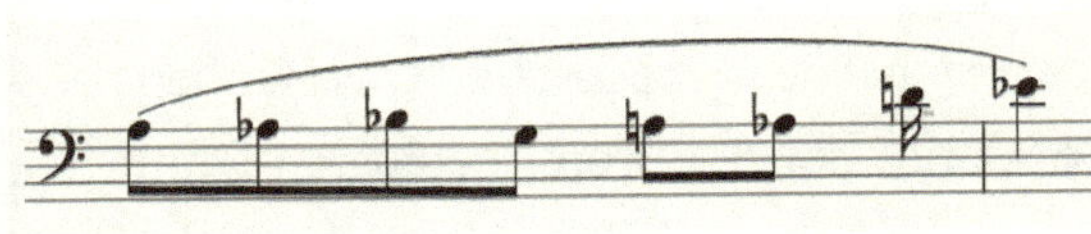

Figure 7.2. "star+cross" motif

In movement eleven, "The First Communion of the Virgin," we hear from the Mary of the Magnificat, her prophetic song (Lk 1:46-55) of

[16]Griffiths, *Olivier Messiaen*, 117.

[17]Dom Columba Marmion, *Christ in His Mysteries: A Spiritual Guide Through the Liturgical Year*, 9th ed., tr. Mother M. St. Thomas of Tyburn Convent (London: Sands & Co, 1939), 155.

wonder at the growing child in her womb. Her song proclaims the past work of God and the future promises of this child. Mary acknowledges that she is blessed and praises God for honoring his promises to Abraham and his descendants. She sings about how the work of the overshadowing Spirit in her conceiving this child will bring justice and good to the world, for the God who "has filled the hungry with good things" has also "brought down rulers from their thrones but has lifted up the humble." Messiaen marks this work through his "theme of God" motif (fig. 7.3), which sounds softly through most of the movement. The descent of the Spirit is also heard, marking the crossing over of the divine into the finite body of Mary. Exchange and crossing are sounded out like starlight, echoing Messiaen's star + cross (fig. 7.2) theme and movement three's exchange. Glory seems to break through in chordal clusters and arpeggios, but it is the sound of the child's heartbeats from Mary's womb sounded out in a section with low repeated Fs in the pianist's left hand. The movement then ends with a section titled "*Embrassement intérieur*" ("interior embrace"), transitioning into a mode of quiet wonder and praise as the theme of God grows quieter, yet still present, to make space for the Word to be made flesh, a foreshadowing of how "Mary treasured up all these things and pondered them in her heart" (Lk 2:18).

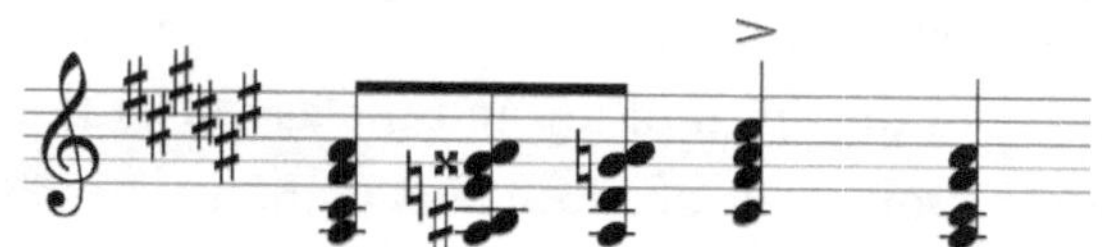

Figure 7.3. "theme of God" motif

The final movement of *Vingt Regards* is a contemplation of the eternal church, "Contemplation of the Church of Love." If, again, the waters of the womb of Mary are connected to the waters of baptism, then the church begins with Mary through the work of the overshadowing Spirit. Mary's body bearing Jesus then becomes a precursor to the church, which becomes the body of Christ in the world. Indeed, Mary's presence throughout *Vingt Regards* is concomitant with the eternal and eschatological church, as sounded by Messiaen. The church of love (*L'église D'amour*), as Messiaen names it, is the eternal life of those in Christ, filled with the Spirit. The major thematic material of this movement is Messiaen's "theme of God," along with echoes of the colorful, chordal exuberance of the Spirit of joy from the tenth movement—akin to the chimes of church bells on Christmas and Easter found in movement thirteen. As one listens, the unraveling of injustice and sorrow and the reweaving of the joy of resurrection throughout creation feels palpable. One can hear both the descent of the Spirit of joy and the ascent of the church into eternity. The final movement of Messiaen's piano masterpiece is about love and consummation, when all that is created joins with the divine love in eternity. Or as Messiaen comments in his notes about this movement, "triumph of love and joy, tears of joy."[18]

The overshadowing Spirit initiates this consummation in and through Mary's womb. As Rogers argues, "The opening of Mary's womb brings the advent of God's realm, a realm traditionally called God's kingdom."[19] He goes on to claim that the annunciation is primarily about consummation, the arc of justice and redemption, the fulfillment of God's promises as a whole. Mary becomes a prophet who sings a song of praise about her child, *the* Word, the one who sets right all wrongs. So, even as the Spirit, through Mary, births the church of the new covenant, so does the Spirit solidify the redemptive and reconciling purposes of God, the bringing about of the consummation of the kingdom or the household of God. Through the work of the overshadowing Spirit, Mary brings the Word into the flesh and births the one who justifies and transforms the cosmos.[20] Messiaen conveys this wonder and hope in his music, as faith, hope, love, and joy burst out like musical fireworks in celebration of the work of the overshadowing Spirit in the advent of the infant Jesus. Perhaps most crucially for our purposes here, Messiaen's decision to center Mary throughout not only further emphasizes the overpowering Spirit's role in reconciling and elevating humanity to familial kinship with Christ. It also opens up through this wonderfully complex exchange of sounds a new imagination of the unexpected mutuality in responding to the Spirit's overshadowing.

[18]Cagdas Soylar, *Messiaen's Musical Language on the Holy Child: A Study of Vingt Regards sur l'Enfant-Jésus, No: XIX: Je dors, mais mon coeur veille, No: XIV: Regard des Anges* (Eugene, OR: Wipf & Stock, 2019), 18.

[19]Rogers, *After the Spirit*, 104.

[20]Rogers, *After the Spirit*, 105.

The Overshadowing Spirit Today

Focusing on Mary, especially the importance of Mary's womb, can seem unconnected to daily Christian life and spirituality. Yet this chapter has emphasized the vital role of human bodies to the ongoing work of the Holy Spirit. Bodies are not secondary in the life of faith; bodies are the location where the Spirit is at work, initiating and perfecting faith within and through particular and collective bodies.[21] The Spirit shows up *because* of one's body, not despite it, just as the Spirit showed up with and through Mary.

On a practical level, what would it look like to make more space in worship spaces for the Spirit to become manifest in and through our bodies as Christians? As Rowan Williams argues,

> Only the body saves the soul. It sounds rather shocking put like that, but the point is that the soul (whatever exactly that is) left to itself, the inner life or whatever you want to call it, is not capable of transforming itself. It needs the gifts that only the external life can deliver: the actual events of God's action in history, heard by physical ears, the actual material fact of the meeting of believers where bread and wine are shared, the actual wonderful, disagreeable, impossible, unpredictable human beings we encounter daily, in and out of church. Only in this setting do we become holy—in a way unique to each one of us.[22]

He argues that believers are initiated into faith through baptism, and every sacrament, every eucharistic meal, reminds and renews in us that we bear Christ within our bodies.[23] The Spirit, then, guides and nurtures our worship through our bodies and material realities as we become the body of Christ in the world. This requires a certain anticipation for the presence of the Spirit as Christians throughout time to worship as the body of Christ in our many forms and denominations. This seems to

[21]See also W. David O. Taylor, *A Body of Praise: Understanding the Role of Our Physical Bodies in Worship* (Grand Rapids, MI: Baker Academic, 2023).

[22]Rowan Williams, *Silence and Honey Cakes: The Wisdom of the Desert* (Kidderminster, UK: Lion, 2004), 94-95.

[23]See also Rowan Williams, *Being Christian: Baptism, Bible, Eucharist, Prayer* (Grand Rapids, MI: Eerdmans, 2014).

expand naturally to creation care, for all of creation groans as in the pangs of childbirth for those who have the "firstfruits of the Spirit" to come fully into our identities and glory as the children of God (adoptees into God's household) and the "the redemption of our bodies" (Rom 8:23). The work of the Spirit and the inclusion of human bodies in the life of worship and faith seem to be intertwined. If we are to sing as Mary sang of the great works of God, we must embrace a full-bodied song of praise. As the psalmist declares, "Open my lips, Lord, and my mouth will declare your praise" (Ps 51:15).

Conclusion

Music has, as Messiaen demonstrates, the capacity to nurture and expand one's theological, liturgical, and aesthetic imagination. Music engages our senses and can open our hearts in anticipation of the work of the Holy Spirit. The work of the overshadowing Spirit prepares bodies and spaces to receive the glory and presence of God. Mary breaks into song after she says yes to the gifts of the overshadowing Spirit. She praises God and wonders at his mysterious ways. By singing prophetically of God's justice and reconciling purposes, she invites all who have come before and after her to prepare the way for the God who fills the hungry with good things and overcomes injustice (Lk 1:46-55).

The overshadowing Spirit gives a picture of where and how the Spirit prepares and enables God's presence to dwell in and with human bodies. Through Mary, the Spirit moves ahead in anticipation of the Word, enabling Christ to become fully human. If we miss out on the initiating work of the Spirit in Christ through Mary, we miss out on how the Spirit continues to work in the church and in our own lives. The clear purpose of the Spirit's overshadowing is to bring about the means, conditions, and possibilities for humanity to become coheirs with Christ, to be adopted into God's household for the "the redemption of our bodies" (Rom 8:23). The Spirit as the overshadowing one, then, invites us into being prepared to bear God in our bodies and in our ministries. The overshadowing Spirit seems to delight in befriending human bodies and initiating the work of reconciliation in the world into the new creation.

8

THE CONVICTING SPIRIT

THE HOLY SPIRIT'S USE OF BLACK MUSIC FOR THE NEW CREATION

Julian Davis Reid

DURING A PIANO PERFORMANCE at a church in 2022, God expanded my understanding of the Holy Spirit's convicting work in the world. The lesson came at the end of *Notes of Rest*, my contemplative-musical ministry that invites the weary to listen for God's transformative rest practiced in the Bible and Black music. To conclude the workshop, I began my customary solo piano rendition of the Negro spiritual "Give Me Jesus," which sends forth the community in the encouragement of my enslaved ancestors: to ultimately find their rest in Jesus no matter what this world gives or takes.

But that night's performance did not go as planned, for I sensed the Spirit prompting me to spontaneously enfold "Holy, Holy, Holy" into "Give Me Jesus." At the time, I found this addition odd and perhaps problematic, because "Holy, Holy, Holy" was written by a White Englishman in a rather different context from the antebellum slave context in which enslaved Black folk composed "Give Me Jesus." By incorporating a hymn of imperial Britain, I worried I was trivializing or even violating this sacred moment that centered the hard-earned wisdom of my enslaved ancestors. Far from accentuating rest in Jesus, including "Holy, Holy, Holy" could very well *disturb* the rest these Black folk prized and that I wanted my audience to hear. But in retrospect, my blending of the two songs demonstrated the capacity of Black musical practice to bear witness to the Holy Spirit who convicts God's people of participating in the old world of oppression that is passing away so that God's new creation can come.

This essay explores the musical, cultural, and theological dimensions of that night to advance the idea of the Spirit as the one who convicts. In the first section, I analyze select scriptural passages in which the Holy Spirit partners with people to convict the community of God of oppression and attempted control of God—of sinful habits that need to die so that the new life of God can break forth. The second section combines that scriptural backdrop with musical analysis to discuss my performance, where I too experienced God's convicting Spirit address oppression and needless control of the moment. The last section considers implications for the church's engagement today with the convicting Holy Spirit as experienced in music. Music in general, and Black music in particular, is a means by which the church can receive the Spirit's generative conviction.

Figure 8.1. Impromptu performance at University Presbyterian Church in Seattle, WA, 2022

Before turning to the scriptural analysis, I invite you to pause your reading and listen to my piano performance. You can click on the QR code to do so. I pray God's Spirit can continue speaking to us through that performance, and this essay, so that we too can partner with the creative, convicting Holy Spirit to enfold the old oppressive world into God's unfolding liberated one.

As you listen, you're invited to pray this prayer: God, show me how to be accountable to the enslaved composers of "Give Me Jesus." Amen.

The Holy Spirit's Conviction in Ezekiel and Luke-Acts

Our first scriptural case study is Ezekiel, whom the Holy Spirit empowers to convict and correct an adrift Israel. We focus on this prophet because (1) Ezekiel identifies the Spirit of Yahweh as the reason for his prophecy, (2) Ezekiel wrestles with the freedom of the Holy Spirit to act when and how God chooses, and (3) the Spirit's mission to convict Israel for their oppression is linked to the divine vision of restoration of Israel into a new, postexilic life.[1]

Ezekiel 11 opens with the Holy Spirit giving Ezekiel a vision in which he sees Judea's disobedience and injustice that led to Babylon's sacking of Jerusalem. In this vision, God brings to Ezekiel's attention two high-ranking officers of Israel, Jaazaniah and Pelatiah, whom Ezekiel, as God's spokesperson, blames for the unjust deaths of many Judeans in Jerusalem's streets (Ezek 11:1). Ezekiel prophesies that God will judge them for their culpability in the death of Judeans who opposed allying with Egypt against Babylon (Ezek 11:5-12). (Ezekiel understands such foreign alliance as contrary to reliance on God.)[2] While Ezekiel prophesies, Pelatiah dies, seemingly enacting God's judgment on Pelatiah's corrupt and deadly political maneuvering.[3] Pelatiah's death drives Ezekiel to cry out to God and question whether God will kill off the remnant of Israel (Ezek 11:13).

It is unclear from the text's tone whether the Spirit killed Pelatiah or whether Pelatiah died for another reason, for the text (in the NRSVUE) simply reads, "Now, while I was prophesying, Pelatiah son of Benaiah died." Either way, Pelatiah's death and Ezekiel's subsequent reaction suggest that the prophecy the Holy Spirit gave Ezekiel was not necessarily what Ezekiel himself wanted. In fact, it is possible that he did not want the corrupt official, notwithstanding his arrogance, to die. Ultimately,

---

[1]Robert L. Hubbard Jr., "The Spirit and Creation," in *Presence, Power and Promise: The Spirit of God in the Old Testament*, ed. David G. Firth and Paul D. Wenger (Downers Grove, IL: IVP Academic, 2011), 86-87.

[2]Joseph Blenkinsopp, *Ezekiel* (Louisville, KY: Westminster John Knox, 2012), 61-62.

[3]Dennis R. Bratcher, "Pelatiah," in *HarperCollins Bible Dictionary—Revised and Updated*, ed. Mark Powell (San Francisco: HarperOne, 2011).

Ezekiel's outcry shows he cannot control God's decision to exact justice as God wished on Israel.

Following Ezekiel's lament, in Ezekiel 11:14-25, God casts a vision for the restoration of exilic Israel to relationship with God and with each other in Jerusalem with the creation of a second temple. Still caught up in his Spirit-inspired vision, Ezekiel writes, "I will give them one heart and put a new spirit within them; I will remove the heart of stone from their flesh and give them a heart of flesh" (Ezek 11:19 NRSVUE). After this vision ends, Ezekiel returns to Babylonia and explains his vision to the exiles.[4]

Similarly to Ezekiel, Luke–Acts also reveals the Holy Spirit to be the one who convicts the community of God of its oppression and its attempts to control God. In Luke 4, Jesus announces in the temple that the Holy Spirit is upon him to announce freedom to the captives and good news to the oppressed. This declaration of his authority first leads to people praising him ("all spoke well of him," Lk 4:22 NRSVUE) but then quickly turns to consternation when Jesus tells them that his prophetic ministry will not fulfill their every wish (Lk 4:23-30). His refusal to capitulate to their desires angers them to the point of trying to stone him to death, which he escapes. The episode reveals their desire yet inability to control the Spirit-led rabbi, a theme which returns in Acts.[5]

In Acts 2:1-13, the Holy Spirit comes without warning and as a swift challenge to life in the community of Jesus as they knew it. As Jesus promised (Acts 1:5), the Paraclete arrives on the gathered Jewish community of Jesus and possesses the people to speak in the mother tongues of the Diaspora gathered in Jerusalem.[6] The Spirit's possession of those gathered leads them to testify to God's goodness in ways that form new connections between these disparate populations of the Roman Empire. Willie Jennings writes, "The Spirit create[d] joining. The followers of Jesus

[4]David L. Petersen, "Ezekiel," in *HarperCollins Study Bible—Student Edition: Fully Revised and Updated*, ed. Harold W. Attridge and Wayne A. Meeks (San Francisco: HarperOne, 2006), 1110-11.

[5]Though John is not narratively tied to Acts and probably was even written after Acts, this doctrine of the Holy Spirit coheres between the two writers sufficiently for my argument.

[6]Jeremy Begbie, *Theology, Music, and Time*, Cambridge Studies in Christian Doctrine 4 (New York: Cambridge University Press, 2000), 242.

[we]re now being connected in a way that join[ed] them to people in the most intimate space—of vice, memory, sound, body, land, and place."[7] Among the onlookers, such joining breeds incredulity—"[H]ow is it that we hear?"—and disbelief—"They are filled with new wine" (Acts 2:8, 13 NRSVUE). But in a beautiful moment of pastoral improvisation, Peter, who has been a part of this gathering, seizes on this novel outbreak of praise to convict the onlookers by educating them about the role of the Spirit in furthering the ministry of Jesus. I highlight the "improvisation" of this moment because, as we will see in my musical performance, being able to confront, in a moment's notice, aversion to intimacy between disparate groups is a mark of the Spirit's dynamism.

In Acts 2:14-36, Peter explains that the people are not drunk, but are filled with the Holy Spirit whom the prophet Joel prophesied would be poured out on all flesh (Joel 2:28-29). The uncontrollable reach of the Spirit means that people from all economic backgrounds are eligible to speak about the goodness of God with authority. As Jennings explains, "The famous Joel passage . . . proclaims a new world order energized by the movement of the Holy Spirit, breaking through on all flesh and destroying social orders that find slavery useful, stable, capable of making fundamental differences of identity between would-be masters and would-be slaves."[8] In the middle of an economic system and political system intent on subjugation and erasure of identity, Peter notes that the Spirit is calling the people to participate in a new life together grounded in a radical kind of giving and receiving toward one another.

For the onlookers at Pentecost, there could be no easy dismissal of the speech of God because of how the Spirit was moving through this diverse array of people. Pricked by this challenge, the listeners ask what they should do (Acts 2:37), a question that indicates they are heeding the challenge from the testifying community. Are the jeers going to turn into humble embrace or turn to a hardening of heart? The listeners answer by joining in droves, and the convicting call gives way to new life.

---

[7]Willie James Jennings, *Acts: A Theological Commentary on the Bible* (Louisville, KY: Westminster John Knox, 2017), 28.

[8]Jennings, *Acts*, 34-35.

Acts 5 plays on the theme of the Spirit's convicting work. In Acts 3–4, the community of Jesus proliferated, and the members sustained the community with their personal possessions. However, by Acts 5, one couple, Ananias and Sapphira, violate this agreement. They sold their land but withheld from the group a portion of the revenue, depriving others of economic support they needed. Peter confronts them for testing the Spirit of God in this way, and after they comprehend their deeds, they die. (It is unclear who is responsible for their death, just like in Ezekiel and Pelatiah. This is to say that the Spirit's creation of new life is not obviously tied to death, at least not in these instances.)

These scenes from Acts 2 and Acts 5 reflect how the Spirit functioned in the church as the Spirit did in Ezekiel with the remnant of Israel: moving beyond human control to convict people of their oppression and to invite members of the community into the new life that God is creating. With this view of the convicting Holy Spirit in mind, we now turn to the Spirit's presence as I experienced it in my performance.

Encountering the Convicting Holy Spirit in My Performance

I had the pleasure of offering Notes of Rest at a church in the heart of Seattle. The congregants were predominantly White and Asian people, with a few Black folk in the number. I assumed many of the attendees were decently middle class given the church's ornate sanctuary and beautiful Steinway concert grand piano. The night flowed with concert-hall attentiveness, which emerged from the European cultural value of listening to "great music." This value stands in contrast to the call-and-response culture of Black life, from which the Negro spirituals, including the song I played that night, and my musical and religious practice emerged. I note this contrast because the European great-music and communal Black musical traditions informed my performance decisions.[9]

I approached that night's performance as an improviser. As has been the case with many improvising musicians before me, I always try to avail

[9]Samuel A. Floyd, *The Power of Black Music: Interpreting Its History from Africa to the United States* (New York: Oxford University Press, 1995), 151.

myself to the Holy Spirit and receive the flow in the moment for the creative activity that will bring new life through my music.[10] I partner with God like the Spirit did with the earth at the beginning of creation and like Peter did with the Spirit in Acts, following God into the unknown. During this performance, that partnership took me to places I had never seen, not only with the inclusion of "Holy, Holy, Holy" at the end of the piece, but also with my initial treatment of "Give Me Jesus" itself.

The performance began with my playing the melody for "Give Me Jesus" *rubato* (1:49:04; *rubato* means "out of time"). I stretched the phrase in keeping with Black improvisational music traditions, creating more drama in the performance than is customary for spirituals. I decided to play *rubato* to heighten the suspense in my listeners, inviting them to lean forward and listen. This was channeling the impulse of the bebop tradition that I stand in as well, in which Black musicians in the 1940s made a distinct departure from the swing music that White people had monopolized in the 1930s. Thelonious Monk, Dizzy Gillespie, Charlie Parker, and other pioneers created a new music with angular melodies, complex rhythms, and "melodic paraphrases" that shifted jazz from being dance-hall music to a listener's music.[11]

After I moved through the first time of stating the melody with alternative harmonies, I picked up speed and filled the song with embellishment. Here I just let go and played. I was so consumed by the moment that I was no longer thinking about the kind of peaceful lilt that typifies the conclusion of most Notes of Rest sessions. On this night, I inhabited the vim and vigor of Black American cultural expression exemplified in the "exploratory rigor" of Bebop.[12] As I soared, it occurred to me that this unprecedented use of speed and complex harmonies was my attempt to connect with the original setting of the song.

Between the original context of plantation slavery in the nineteenth century and me in the twenty-first century sat the expanse of musical

---

[10]Jason Bivins, *Spirits Rejoice! Jazz and American Religion* (New York: Oxford University Press, 2015), 208-9.

[11]Floyd, *Power of Black Music*, 158.

[12]Eric Lott, "Double V, Double-Time," in *The Jazz Cadence of American Culture*, ed. Robert O'Meally, (New York, NY: Columbia University Press, 1998), 462.

development in Black music, specifically the concertized spirituals and the instrumental jazz tradition. The Negro spirituals emerged in a call-and-response culture in a setting where they were sung for the survival of those who worked the fields, not primarily for performance to fascinated crowds. However, after the Civil War, Black musicians such as the Fisk Jubilee singers adapted these songs for the concert-hall audiences that they could now command with their incredible performance. But this change was not without its cost. Samuel Floyd writes, "The Jubilee Singers had adapted the slave songs to fit the vocal and expressive requirements of their European-style choral training. . . . In the Jubilee Singers' renditions, the powerful Negro spiritual has been transformed into a fine imitation of itself."[13] Though I am not a singer, the Jubilee treatment of the song as a meticulously created performance in a concert venue shaped my approach as a pianist to "Give Me Jesus," furthering the distance between me and the original context of it as survival music created amid plantation life.

Jazz complicated my relationship to the spirituals even more. As Black folk started exploring new forms of freedom in music in the nineteenth and twentieth centuries, they took the blues and innovated on its rhythms by blending it with new harmonic structures and tempos that came from Europe.[14] Moreover, they did much of this through instrumental music, either writing music that had no lyrics to begin with—as was often the case in bebop—or playing word-based music on wordless instruments—e.g., John Coltrane's seminal rendition of "My Favorite Things." I would apply the latter strategy to "Give Me Jesus," playing it as an instrumental piece with great harmonic dissonance and elongated rhythm.

Notwithstanding these enduring differences, in the performance I could feel myself being convicted by the Spirit to remember my ancestors who composed this song and to remember those most violently experiencing anti-Blackness now. When I broke ties with the smooth, mellifluous beginning and started playing vigorously, I was signifying the break in predictability for Black folk in the United States. Black life in this

---

[13]Floyd, *Power of Black Music*, 61.

[14]Floyd, *Power of Black Music*, 158.

country has always been enshrouded in uncertainty, except for Black death and erasure: "the immanence of death as 'a predictable and constitutive aspect of this democracy.'"[15] As such, I disrupted the flow of the song to express the ongoing rupture that is Blackness. I hoped then and hope now that this approach to the music might help the congregation and myself hear the cries from the Black folk whose economic, physical, and social precarity in society today is most akin to that of the original composers. And to be clear, though all Black folk in the United States are subjected to the throes and woes of anti-Blackness, the degree to which I am personally subjected is attenuated vis-à-vis others given my socioeconomic standing and my training in music. Using Ananias and Sapphira as a cautionary tale, I want to hear the Holy Spirit's convicting word to me that I, given my access to abundant resources, am responsible to the life of the greater Black community. This performance in Seattle holds me accountable to my people as we navigate the continued precarity of anti-Black modern life and yet participate in God's new life for Black flourishing unfolding amid the oppressive status quo we endure.

The change in tempo and feel also reflected the heft of the song's lyrics. Below is an abridged version of the song's verses I had in mind while playing:

> In the morning when I rise (3×) / Give me Jesus . . . you can have all (of) this world, give me Jesus
>
> When I come to die / When I come to die / When I come to die, give me Jesus. . . . You can have all of this world, give me Jesus

These lyrics are a prophetic critique of the offerings of the so-called New World. Music critic Amiri Baraka notes that the Black slave had routinely been offered inclusion in the White world, but after the Civil War we realized the country would systemically deny us equality. We put our resulting disappointment into song. Baraka called such musicians "blues people," for they responded to the creation of this insurmountable chasm between Black folk and White folk with a uniquely sorrow-laden music.

---

[15]Christina Sharpe, *In the Wake: On Blackness and Being* (repr., Durham, NC: Duke University Press, 2016), 15.

He argues that the realization of the chasm, and the turn to our own resources to create music in response, is what has defined the "logic and beauty" of Black music in the United States ever since.[16]

This brisk portion of the spiritual was my inhabiting the blues-people ethos. In the twenty-first century I still lament how the chasm and the disappointment of the Reconstruction era persists. However, this part of the performance was a way for me to celebrate the joy of the Lord in my life. With reverence, praise, and joy I played the refrain, "Give me Jesus (2×) / You can have all this world / Give me Jesus." I was singing with my ancestors out of deep gratitude that God was present to us. My impulse to play "Give Me Jesus" briskly felt to be a conviction of the Holy Spirit for too often playing the spiritual morosely. Even in a world where Black people have been marked as "afterlife of property" in the wake of slavery, the Holy Spirit has given us a reason to get happy in our souls nonetheless, to "have a vibrant affirmation of life."[17] The declaration that Jesus was worth having no matter what this death-dealing world inflicted or confiscated was cause for my joy.

Then I began to tarry (1:51:35). As I was finishing my second pass through the song, I looped the ending by extending the final melody with flourishes on the melodies and eluding the home chord. By now I had left the *vivace (bright and quick)*, *fortissimo (very loud)* segment and had instead settled into a steady, flowing *mezzo forte (mildly loud)* pace, allowing the audience to settle into a period of uninterrupted playing. Ironically, I did not feel this calm on the inside because I did not sense a call to end the piece yet. This uncertainty was atypical because usually I played the song twice and then concluded on a simple tonic chord. In that moment, however, I sensed the Spirit come upon me again to draw to my attention "Holy, Holy, Holy."

As mentioned in the introduction and scriptural analysis, I found this pivot disorienting, which is why I resonated with Ezekiel when he was on his knees crying out about God's freedom to move as God wanted.

---

[16]Amiri Baraka, *Blues People: Negro Music in White America* (New York: William Morrow, 1963), 80.
[17]Sharpe, *In the Wake*, 15; James Cone, *The Spirituals and the Blues*, 4th ed. (Maryknoll, NY: Orbis, 1997), 31.

Initially I wanted to play "Give Me Jesus" without interruption to keep the focus on enslaved Black folk. But in that split-second decision to shift to "Holy, Holy, Holy," I sensed a new perspective emerging, which I attribute to the presence of the Spirit just like Peter provided new perspective in Acts. (Recall that the improvisational capacity of the Spirit makes conviction all the more possible in moments of surprised joining of disparate groups.)

In the moment, I decided to pivot for two reasons. The first reason I played "Holy, Holy, Holy" was to extend the close of "Give Me Jesus." "Holy, Holy, Holy" fit the tempo and chord progression enough such that I could flow without rhythmic hiccups. The second reason was that I knew the song would be recognizable to the people in the room. "Give Me Jesus" was a song that was recognizable to me and fit thematically with the vision of rest I had been casting throughout the night, but the majority White and Asian congregation might not have resonated. "Holy, Holy, Holy," however, would probably be familiar to them given its ubiquity in the hymnody of this church's denomination. I played it so they could praise God in their own tongue, just like in Acts 2. In choosing to use a shared language, I followed the Spirit in participating in the "revolution in the intimate" between this congregation and myself.[18]

Those were the hasty reasons for the decision at the time. But now in retrospect I see that the foundational reason to join these songs together was that the Spirit was prompting me to provide a convicting yet generative word to myself and the congregation about the oppression Black folk continue experiencing in society and the way in which God is taking us forward into new life. Before analyzing the performance itself, an analysis of the songs' lyrics illuminates this perspective on the Spirit's work.

Each song begins with an address to God in the morning—the second line of "Holy, Holy, Holy" has "early in the morning," and "Give Me Jesus" begins, "In the morning when I rise." However, the two morning risers meet the day differently. "Give Me Jesus" adopts the posture of one who is seeking to deny the world. "The world" here means the one in John 16:13

[18]Jennings, *Acts*, 27.

that needs to be convicted of its sin by the Holy Spirit: "And when he comes, he will prove the world to be in the wrong about sin and righteousness and judgment" (NRSVUE). In the case of "Give Me Jesus," it is the sin of Whiteness. The singer tells their imagined interlocutor that they can have this world. This is probably because the world to which the slave daily rises is one that subjects all Black folk to the "visual, discursive, state, and other quotidian and extraordinary cruel and unusual violences" of anti-Blackness, a violence that continues to perpetuate further violence.[19] So the composers declare, "You can have all this world, give me Jesus."

But Anglican Bishop Reginald Heber, the composer of "Holy, Holy, Holy," does not deny this world built on oppression. He instead rises in the morning to embrace and subdue it, claiming Christianity as a civilizing force wherever it went, including India, where he would serve as bishop.[20] Heber is recorded as having prayed for God to sanction Britain's imperial incursion into India: "Bless likewise, Oh Lord, all the potentates and former rulers, all the subjects and people of this land; that the loss of earthly dominion may be repaid by a Heavenly heritage, and that they may have cause to rejoice in that dispensation of Thy providence which hath made strangers to be Lords over them."[21] The Lord addressed in "Holy, Holy, Holy" is the God whose workmanship redounds to God's glory that Britain furthers: "All thy works shall praise thy name in earth and sky and sea." My performance in Seattle animated this tension between Heber composing a world-affirming song and the enslaved Black folk composing a world-denying one.

I approached "Holy, Holy, Holy" as a sad, dissonant lullaby. The song started at the top of the piano in the C5 octave and did not progress with the stately tempo customary in congregational settings. (Of course, nobody here was singing along, given the concert-hall setting.) When I landed on the lyrics "our song shall rise to thee," I play a D5 chord open and then a D7b9 chord. Typically, that landing chord before the return to

---

19Sharpe, *In the Wake*, 116-17.

20Geoffrey Cook, "'From India's Coral Strand': Reginald Heber and the Missionary Project," *International Journal of Hindu Studies* 5, no. 2 (2001): 131-32.

21Cook, "'From India's Coral Strand,'" 136.

the tonic chord (C major) is a straightforward G7 chord (or perhaps a G suspension to a G7 chord), which connoted more stability than what I played. But I injected more tension into this moment to show that "Holy, Holy, Holy" is not being sung with the stable joy coursing through Heber's text. Rather, this song of divine praise was taking its harmonic cues from the sorrowful joy of the singers of "Give Me Jesus," whom Bishop Heber's fellow churchmen in Europe and America had subjected to the hell of chattel slavery.

I continued this approach when I moved past the dominant harmony to the next line of the song, which again praises the God who is three times holy.[22] Instead of coming back to the C major tonic, I inserted a deceptive cadence and moved to the minor 6 harmony, further emphasizing this trace of sorrow inside the praise. And as soon as I get to the end of that line of text ("Lord God Almighty"), I moved back to the spiritual's line, "you can have all of this world / give me Jesus." That is, I elided the end of Heber's hymn, such that the God who receives our "holy, holy, holy" in Revelation 4:8 (NRSVUE) is also the God we petition to accompany us in the sorrow of the world that slavery has built.

I returned to "Holy, Holy, Holy" and progressed through the hymn again. (I am not sure what verse I had in mind, as this was all happening so fast that I was just trying to keep up with the chord changes!) This time the melody was played in the C4 register, meaning the middle of the piano, and is more confidently stated. I wanted to model praising God with the conviction of the proud Black folk who built this country that this world will not break us even amid our sorrow. I approached the end of the second line of text of the second verse—"casting down their golden crowns in earth and sky and sea"—with the more standard G7 chord that set me back up for the strong tonic chord, C major. But again, I only moved through half the verse before I felt whisked back to the refrain from "Give Me Jesus."

The unannounced quick movements from "Holy, Holy, Holy" back to "Give Me Jesus" added to my sense of living on my knees before the

[22]I am grateful to my dear friend and colleague Rev. Dr. R. Nick Peterson for this colorful naming of God.

uncontrollable Spirit, just like Ezekiel. Before that performance, I had rarely stitched songs together in such an unpredictable fashion. But doing so in this case allowed me to access the melodies of each respective song in new ways that made for a unique musical performance experience, one that resonated with the way the Spirit moved unpredictably in Luke 4 with Jesus. In Luke 4, Jesus convicts people of oppression and eludes control, and so did I here. Moving that quickly between the two was also a reminder to me and to the congregation that the theological vision of "Holy, Holy, Holy" was inside that of "Give Me Jesus." The majority non-Black audience was invited to hear something new of God's generative work in the world by hearing their familiar triumphant hymn turned into a lament, sung from the vantage point of the slave.

The performance could have ended with either hymn, but I found it fitting that I ended with "Give Me Jesus," and that I did so calmly. Ending with "Give Me Jesus" ensured "Holy, Holy, Holy" remained accountable to Black pain. Just like Jesus' declaration in Luke 4 of Isaiah 61, the Spirit of the Lord being upon me kept me mindful of the oppressed and the captive who needed (and needs) to hear good news. Moreover, after the whirlwind of a medley, ending with calm resolution was an affirmation of God's goodness to us amid it all. James Cone corroborates my decision: "Through [spirituals], black people were able to affirm that Spirit who was continuous with their existence as free beings; and they created a new style of religious worship."[23] It has been the Spirit who has walked with my people in our pain (as with, for example, the Fisk Jubilee singers) in such a way that we could reinterpret songs from the colonial powers over us and invite others to do the same. My hope was to prick the heart of the listeners, just like Peter's improvised speech did in Acts 2 or his confrontation did in Acts 5, to have them think about to whom this Black music made them accountable.

Holding the congregation accountable to Black pain is one level of the Spirit's work, but there was a deeper level for me. Recall that my initial aversion to adding a British imperial hymn was that it seemed irrelevant

[23]Cone, *Spirituals and the Blues*, 29.

to this moment focused on Black pain and hope. But the Spirit was convicting me of how my thinking needed to widen on how the Spirit moves. The Holy Spirit was bound neither to Ezekiel's concern, nor to the crowds around Jesus (in Luke) or Peter (in Acts), nor to me onstage. As the song unfolded before me, I felt convicted by the Spirit who, like in Joel, was imbuing the enslaved with the capacity to praise God's name with whatever song God pleased—in this case, a remix of "Holy, Holy, Holy."

To be sure, having grown up in Black United Methodist churches, I had seen my Black elders do just that—namely, adopting Charles Wesley, Isaac Watts, and Bishop Heber hymns to our own lives.[24] But on that special night in Seattle, my initial aversion revealed to me that I still had to practice releasing control and following the Spirit. The Spirit was not only convicting all of us of the horrors of slavery, but also convicting me of my need to grow my imagination about how God brings together the death of the old world into the life of the new creation, just like Israel's restoration into the temple.[25] In this new world, as revealed in Acts, the oppressor's melody finds voice within the song of the oppressed.

Implications for the Church Today

Our journey through this performance has shown how the Holy Spirit can use Black music to convict us should we listen for it. Black music can bring us forward into new life in God wherein oppression and corruption can be transmuted into healing, such as healing between those descendant from the "Give Me Jesus" composers and those descendant from the "Holy, Holy, Holy" composer. And as the lament version of "Holy, Holy, Holy" showed, the convicting Holy Spirit enacts this healing to overcome the evils of the world. Womanist theologian Karen Baker-Fletcher

[24]Willie James Jennings analyzes the supersessionist work of Isaac Watts hymns, whereby Britain replaces biblical Israel in the Psalter as God's chosen nation. Watts' imperial theology from the seventeenth and eighteenth centuries rhymes with fellow Englishmen Heber's in the nineteenth century. Yet, Black folk have appropriated Watts hymns in all kinds of ways to speak to our circumstance too. We sing joy to the world, for the Lord has indeed come. Cf. Willie James Jennings, *The Christian Imagination: Theology and the Origins of Race* (New Haven & London: Yale University Press, 2010), 211-19.

[25]For an expansive vision of redemptive art in the new creation, see Makoto Fujimura, *Art and Faith: A Theology of Making* (New Haven, CT: Yale University Press, 2021).

explains this vision of Spirit-empowered healing in her description of iconic Black American women freedom fighters: "Women like Mother Mamie Till-Mobley, Mother Rosa Parks, Mother Ella Baker, and First Lady Coretta Scott King could have hated, but walked in love. They could have sunk to violent rage, but instead they walked in holy indignation and holy dignity. They led others as they followed Christ in the comforting, encouraging, and healing power of the Holy Spirit."[26]

At a time when the US church is contending with problems that call for massive overhaul of our theologies and practices, we can use Black music in our churches to practice hearing the wisdom of God lodged in the throats of the oppressed, whose cries can usher in God's healing. The new creation yet breaks forth.

Related to that, my analysis invites us to discern how harmonic and rhythmic decisions can reinterpret the meaning of songs. I invite you to consider remixing music in your churches such that praise songs become self-aware lament songs and vice versa. When we do our historical homework, all our music, Black and otherwise, serves as fertile space to hold together the world-denial and world-affirmation to which the Spirit calls us. May this essay inspire creativity in your churches as you listen to the Spirit who is trustworthy to convict the world of sin so that new life may come. No matter your color, I pray we remember the convicting call of the Holy Spirit as animated by the voice of the enslaved African in these lands. Lord, give us Jesus as we cry holy. Amen.

---

[26]Karen Baker-Fletcher, *Dancing with God: The Trinity from a Womanist Perspective* (St. Louis: Chalice, 2007), 161-68.

9

THE SPIRIT AS THE BOND OF PEACE

ENACTMENT OF AND PARTICIPATION IN SPIRITUAL SONG

Amy Whisenand Krall

THROUGHOUT THE EPISTLE TO THE EPHESIANS, we find the Spirit present and working in a multiplicity of ways. The author writes that the letter's audience has been "sealed with the Spirit"[1] in both Ephesians 1:13 and Ephesians 4:30. The author prays that the audience may be "given the Spirit of wisdom and revelation" in Ephesians 1:17.[2] Through Jesus Christ and in "one Spirit," they—both Jew and Gentile—now have access to the Father (Eph 2:18). The mystery of Christ is revealed through the Spirit (Eph 3:5), and the congregation is strengthened through the Spirit (Eph 3:16). The author admonishes the congregation to "keep the oneness of the Spirit in the bond of peace" (Eph 4:3) and reiterates that there is one Spirit (Eph 4:4). Later in the letter, the congregation is exhorted to "be filled with the Spirit" (Eph 5:18). They are to take up the "sword of the Spirit" (which the author points out is the "word of God" [Eph 6:17]) as well as to pray in the Spirit (Eph 6:18).[3]

---

[1] All translations of the biblical text are my own unless otherwise noted.

[2] For more on the translation of "the Spirit" instead of "a Spirit," see Gordon D. Fee, *God's Empowering Presence: The Holy Spirit in the Letters of Paul* (repr., Grand Rapids, MI: Baker Academic, 2012), 675-76.

[3] The word for *spirit* occurs in Eph 2:2 and Eph 4:23, though not in reference to the Holy Spirit in Eph 2:2 and likely not in reference to the Holy Spirit in Eph 4:23. For more on this topic, see Fee, *God's Empowering Presence*, 679-80 and 709-12.

To ears within the modern North American context, the exhortation in Ephesians 4:3 to "keep the oneness of the Spirit in the bond of peace" brings up particular questions. A word such as *oneness* might sound like a move towards homogenization; the language of the Spirit as a *bond* could sound like restriction, and *peace* might even seem like an erasure of particularity in favor of uniformity and abandonment of difference. What kind of oneness, bond, and peace should we hear in this admonition and invocation of the Spirit? What does that language mean for the way the Spirit works within the church community?

The contemporary choral work "Hope for Resolution," a piece that integrates ancient plainsong chant and a South African protest song, can help us hear anew the emphasis in Ephesians on the Spirit's capacity to bring/bind these members of the church together, and particularly to enact a peace that does not negate particularity or difference but rather brings about a new creation.[4] Furthermore, attention to this choral work and to the scriptural activity of the Spirit presses us to expand our imagination for the adjective *spiritual* (*pneumatikos*), specifically with respect to "spiritual song" in Ephesians 5:19.[5] There is a trajectory of interpretation in both biblical scholarship and theology of worship that takes "spiritual song" as a reference to songs that are composed spontaneously in the Spirit. In this context, *spontaneity* becomes a key attribute of the adjective *spiritual*, and the phrase "spiritual song" corresponds to music making in the church that is unpremeditated and unplanned by humans. However, scriptural exegesis and musical interpretation retune our understanding of the adjective *spiritual* to hear it together with the "bond of peace." The adjective *spiritual*, specifically in the context of "spiritual song," denotes the enactment of the bond of the Spirit—the bond that draws together the new humanity brought into community through the life, death, resurrection, and ascension of Jesus Christ.

---

[4]An excellent recording of "Hope for Resolution" can be found on YouTube. See "Hope for Resolution (Arr. S. Ivory & P. Caldwell)," St. Olaf Choir – Topic, February 4, 2021, YouTube video, 6:07, www.youtube.com/watch?v=8a5NWASPU50.

[5]This essay primarily focuses on Ephesians. However, due to their similarities, Ephesians and Colossians are often read together as a literary pair, especially when it concerns the exhortations about "psalms, hymns, and spiritual songs" in Eph 5:19 and Col 3:16.

The following essay will begin by tracing the activity of the Spirit in Ephesians in concert with the choral work "Hope for Resolution," helping us to hear anew the "oneness of the Spirit in the bond of peace" (Eph 4:3) as the formation of new creation without erasure of particularity. The second part then explores how such revocalization of the bond of peace puts pressure on interpretations that limit the definition of "spiritual song" to "unpremeditated spontaneous music making." The final section of the essay will then draw out how the revocalization of "bond of peace" (from the first part of the essay) can expand our imagination for "spiritual song" in Ephesians 5:19—particularly as an enactment of and participation in the bond of peace. In short, "Hope for Resolution" helps us hear anew the exhortation in Ephesians 4:3 as a call to unity that does not erase particularity as well as to hear "spiritual song" as an enactment of and participation in the formation of the new creation.

The "Bond of Peace"

When the author of Ephesians exhorts the audience to "keep the oneness of the Spirit in the bond of peace" (Eph 4:3), the question of what happens to difference and particularity arises (and matters) because, according to the witness of Ephesians in particular and the New Testament more broadly, the Spirit draws together people from across ethnic and socioeconomic boundaries. This is a repeated movement across the book of Acts—from Pentecost (Acts 2:1-47), to the outpouring of the Holy Spirit on Cornelius and his household (Acts 10), to the Jerusalem Council (Acts 15), to the baptisms of Lydia and the Philippian jailer (Acts 16:11-34), to name a few examples. We find this pattern again in Paul's admonitions to the Corinthians—the congregation draws from a diversity of socioeconomic locations (1 Cor 1:26). The letters to the Ephesians and Colossians imply the presence of both Greeks and Jews among the church community (Eph 2:14-18; 4:3; Col 3:10; 4:15). As summarized in the letter to the Colossians, "Greek and Jew, male and female, enslaved and free" now live "in Christ" (Col 3:11).

What happens, then, to difference and particularity? Within Ephesians, because of the work of Jesus Christ (Eph 2:14-18) and the acting of the

Spirit (Eph 4:3), these diverse peoples now find themselves together worshiping and living in community. Because of the Spirit, they participate in the "new human" (see Eph 4:24; Col 3:10). Here, the divisions between Jew and Gentile have been torn down by Jesus Christ, who brings about peace (Eph 2:14-18). They have reconfigured social relationships—new social bonds.

Significantly, Ephesians makes no mention of Jews either becoming or becoming "like" the Gentiles, or the Gentiles becoming or becoming "like" Jews. In fact, texts such as Acts 15 and the account of the Jerusalem Council press against the notion of Jews and Gentiles assimilating to one another. In Ephesians, the peacemaking accomplished in Jesus Christ enables both Jew and Gentile to have access to God (Eph 2:18). It is in the context of this new reality that the author of Ephesians admonishes the audience to "keep the oneness of the Spirit in the bond of peace" (Eph 4:3). However, does this new unity mean neither Jews nor Gentiles retain their own particularity? Put another way, do they each assimilate to a third group that negates or erases their uniqueness?

Attention to "Hope for Resolution: A Song for Mandela and deKlerk" by Paul Caldwell and Sean Ivory can help interpret the oneness, bond, and peacemaking of the Spirit by providing a rearticulation or revocalization of the possibility for unity without erasure. "Hope for Resolution" can help us hear how both Jew and Gentile can now participate in community together such that their unique social histories are not erased while a new history can yet begin in relationship with one another.

In the choral arrangement we find two songs, "Of the Father's Love Begotten" and "Thula Sizwe." These two songs come from two different styles, two distinct musical traditions, and two unique languages. "Of the Father's Love Begotten" is sung in English. It is a translation from the 1850s by J. M. Neale and H. W. Baker of a Latin hymn composed by Marcus Aurelius Clemens Prudentius during the christological controversies of the fourth century CE. The tune, *Divinum Mysterium*, is a plainsong chant that derives from twelfth- to fifteenth-century manuscripts of the *Divinum Mysterium* text. "Thula Sizwe" is sung in Zulu—it translates into English as, "Be still, nation. Do not cry / Your Jehovah will fight for you." During anti-apartheid protests in South Africa, it was one of the songs used to unite and uplift the protesters. "Hope for Resolution" as a choral arrangement lyrically and musically binds together these two songs while being a composition in itself as a choral arrangement.

Lyrical analysis of "Hope for Resolution." "Thula Sizwe" was originally a lullaby, expressing faith in the protection of God. In its reception, this lullaby participates in the tradition of incorporating lullabies for lament and protest of oppression.[6] The words of the lullaby-as-protest-and-lament assure the listeners that God will indeed intervene and protect them. "Of the Father's Love Begotten" describes how Christ was "begotten before all worlds" of the Virgin Mary and deserves praise, "hymn and chant and high thanksgiving." It is a lyrical, doctrinal argument for the incarnation, God's entrance into our world, and God's deep care and love for humanity, as well as God's worthiness of worship.

Together, the two individual songs play off each other while retaining their own language and message. The interplay of the two songs brings out new meaning from each. "Thula Sizwe" fills out the reflections of "Of the Father's Love Begotten"—the God who has entered into the world out of love also intervenes on behalf of the oppressed. This new composition tells of the character of God, who enters into the human world and protects the vulnerable. As such, the listeners can be reassured and confident in the protection of God as they seek freedom. In this interplay—a sustained playing off each other—we find something new, a third song, "Hope for Resolution."

Musical analysis of "Hope for Resolution." Musically, we find that the arrangement preserves the distinctness of each song, even as we witness the presence of a new musical composition. While the melodies of the two distinct songs intertwine, each retains its integrity—the listener can recognize them as their original tunes. Yet, each of the two songs is also set—bound together—in a new, reconfigured arrangement.

As "Hope for Resolution" begins, we hear the simple melody from the plainsong chant of "Of the Father's Love Begotten." The composers have

[6]Thank you to Johann Buis, who pointed out this aspect of the song to me.

noted that the opening choir is to be sung by a children's choir (measures 10-90).[7] The children begin by singing the first verse in unison (measures 10-29) and the second and third verses as a round (measures 30-49, 70-89). Between the second and third verses, the piano breaks in, echoing the melody and harmonizing. The third verse also introduces flute with a countermelody.

Then there is a brief pause/break/breath. The adult choir (soprano, alto, tenor, and bass) breaks in with the words of "Thula Sizwe" (measure 91). The percussion begins in the very next measure (measure 92). The adult choir sings two verses of "Thula Sizwe" (measures 91-106/107), and then the piano echoes the melody with another interlude.

After this brief piano interlude, the adult choir divides. One choir leans into the pickup to begin the first verse of "Thula Sizwe" again (measure 125), while this time the other choir—doubled by soprano sax—begins verse one of "Of the Father's Love Begotten" on the downbeat of the next measure (measure 126). The choirs continue to sing the two songs simultaneously for the next several measures (measures 126-54). In measure 154, the composers indicate an optional semichorus (within the adult choir), which sings harmony on "Thula Sizwe" to the end (measures 154-65).

What is happening musically in the combining and intertwining of these two pieces? These two pieces retain the characteristics of their musical tradition; "Of the Father's Love Begotten" is musically linear, while "Thula Sizwe" is musically circular and repetitive.[8] Yet the two pieces join together into a third distinct piece of music as its own entity. In the intertwining of these two songs, we find uniqueness and yet synchroneity—difference and sameness as well as diversity and unity.

Music has this capacity for difference and sameness, or, as Jeremy S. Begbie writes in "Room of One's Own?," for interpenetration. Drawing on Victor Zuckerkandl, Begbie writes, "When one tone is heard along with a different one, it does not drive the first away, nor is it in a different place,

---

[7]When I have heard this song performed, women's voices have sung this first part instead of a children's choir.

[8]Thank you to Johann Buis for pointing out these important differences between the two pieces.

nor does it merge with the first to create a new tone. Both are heard as full and distinct. . . . They can be *in* one another, while being heard *as* two distinct tones."[9] In "Hope for Resolution," we find two different songs from two different traditions sounding at the same time with their own unique characteristics. While set, configured, and bound together to the other song in a new setting/arrangement, each song retains integrity and is recognizable as itself. Each retains its own unique identity. At the same time, the composers have joined the two songs such that together they are a new piece of music. When the choir sings this choral arrangement, we encounter a new song with its own particularity. The unity of the two pieces, and of the singers voicing the musical lines, presents us with a third piece of music—the bond between the two pieces, which is yet again something itself.

Lyrically and musically, "Hope for Resolution" embodies and witnesses to the specific characteristic of "oneness of the Spirit in the bond of peace" in Ephesians 4:3. The Spirit brings about unity between different voices/groups, creating something new. The peacemaking of the Spirit is generative of a new creation. Those in Jesus Christ live as the "new human" (Eph 4:24; Col 3:10). In this new creation, particularity and difference are not erased—they continue to persist in the retelling of the story of peacemaking (Eph 2:14-18). Particularity and difference are bound up in God's saving work.

The Bond of Peace and Spiritual Song

Hearing the exhortation "to keep the oneness in the bond of the peace" in Ephesians 4:3 in concert with "Hope for Resolution," we turn to the adjective *spiritual* (*pneumatikos*), specifically with respect to "spiritual song" in Ephesians 5:19.[10] The revocalization of the bond of peace can expand our imagination for spiritual song. The third and final section of this essay will develop this claim and attend to the ways that spiritual song

---

[9]Jeremy S. Begbie, "Room of One's Own? Music, Space, and Freedom," in *Music, Modernity, and God: Essays in Listening* (Oxford: Oxford University Press, 2013), 141-75, especially 159.

[10]This argument also has implication for the parallel exhortation in Col 3:16. However, in this essay I focus on Eph 5:19.

becomes an enactment of and participation in the bond of the Spirit. However, hearing spiritual song through the bond of peace (together with "Hope for Resolution") puts pressure on certain interpretive trajectories in both biblical scholarship and theologies of worship in contemporary North American Protestant contexts. This section addresses these interpretive moves.

In these interpretive trajectories, the adjective *spontaneous* becomes an implicit and even sometimes explicit complement/characteristic of the adjective *spiritual*. As such, "spiritual song" is understood as "spontaneous song," especially in applications of Ephesians 5:19 (Col 3:16). Significantly, *spontaneous* here means "unpremeditated," even "unexplained from a human perspective." It is important to note that by *spontaneous* these commentators do not mean "improvisational." Improvisation depends on listening to one's fellow participants (whether musical or theatrical) and responding to others—playing off them—in the moment. Improvisation, while created in the moment, still results from human activity, with attention to both present musical action and deeply ingrained musical knowledge and habits derived from practicing with and without others.[11]

However, these commentators use the word *spontaneous* to denote activity with a nonhuman origin—and thus divine origin. One sometimes gets a picture of a Spirit purposefully avoiding human structures and organizations. To consider two examples among biblical scholarship: Ralph Martin expresses hesitation in distinguishing between the "psalms, hymns, and spiritual songs," in Ephesians 5:19 and Colossians 3:16. Yet he also posits that psalms take inspiration from the Old Testament Psalter, while hymns are "longer compositions." He proceeds to hypothesize that spiritual songs "refer to snatches of spontaneous praise which the inspiring Spirit placed on the lips of the enraptured worshipper as 1 Corinthians xiv, 15 implies"—and he adds, "These 'inspired odes' would no doubt be of little value, and their contents would be quickly forgotten."[12]

---

[11]Thank you especially to Julian Davis Reid for sharpening my thinking on this point.

[12]Ralph P. Martin, *Worship in the Early Church* (Grand Rapids, MI: Eerdmans, 1974), 47; see also 43, 137.

Likewise, in a comprehensive study of the Spirit (and its related lexical forms) across the New Testament, Gordon Fee puts forth the idea that spiritual songs could refer to "spontaneous song" when he discusses Colossians 3:16 (and later references his treatment of Col 3:16 when he discusses Eph 5:19). While Fee (like Martin) expresses reservation about assigning definitions to each of the three terms "psalms, hymns, and spiritual songs" as specific types of musical compositions, he concludes that the adjective *spiritual* (*pneumatikos*) modifies *song* (rather than all three terms—*psalms*, *hymns*, and *songs*).[13] With respect to the use of the adjective *spiritual* (*pneumatikos*), he comments, "We are dealing with songs that are inspired by the Spirit. As noted on 1 Cor 14:15-16 and 26, this most likely indicates a kind of 'charismatic hymnody' in which Spirit-inspired, and therefore often spontaneous, songs were offered in the context of congregational worship."[14] While this connection between spiritual songs and spontaneity is not universally held, it still represents a significant interpretive trajectory in understanding "spiritual song" in Ephesians 5:19 (and Col 3:16) and a significant interpretation of how the Spirit works in the life of the congregation.[15]

---

[13]When expositing the meaning of "psalms, hymns, and spiritual songs" in Eph 5:19 and Col 3:16, biblical scholars often divide the three terms into three types of song. To be sure, many biblical scholars hesitate to make distinctions between psalms, hymns, and spiritual songs. See, for example, Heinrich Schlier, "ᾄδω ᾠδή," in *Theological Dictionary of the New Testament*, ed. Gerhard Kittel and Gerhard Friedrich, trans. Geoffrey W. Bromiley (Grand Rapids, MI: Eerdmans, 1964–1976), 1:163-65; Eduard Lohse, *Colossians and Philemon*, trans. William R. Poehlmann and Robert J. Karris, Hermeneia (Minneapolis: Fortress, 1971); Eduard Schweizer, *The Letter to the Colossians: A Commentary*, trans. Andrew Chester (Minneapolis: Augsburg, 1982), 210. By contrast, Barth and Blanke see *spiritual* as referring to all three terms, and they do not distinguish between the terms. See Markus Barth and Helumt Blanke, *Colossians: A New Translation with Introduction and Commentary*, trans. Astrid B. Beck, Anchor Bible 34B (New York: Doubleday, 1994), 427-28.

[14]Fee, *God's Empowering Presence*, 653.

[15]For example, R. McL. Wilson, *A Critical and Exegetical Commentary on Colossians and Philemon*, International Critical Commentary (London: T&T Clark International, 2005), 267-69. Here again, we find another biblical interpreter who connects *spiritual* with *spontaneous*.

In her commentary on Ephesians and Colossians, Margaret MacDonald also points out the dependence of the phrase "psalms, hymns, and spiritual songs" on the Spirit (Eph 5:18-19). She argues that in Colossians the instructional nature of the phrase is drawn out, while in Ephesians the connection to the Spirit is highlighted. Regarding Colossians, MacDonald says we cannot distinguish between the three terms "psalms, hymns, and spiritual songs" (following Lohse and Meeks). However, she says that spiritual songs likely denote the gift of tongues and the inspiration of the Spirit (referencing 1 Cor 14:15). See Margaret Y. MacDonald, *Colossians and Ephesians*, Sacra Pagina 17 (Collegeville, MN: Liturgical Press, 2000), 143.

A similar connection between *spiritual* (*pneumatikos*) and *spontaneous* finds expression in literature about worship by theologians of worship. Here I take David Blomgren and his book *Song of the Lord* as a helpful snapshot of significant influences in contemporary praise and worship music.[16] Blomgren's book contains musical techniques that became standard—especially as relates to flow in worship. Given the window into musical practice that Blomgren's work provides, it is helpful to consider what he writes about "spiritual song" and to explore his exegesis.

Blomgren writes about "psalms, hymns, and spiritual songs" as a guide for worship leaders, and he breaks down the three terms as signifying distinct categories of songs for worship. *Psalms* designate "Songs of Praise from Scripture or songs in the character, spirit, or manner of O.T. Psalms," and they are directed primarily to God. *Hymns*, on the other hand, denote "Songs of Praise of Human Composition on Christian Themes." Such hymns are directed at other worshipers in praise of God for the purpose of supporting others in worship. Finally, and most importantly for our purposes, Blomgren defines "spiritual songs" as praise-oriented songs of

---

Additionally, in his commentary on Philemon, Colossians, and Ephesians, Ben Witherington III conjectures that the term "psalms" (*psalmos*) refers to "praise with accompaniment," the term "hymns" (*hymnos*) to prewritten, liturgical, a cappella pieces, and "spiritual songs" to spontaneous songs prompted by the Spirit. See Witherington, *The Letters to Philemon, the Colossians, and the Ephesians: A Socio-rhetorical Commentary on the Captivity Epistles* (Grand Rapids, MI: Eerdmans, 2007), 312). In his discussion of the parallel phrase "psalms, hymns, and spiritual songs" in Col 3:16, Witherington writes, "Of the three types of songs, psalms would presumably refer primarily to the OT songs we find in the Psalter, hymns to the king of Christological material we find in Colossians 1 (it certainly refers to something sung to a deity), and spiritual songs to songs prompted by the Holy Spirit, perhaps spontaneously" (181).Witherington references James Dunn in support. Regarding the phrase in Col 3:16, James Dunn also argues that the adjective *spiritual* qualifies *song* such that it refers to something sung under the influence of the Holy Spirit. See James D. G. Dunn, *The Epistles to the Colossians and to Philemon: A Commentary on the Greek Text*, New International Greek Testament Commentary (Grand Rapids, MI: Eerdmans, 1996), 239. However, Witherington does qualify his claims by saying, "We cannot be certain about any of this (cf. Col 3:16). It could just be part of the Asiatic style with its proclivity for 'piling up near synonyms'" (*Letters to Philemon, the Colossians, and the Ephesians, 181*). Nonetheless, Witherington does cautiously suggest the connection between *spiritual* and *spontaneous*.

[16]Lester Ruth and Lim Swee Hong, *A History of Contemporary Praise and Worship: Understanding the Ideas That Reshaped the Protestant Church* (Grand Rapids, MI: Baker Academic, 2021), 61-65. As Ruth and Lim note, "It would be wrong to say either that Blomgren's book was *the* book that launched the discussion of how to do periods of congregational singing or that it was *the* book that all future worship leaders referenced for proper technique. However, it is a good window into Praise & Worship musical technique" (64, emphasis original).

"a spontaneous or unpremeditated nature with unrehearsed melodies, sung under the impetus of the Holy Spirit."[17] Blomgren describes these spiritual songs as directed both to God and to other humans for edification.

Significantly, the notion of spontaneity takes precedence in this categorization. According to Blomgren, the adjective *spiritual* (*pneumatikos*) refers to the inspiration of the Holy Spirit and the charismatic gifts of the Spirit named in 1 Corinthians 12:1. He argues that the adjective (*pneumatikos*) does not refer to the charismatic gifts in general but specifically to the gift of speaking by the Spirit in tongues and prophecy.[18] So, "spiritual songs" are songs through a human singing in the Spirit. Moreover, Blomgren connects spontaneity with the activity of the Spirit by taking spontaneity as evidence of a nonhuman origin. He writes that spiritual songs have an "unpremeditated nature, with unrehearsed melodies," and they "are more than the natural creative inspiration of a Christian musician. They are songs birthed spontaneously under the impetus of the Holy Spirit."[19] While Blomgren does not use the word *unexplained* to illuminate the adjective *spiritual* (*pneumatikos*), his exposition points in that direction. The unexplained becomes evidence of something beyond the natural world, evidence of God and the work of the Spirit. In a secular world, humans need evidence of something transcendent. God's activity is reduced to the unexplained actions that occur in the moments that humans do not plan and/or cannot account for.

While Blomgren wrote several decades ago, we still find similar thoughts about the work of the Spirit and spontaneity at play in discussions about worship today. For example, in his writing about worship planning, Zac Hicks first identifies an approach to worship planning that conceives of the Spirit as the one who fills in the gaps for humanly planned worship.[20] Hicks then argues for a balance of planning and openness to spontaneity

[17]David K. Blomgren, *Song of the Lord* (Portland, OR: City Bible, 1989), 10-11. All quotation in this paragraph come from these two pages.

[18]Blomgren, *Song of the Lord,* 57. See footnote on his explanation of the grammatical gender here. Blomgren supports his point by turning to 1 Cor 14:37 (as well as Gal 6:1; 1 Cor 2:15).

[19]Blomgren, *Song of the Lord, 11,* 57-58.

[20]Zac Hicks, "Spontaneity, Planning, and the Holy Spirit in Worship," July 20, 2015, https://zachicks.com/spontaneity-planning-and-the-holy-spirit-in-worship/.

and cites Constance Cherry for support. Cherry points out, "Though the Holy Spirit may appear to us to act spontaneously, this is because we are often unaware of the Spirit's action until it occurs, for we are not often privy to God's actions in advance. Therefore it is a leap in logic to assume that the Spirit primarily acts spontaneously and is therefore the preferred mode for the ordering of worship events."[21] While Cherry argues against understanding *spiritual* as only or merely "spontaneous," and while Hicks too presses toward a balance of planning and spontaneity, the fact that they each address an understanding of *spiritual* as "spontaneous" shows the continued popularity and prevalence of this view.

Spiritual Song as Enactment of and Participation in the Bond of Peace

However, attention to the "oneness of the Spirit in the bond of peace" (Eph 4:3)—as heard through "Hope for Resolution" and with the larger themes of Ephesians and the New Testament—challenges us to broaden our imagination for what *spiritual* (*pneumatikos*) means in the context of "spiritual song" and thus also what "spiritual song" could be. In the New Testament, we find the adjective *spiritual* (*pneumatikos*) peppered across the Pauline letters (Rom 1:11; 7:14; 15:27; 1 Cor 2:13, 15; 3:1; 9:11; 10:3-4; 12:1; 14:1, 37; 15:44, 46; Gal 6:1).[22] The occurrences of the word show that it serves to describe something "pertaining to the Spirit." Moreover, in Ephesians, the admonition to incorporate "spiritual song" serves to illustrate how "being filled with the Spirit" comes about (Eph 5:18).

And what does the Spirit do? As discussed earlier, the Spirit, as the "bond of peace," brings about a new creation in which the particularities of those brought together are not erased. The adjective *spiritual* then describes the effects of the characteristic of Spirit as the one who brings

---

[21]Constance Cherry, *The Worship Architect: A Blueprint for Designing Culturally Relevant and Biblically Faithful Services* (Grand Rapids, MI: Baker, 2010), 41. Cherry continues, "I am not suggesting that there should not be room for unexpected movements of God's Spirit in worship; these should be expected and welcomed when they occur. Yet there is no biblical evidence that the Holy Spirit is especially available as an antidote for inadequate worship planning" (41).

[22]We may include Ephesians and Colossians in the Pauline corpus whether or not they are written by Paul. It is generally conceded that they are significantly influenced by Paul, and if they are not Pauline, that the author strives to imitate Paul.

about unity and who binds together without obliterating particularity. *Spiritual* names the social implications of the enactment of and participation in this bond of peace.

Some arguments in contemporary biblical scholarship can lend support to emphasizing such social dimensions of the adjective *spiritual*. In his article "Πνευματικός in the Social Dialect of Pauline Christianity," John Barclay argues that the word *spiritual* (*pneumatikos*) reflects the early Christian "social dialect"—that is, ways of using language that reflect a community's interpretation of events and the world.[23] Within this Christian social dialect, the adjective *spiritual* (*pneumatikos*) denotes the kind of people who are "in Christ"; it describes the members of the early church community as "Spirit-people."

Barclay argues that the early Christians took this adjective and infused it with special meaning. The adjective occurs in usage outside the New Testament, though only rarely outside Jewish Greek. When Paul uses the adjective in his letters, he uses it without explanation. Barclay points out that this lack of explanation of the word shows that Paul is not developing an "idiolect," that is, speech that has meaning only particular to Paul's own usage. Rather, the word reflects a particular use and has a specific meaning within the early Christian community. The adjective "describes people . . . in relation to their new status as graced by the Spirit of God." Put another way, the adjective *spiritual* denotes a certain group of people unified by a certain experience. It is a social designation.[24]

We can press Barclay's conclusions still further with respect to the use of the adjective in Ephesians. If the adjective *spiritual* identifies a specific social group or community (one defined by the work of the Spirit), then the "oneness of the Spirit in the bond of peace" (Eph 4:3) should also shape our understanding of the adjective *spiritual* (*pneumatikos*) as a "social designation" for "those who are in Jesus Christ." We should thus

[23]John M. G. Barclay, "Πνευματικός in the Social Dialect of Pauline Christianity," in *The Holy Spirit and Christian Origins: Essays in Honor of James D. G. Dunn*, ed. Stephen C. Barton, Bruce W. Longenecker, and Graham N. Stanton (Grand Rapids, MI: Eerdmans, 2004), 159.

[24]Barclay, "Πνευματικός in the Social Dialect," 161, 167.

also expect the adjective to denote the capacity and characteristic of the Spirit to bind together God's people in love for the purpose of unity.

As we explored in the first section of this essay, "Hope for Resolution" as a choral arrangement lyrically and musically helps us hear this kind of unity. In the musical arrangement of these two unique pieces, we find a third piece. The two unique pieces come together—retaining their uniqueness and particular qualities—to participate in something new, a piece of music in its own right. This choral work helps us hear the nature of the oneness, bond, and peace in Ephesians 4:3. It helps us hear the adjective *spiritual* as a social designation for the people of God, one that witnesses to the Spirit's capacity to bind together without erasure of difference.

This way of understanding the adjective *spiritual* should in turn shape and infuse our interpretation of "spiritual song" in Ephesians 5:19.[25] "Spiritual song" more broadly denotes corporate singing that binds diverse followers of Jesus Christ together. We can extend our understanding of "spiritual song" to a range of corporate song (not only spontaneous and unwritten melodies) that builds and strengthens the bond of the members of the church together in Christ.

The act of corporate singing in itself can embody this characteristic to bring about social bonds. Studies in music psychology provide such evidence. For example, Ian Cross, Felicity Laurence, and Tal-Chen Rabinowitch write about the power of corporate music to cultivate empathy between participants and to forge new social connections. Other writers make similar observations.[26] Singing together forges new social bonds through musical entrainment—the coordination and synchronization of individuals to a common beat. This phenomenon of entrainment can lead to the building of new bonds.[27] Individuals maintain their unique

---

[25]Barclay, "Πνευματικός in the Social Dialect," 167.

[26]Ian Cross, Felicity Laurence, and Tal-Chen Rabinowitch, "Empathy and Creativity in Group Musical Practices: Towards a Concept of Empathic Creativity," in *The Oxford Handbook of Music Education*, 2nd ed., ed. Gary E. McPherson and Graham F. Welch (New York: Oxford University Press, 2012), 2:337-53. See also William H. McNeill, *Keeping Together in Time: Dance and Drill in Human History* (Cambridge, MA: Harvard University Press, 1995), 1-35, 48, 83, 152.

[27]See Martin Clayton, "What Is Entrainment? Definition and Applications in Musical Research," *Empirical Musicology Review* 7, nos. 1-2 (2012): 49-56. Martin Clayton, Rebecca Sager, and Udo

particularity, and yet they participate in connection with others, even with new social cohesion. Even in their particularity, they experience a new formation of relationship and connection.[28]

To be sure, corporate song that is spontaneous can participate in and evince such social bonds. In his book *A Body of Praise,* W. David O. Taylor presents a theological case for the edification of spontaneity in worship.[29] And as Lester Ruth and Lim Swee Hong describe in their work on the history of contemporary praise and worship music, corporate instances of spontaneous song can show forth connection between worshipers as well as bind them together. To return briefly to Blomgren's work, while he does reduce the adjective *spiritual* to mean "spontaneous," Blomgren also stresses that "spiritual songs" are directed both to God and to other worshipers.[30] This explication of spiritual songs shows that they have a part in edification within the worshiping church. Thus, his work also points us in the direction of understanding "spiritual song" as edification of the community for the worship of God.

Far from rejecting spontaneous song as evidence of the work of the Spirit, then, this essay has attempted to demonstrate that "spiritual song" has a greater range of meaning and that this kind of bond can take place through other modes of corporate song as well. As argued above, a carefully constructed, prewritten choral arrangement such as "Hope for Resolution" can also provide occasion for such bonding. I know this from personal experience: I first encountered this musical work in seminary, where members of the choir came from different social, economic, ethnic, and even theological backgrounds. Singing this piece together became a

---

Will argue along these lines in "In Time with the Music: The Concept of Entrainment and Its Significance for Ethnomusicology," *ESEM CounterPoint* 1 (2004): 3-75, esp. 4. See also Ian Cross, "Music and Meaning, Ambiguity and Evolution," in *Musical Communication*, ed. Dorothy Miell, Raymond MacDonald, and David J. Hargreaves (Oxford: Oxford University Press, 2005), 27-44; Cross, "The Nature and Evolution of Music," in *The Oxford Handbook of Music Psychology*, ed. Susan Hallam, Ian Cross, and Michael Thaut (Oxford: Oxford University Press, 2009), 3-13; Nathan Myrick, "Relational Power, Music, and Identity: The Emotional Efficacy of Congregational Song," *Yale Journal of Music and Religion* 3, no. 1 (2017): 77-92, https://doi.org/10.17132/2377-231X.1060.

[28]I argue this point more robustly with respect to Col 3:16 in *Singing Reconciliation: Inhabiting the Moral Life According to Col 3:16,* Biblical Interpretation Series 217 (Leiden: Brill, 2023).

[29]See W. David O. Taylor, *A Body of Praise: Understanding the Role of Our Physical Bodies in Worship* (Grand Rapids, MI: Baker Academic, 2023).

[30]Blomgren, *Song of the Lord,* 56-68.

way for us as a community to embody unity and a bond—a bond that could easily fracture when we discussed our differences in the classroom or the cafeteria. Yet, as we sang, we maintained those differences while participating in song together. As we sang, we could hear our individual voices, our unique melodic lines, drawn together into a bond that allowed us to hear one another's song—and practice enacting—new creation.

Hearing and attending to Ephesians through "Hope for Resolution" presses against a move toward homogeneity and sameness. Such attention holds out hope for the enactment of difference in an eschatological horizon of reconciliation across time and space, for a community that can hold together thanksgiving and lament, praising God and protesting injustice, and for a bond that paradoxically liberates, that breathes out audible unity in the Spirit.

10

THE FREEING SPIRIT

RESIGNATION AS CREATIVE FREEDOM IN THE HYMNS OF CHARLES WESLEY

Shannon Steed Sigler

For many artists today, the blank canvas can be a completely debilitating encounter; it can feel, in fact, like an impossible burden. In seeking to understand this challenge, Sarah Schumacher argues that the artistic burden in our current art climate is not what we might suppose. The burden that artists bear, she argues, is the idea of absolute autonomy. She writes, "this statement—'You can do whatever you want'—comes from a misconstrued understanding of who the artist is in relation to the world around her. The modern art era heralded the autonomy of the artist, 'liberating' artists to new heights of near divinity as in their autonomy they had unique access to the Other—(the spiritual) that which is not ourselves."[1] Schumacher references Wassily Kandinsky's understanding of the autonomous artist as the top of the "spiritual pyramid" and a guide to others into spiritual freedom. And yet, such elevated depictions of the autonomous artist as "free" prompts the question: Is the autonomous artist truly free? And in what way might Christian theology interrogate the assumptive link between autonomy and freedom so beloved in the modern era?[2]

[1]Sarah Schumacher, "The Burden of Autonomy," *Transpositions Blog*, accessed October 2, 2023, https://itiablog.wordpress.com/2010/07/15/the-burden-of-autonomy/. Parenthetical phrase added by the author.

[2]Schumacher adds this note: "As humans, I don't think we are meant to carry the weight of autonomy that has been given to artists." Then, offering a distinctly Christian perspective, she summarizes William Dyrness, who "reminds us that artistic autonomy is a fairly recent idea, instituted

Though little has been written on aesthetics from the lens of Wesleyan theology, I argue here that a Wesleyan pneumatology provides a fresh lens through which to view the burden of the creative process and the possibilities of finding freedom therein. In contrast to the dominant assumption of the contemporary art world that "unconstrained" autonomy is required in order to be truly free, a Wesleyan pneumatology insists that it is the Holy Spirit's free and loving initiative and our subsequent free response to that divine initiative that creates a true condition for freedom in creative practice. A Wesleyan pneumatology, in other words, offers an anchor for the creative process as the artist yields herself to her "beloved" identity in Christ through the indwelling presence of the Holy Spirit, the Spirit of Freedom.

This essay examines the life and work of the poet Charles Wesley in relation to the way the Holy Spirit drew him into active surrender for the sake of freedom: freedom both in his spiritual life and in his artistic practice.[3] In this essay, we look first briefly at how the Spirit brought freedom within the context of Wesley's faith journey. Second, we examine the twin Wesleyan pneumatological ideas of "call and response" and "resignation" in Charles Wesley's writings as a way to discern the activity of the Spirit in Wesley's creative practice. And, finally, drawing on Julie Lunn's superb study, we engage a close reading of the hymn "The Resignation" to reflect on the implications of a Wesleyan pneumatology for creative freedom in the life of practicing artists today.

---

by the Romantic movement and then built upon by later art movements. Before the Renaissance, artists were not called 'creative'. Instead, artistry was 'seen as a kind of stewardship of the creative order, or the religious tradition, not absolute creativity' (115)."

[3]Charles Wesley, the lesser-known Wesley brother, is often overshadowed by his brother John in historic and scholarly sources. Recent developments in Charles Wesley scholarship have, however, provided us a glimpse into this younger brother's theology, life, and creative output. Author of over nine thousand hymns and poems, it is notable that Charles Wesley has rarely been examined as an artist, but has been limited to the confines of liturgical or musical theology. As I craft a preliminary Wesleyan aesthetic, I understand Charles Wesley as an artist, even though this would not have been a title he would have used to describe himself in his own time. While this exploration does engage some history, the historical dimensions are meant as support to an aesthetic argument. Meaning, when I position Charles Wesley as artist, I do not attempt to make a cultural-historical defense of this label, but rather an aesthetic case. By understanding Charles Wesley as a poet, or "maker" I examine his life and writings through the lens of theological poetics and seek to understand the mechanics of what is happening in both his spiritual life and creative processes.

From Anxiety to Freedom: Charles Wesley's Spiritual Journey

Charles Wesley's spiritual journey was marked by an extreme desire for an assurance of his salvation.[4] The Oxford Methodists of his time wholeheartedly embraced rigorous Christian practices in every moment of their lives in their pursuit of salvation and sanctification. Frank Baker notes, "[Charles'] finger was constantly on his spiritual pulse."[5] Notably, Wesley did not begin writing poetry regularly until after his moment of assurance of salvation, often called the "second work of grace," on May 21, 1738—Pentecost day.[6] For early Methodists, this work was seen as the Holy Spirit's testimony to the believer's heart that one was in fact saved and adopted as a child of God. Up until the point of his assurance of salvation, Wesley's spiritual journey was marked by difficulties with the rigorous nature of the spiritual practices that the early Methodists at Oxford College committed themselves to.[7] Anxiety became a common experience for Wesley during his early ministry at Oxford and then during his failed mission work in the United States in Georgia. He also consistently struggled with physical maladies, suffering in both body and mind in his pursuit of assurance of salvation.

Wesley is speculated to have struggled with mental health issues that would likely have received a clinical diagnosis in our contemporary context, and it seems that his struggles in the midst of his pursuit of salvation may have been more substantial than simply affirming his place in the cultural construct of the early holiness movement.[8] His specific

---

[4]Early Methodism was shaped deeply by the Pietists, Puritans, and Non-Jurors. Each of these religious movements emphasized spiritual rigor as the trajectory toward salvation.

[5]Frank Baker, *Charles Wesley as Revealed by His Letters* (Eugene, OR: Wipf & Stock, 2017), 13.

[6]See S. T. Kimbrough Jr. and Kenneth G. C. Newport, *The Manuscript Journal of the Reverend Charles Wesley, M.A.* (Nashville: Abingdon, 2008), 1:106-9.

[7]The means of grace are defined many times by the Wesleys but most notably in John Wesley's sermons.

"By 'means of grace' I understand outward signs, words, or actions, ordained of God, and appointed for this end, to be the ordinary channels whereby he might convey to men, preventing, justifying, or sanctifying grace." These practices include reading and hearing the Word of God, public and private prayer, receiving the sacraments, and fasting. From John Wesley, "The Means of Grace," Sermon 16, in *The Works of John Wesley: Volume 1*, ed. Albert C. Outler (Nashville: Abingdon, 1984), 198-99.

[8]Joanna Cruickshank affirms the importance of cultural location in seeking to understand Charles Wesley's experience of suffering: "The study of suffering . . . requires an awareness of the historical

psychological challenges were likely exacerbated by the cultural expectations of the movement he helped shape. Pauline Watson notes, "Before his 'conversion' he suffered significant bouts of depression, with guilt, and wished that he could die. He would become physically ill under stress, as he did in his mission work in Georgia. When he did not deal with disturbing feelings consciously, they would manifest themselves physically."[9] Charles's own writings offer a glimpse into the severity of his suffering. For example, in a stop in Boston on his way back to England, he wrote to his brother John: "Though I am apt to think that I shall at length arrive in England . . . yet I do not expect, or wish for, a long life. How strong must the principle of self-preservation be, which can make such a wretch as I am willing to live at all! Or rather unwilling to die; for I know greater pleasure in life, than in considering that it cannot last forever."[10]

In May of 1738, with a weakened body and a desperate emotional state, Charles Wesley began seeking spiritual guidance from friends and mentors, who emphasized the importance of an "inner religion"—not exclusively dependent on works—for salvation. On the surface, it may seem that Wesley gave up on spiritual practices entirely in the shadow of failure in Georgia; but in fact his commitment to both spiritual practices and a surrender in faith to the work of the Spirit seemed to have worked together to bring him to this point in his spiritual journey. On Pentecost day, he received the so-called second work of grace, his assurance of salvation; shortly after, a friend prayed words of physical healing over him. He wrote in his journal, "Still I felt a violent opposition and reluctance to believe. Yet still the Spirit of God strove with my own and the evil spirit, till by degrees he chased away the darkness of my unbelief. I found myself convinced—I knew not how, nor when—and immediately fell to intercession."[11]

---

and cultural contexts in which individuals experience and interpret the hardships they encounter." Cruickshank, *Pain, Passion and Faith: Revisiting the Place of Charles Wesley in Early Methodism* (Lanham, MD: Scarecrow, 2009), 3.

[9]Pauline Watson, *"Two Scrubby Travellers": A Psychoanalytic View of Flourishing and Constraint in Religion Through the Lives and John and Charles Wesley* (London: Routledge, 2018), 153.

[10]Letter from October 17, 1736. Shorthand translated and reprinted in Frank Baker, *Charles Wesley as Revealed by His Letters* (Eugene: Wipf and Stock, 2017), 27.

[11]Kimbrough and Newport, *Manuscript Journal*, 1:107 (Sunday, May 21, 1738).

From Spiritual Freedom to Creative Freedom

Even such a brief biographical sketch of how Charles Wesley experienced freedom from mental and physical illness serves, I suggest, to illustrate that his pneumatology is inextricably linked to soteriology.[12] For both Wesleys, the *telos* of salvation is the entire sanctification in the life of the believer. In many early Methodist writings, this trajectory is called the "indwelling of the divine nature" and is a direct result of the work of the Holy Spirit. For Charles Wesley in particular, the whole of life is a gift mediated by the Holy Spirit: both the gift of saving faith and the gift of sanctification, or purification of the heart, mind, and soul. Jason Vickers remarks, "Charles Wesley invokes the Holy Spirit as the divine personal agent who brings persons to faith initially, who empowers persons to love God and neighbor, and who indwells persons, enabling them to become 'partakers of the divine nature.'"[13]

Indeed, Wesley's sermons regularly demonstrate both the epistemological necessity and expansive nature of the Holy Spirit's work in the Christian life. To take just one example, Sermon 7 explicitly illustrates Vickers's three qualities of Wesley's pneumatology: revelation, purification, and indwelling. First, the necessity of the Spirit's work for humanity to know the things of God: "They only believe, to whom it is given to know the mind of Christ. Eye hath not seen, nor ear heard, neither have entered into the heart of man, the things which God hath prepared for them that love him. But God hath revealed them unto us by his Spirit, for the Spirit searcheth all things, yea, the deep things of God."[14] In essence, one cannot

---

[12]Wesleyan theological distinctives are broadly the result of a combination of influences—pulling from Anglican, Pietist, and even Eastern sources forms a unique scaffolding for their theologies. While the Wesleys themselves were quick to emphasize that their doctrines were not unique compared to others of the day, their emphasis on salvation broke that mold. Randy Maddox can help us: "In this same vein, the Wesley brothers typically rejected attempts to define Methodism by its distinctive doctrines, emphasizing instead a distinctive concern for spiritual life. At most, they were willing to concede that Methodists placed a special emphasis on certain traditional doctrine, particularly in the area of soteriology. Their characteristic concern in this area was to reclaim a more holistic account of the human problem and of God's salvific response." Maddox, "Theology of John and Charles Wesley," in *T&T Clark Companion to Methodism*, ed. Charles Yrigoyen Jr. (New York: T&T Clark, 2010), 20-35.

[13]Jason Vickers, "Charles Wesley's Doctrine of the Holy Spirit: A Vital Resource for the Renewal of Methodism Today," *Asbury Journal* 61, no. 1 (2006): 48 (quoting 2 Pet 1:4).

[14]Kenneth G. C. Newport, ed., *The Sermons of Charles Wesley: A Critical Edition, with Introduction and Notes* (Oxford: Oxford University Press, 2001), Sermon 7, p. 201.

receive revelation from God or become a Christian without the work of the Holy Spirit in one's life. Accordingly, one also cannot live a Christian life without the work of the Holy Spirit, and this work comes first through the purification of the heart:

> You can demonstrate, as may every thinking man, that Christianity must be of God, but if you think you therefore believe, you deceive your own souls, and the truth is not in you. "The natural man receiveth not the things of the spirit of God: faith is the gift of God; no man can call Jesus the Lord but by the Holy Ghost; flesh and blood cannot reveal it unto him. Faith standeth not in the wisdom of man, but in the power of God. It must be wrought by a stroke of omnipotence. It is the Holy Ghost alone who purifies the heart by faith."[15]

The third of Vickers's qualities—the indwelling of the Holy Spirit in the life of the believer—is also seen in Charles Wesley's Sermon 7:

> This is the greatest and most glorious privilege of the true believer: whosoever shall confess that Jesus is the Son of God, God dwelleth in him and he in God: and hereby knoweth he that God abideth in him, by the Spirit which he hath given him. He that believeth hath the witness in himself, even the Spirit of God bearing witness with his Spirit that he is a child of God. Christ is formed in his heart by faith. He is one with Christ and Christ with him. He is a real partaker of the divine nature. Truly his fellowship is with the Father and the Son. The Father and the Son are come unto him and make their abode with him, and his very body is the temple of the Holy Ghost.[16]

These three qualities can be noted in Wesley's assurance-of-salvation moment in 1738, and each of these begins to lay the groundwork for a call-and-response relationship to the Holy Spirit in Wesley's creative practice. Perhaps most crucially, this promise of becoming "a real partaker of the divine nature," by way of the Holy Spirit's indwelling, offers a clear

---

[15]Newport, *Sermons of Charles Wesley*, Sermon 5, pp. 159-60. The paraphrases of Scripture include Mt 16:17; 1 Cor 2:5; Acts 15:8-9.

[16]Newport, *Sermons of Charles Wesley*, Sermon 7, p. 203. The paraphrases of Scripture include 1 Jn 4:15; 3:24; 4:13; 5:10; Gal 4:19; 2 Pet 1:4; 1 Jn 1:3; Jn 14:23; 1 Cor 6:19.

vision of what Wesley means by freedom: not autonomy but true "fellowship with the Father and the Son."

Toward an Aesthetic of Freedom: Wesley and Resignation

In a distinctly Wesleyan vision of human freedom, freedom is not the capacity to exert individual human will but the capacity to give oneself over fully to the love of God and others. We know that Wesley was shaped by Martin Luther's soteriology (in his commentary on the book of Galatians) just before his assurance moment, even calling Luther's understanding of justification by faith alone "new doctrine" in his journal. For Luther, freedom is a freedom *for* God, and not *from* God.[17]

Accordingly, the freedom Charles finds to follow God can be linked to Julie Lunn's examination of Wesley's use of the word "resignation," which involves a kind of *active passivity* in the reception of the gifts of salvation and sanctification. In turn, this response to the Spirit's gift is followed by an indwelling of the Spirit that provides strength and agency to follow Christ. Lunn's understanding of the role of resignation for Wesley parallels Vickers' three phases of revelation, purification, and indwelling. She writes: "For Charles active resignation is the predominant process through which the believer can prepare to receive God's gift of sanctification. However, for Charles resignation is not only the process toward sanctification, it is also an indication of the state of sanctification itself."[18] After Charles' assurance experience, he is propelled forward by consistent acts of resignation, invited by his continued struggles with emotional and health issues, and fueled by the presence of the Holy Spirit experienced in spiritual practices, or "the means of grace."

Resignation is a repeated tipping point in Wesley's journey of sanctification, and this repetition is seen in both his creative process and his creative product. We see herein the call and response between the Spirit and the believer, in the form of continual opportunities to respond to the

[17]Martin Luther, *Three Treatises*, 2nd ed. (Minneapolis: Fortress Press, 1990), 261.

[18]Julie A. Lunn, *The Theology of Sanctification and Resignation in Charles Wesley's Hymns* (Routledge: New York, 2019).

Spirit's work. It is interesting to note, as Lunn does, that the theme of resignation appears less often in his sermons and letters than in his more personal texts—journals and hymns. She suggests "that this is due to [resignation's] affective nature" and continues, saying that "Charles uses resignation as an expression of the state of his own soul."[19] Thus, this continued dynamic of "active surrender" accurately describes, I believe, not only the nature of freedom in Wesley's artistic practice but its inextricable relationship to sanctification.

Indeed, the spiritual transformation that Wesley experienced gave rise to a profound freedom in his creative, poetic, lyrical work as an artist, and he seems to have undergone an unleashing of his own productivity immediately following his spiritual transformation in 1738. Charles Wesley's assurance-of-salvation experience was, in Lunn's words, "a new horizon moment," a tipping point between time and eternity in which the Holy Spirit testified to his spirit that he was a child of God. Words poured forth from his pen. It is this assurance—this rootedness in Wesley's identity as a child in "true fellowship with the father and son" and not in artistic autonomy—that supports the freedom we see emerge in his creative practice.

It is clear, moreover, that this burgeoning of artistic creativity is never untethered but remains rooted in patterns of "call and response" as we begin to see the give and take of temptation and a new freedom emerge in his journal writings. Two days after his assurance experience, he narrates his hymn-writing for the first recorded time, and notes struggles with pride: "At nine began a hymn upon my conversion, but was persuaded to break off for fear of pride. Mr Bray coming encouraged me to proceed in spite of Satan. I prayed Christ to stand by me and finished the hymn." He subsequently describes his assurance that God "can defend [him] from [pride], while speaking for him," through hymn-writing. He writes that he "rejected the thought [of not writing hymns] with honor, and remained more than a conqueror through him that loved [him]."[20]

---

[19]Lunn, *Theology of Sanctification and Resignation*, 59.

[20]S.T. Kimbrough Jr, and Kenneth G. C. Newport, *The Manuscript Journal of the Reverend Charles Wesley, M.A. Vol. I*, (Nashville: Abingdon Press, 2008), 110.

Thus, he began writing what would ultimately amount to over nine thousand hymns and poems over the course of his remaining years. This dynamic bursting forth of creative energy can also be seen in his writing methods; he often composed while walking or on horseback, seemingly scribbling Spirit-inspired, pre-composed poems from his mind on scraps of paper, envelopes, or bulletins.[21]

Crucially, this ongoing dynamic of call and response achieving freedom through active resignation to the Spirit's work is reflected in the creative product as well—not merely in its content, but in its formal, lyrical qualities as well. In her volume on resignation in Charles Wesley's works, Lunn's examination of Wesley's hymn "The Resignation" reveals a call-and-response relationship in both the personal life of the author and in the art form itself.[22] We see Wesley's affections on full display as he wrestles with the Spirit for his own transformation. As in much of Wesley's hymnody, the medium is the message: what is happening in Charles Wesley's person is reflected in both his creative process *and* his creative product. As we examine the hymn here, we will look for our three pneumatological themes (revelation, purification, and indwelling) as well as reflect on how his use of seemingly contradictory imagery is itself witness to the ongoing way in which the Spirit enables within Wesley a resignation which brings both spiritual and artistic freedom.

Wesley's lyrical language here is often characterized as a paradox, but upon deeper reading, *paradox* may not be a sufficient descriptor. The seemingly opposing concepts in Wesley's hymnody offer, as noted by Stephen Wright in an unpublished article, "a different mode of paradox—not a final limit to inquiry, but a beginning of thought."[23] For Wright, Wesley's hymnody uses language that is not a halting of theological inquiry or understanding, but an opening up of dialogue. He writes, "What

---

[21]John Tyson writes, citing Wesley's journal: "On at least one occasion, Charles surprised his Christian friends by riding his horse through their garden and directly to the front door, through which he burst shouting: "Pen and ink! Pen and ink!" After having writing implements produced for him, he sat down and rapidly wrote down the hymn he had been composing in his head while he rode." From John Tyson, *Assist me to Proclaim: The Life and Hymns of Charles Wesley* (Grand Rapids: Eerdmans, 2007), 255.

[22]Lunn, *Theology of Sanctification and Resignation*, 65-68.

[23]Stephen Wright, "Widest Extremes to Join" (unpublished), 7.

appears as paradoxical—the contrasting predicates of Christ's two natures—turns out to be precisely the form of utterance that the hypostatic union enables."[24] In other words, the very capacity to speak in "contrasting predicates" might itself be a sign of the Spirit's indwelling.

Thus, I suggest that the term "dialectic companion themes" offers a better description than "paradox" of Wesley's theological pairings. Rather than a marriage of concepts that stumps our minds, Wesley's dialectic companion themes create space for deeper understanding, and even transformation, while evidencing his own creative freedom. He reached a new horizon in his creative practice—an expansion in his spiritual capacities to hold opposing concepts and emotions inside himself. And I suggest that the power found in the companionship of themes (like resignation and freedom) we witness in his hymnody is both a technical poetic device and the result of the "call and response" with the Holy Spirit in his life demonstrating his new creative horizon.

Demonstrating Freedom in "The Resignation"

In the second half of the sixth stanza, the speaker in Wesley's "The Resignation" makes a striking declaration:

Lord, at thy feet I fall,
  I groan to be set free,
I fain would now obey the call,
  And give up all for thee.

In stark contrast to a culture which might assume that artistic "freedom" means autonomy and the absence of restrictions, the speaker who throws himself at his Lord's feet, gladly obeying the call and willfully giving up everything, reveals he does so precisely because he longs "to be set free." It's difficult to imagine artists in popular culture even gesturing towards notions of obedience or submission, but for the speaker (who we can reasonably assume also speaks for Wesley), freedom is found in complete surrender.

Fascinatingly, however, this statement declaring the speaker's resignation comes at the literal center of Wesley's eleven-stanza poem. And

[24]Wright, "Widest Extremes to Join," 1.

immediately preceding it in the first half of the stanza is a declaration of the addressee's ("Jesu," "Savior," "my offended Lord,") prior freedom:

Thy condescending grace
  To me did freely move:
It calls me still to seek thy face,
  And stoops to ask my love.

The stanza thus leaves no doubt that the speaker's resignation is dependent on and always only in response to God's prior, freely given gift—a gift which is both freeing and free, precisely because it is given freely. In a remarkable echo of Wesley's Sermon 7 describing the prior revealing, purifying, and sanctifying work of the Holy Spirit, God's freedom begets freedom in those who respond to the call.

To be sure, at this point in the hymn, the speaker has not yet experienced anything like absolute freedom and still longs to be "set free." And yet, as we attend closer to the parallel movements here, we see that the speaker's bowing low before his master's feet is itself a mirroring of that "condescending" grace which "stoops" in freedom toward the speaker. In other words, it's quite possible that the speaker's prostration is not merely a precursor to the freedom he desires, but is itself a testament to the freedom he already possess in so far as he imitates the Son, who by the power of the Spirit, proclaims his perfect fellowship with the Father in the very act of humbling himself (Phil 2:5-8).

Thus, I would suggest that this stanza, which lies at both the literal and figurative center, offers a lens through which we can not only understand the rest of the hymn but also Wesley's creative process more generally. The rest of the hymn, in various ways, mirrors this ongoing process of a speaker both responding to God's activity while still imploring God to continue freeing him from that which holds him captive. And, as with the task of Christian theology more generally, it often involves holding seemingly contradictory concepts in concert with one another: among them a falling which is a lifting up and a constraint which is liberating.

The hymn begins with two key questions that set the stage for where the hymn will take us: "And wilt thou yet be found? / And may I still draw near?"

As readers, we might wonder what precedes the "And" and we don't yet know who is being addressed. Even so, it subtly suggests that knowing someone's location is not the same thing as being near; this is a hymn in search of not just certainty, but intimacy. What follows are series of tentative imperatives which are less commands than supplications: "*listen* to the plaintive sound [. . .] thine aid *afford*, / [. . .] *Lift* up an helpless heart." The "poor sinner" is addressing "Jesu," his "Lord,", and already we begin to see a pattern emerging for the way the rest of the hymn will proceed: "listen to [me] . . ." and "To thee I look." Before the speaker can become the grammatical subject of the preposition "to" he is always first its grammatical object.

Stanzas 2-4 then reveal the depths of Wesley's affliction as he longs to be saved, and we begin to see that freedom, for him, is found in being completely surrendered to God. In the third stanza, he uses two water metaphors to describe the violent movement inside him ("the stream of nature's tide" and "bid the tempest cease"), and then moves on in stanza 4 to images of heat/fire ("purging fire" and "fever of desire"). The stanza closes however, with another water reference which entirely transfigures the previous negative, tempestuous association: "Thy Spirit I implore / The living water of thy grace, / That I may thirst no more." This interweaving of water and fire imagery is clearly suggestive of the Spirit's work of purification, but it also emphasizes the life-giving end in which the speaker's ultimate desires have been transfigured and satiated.

Stanza 5 then presents a second round of questions:

When shall thy love constrain,
  And force me to thy breast?
When shall my soul return again
  To her eternal rest?

Ah! What avails my strife,
  My wand'ring to and fro?
Thou hast the words of endless life,
  Ah! Whither should I go?

In the first set, readers are again confronted with a seeming contradiction: the possibility of a love which through constraining, even force, leads to rest. To be sure, out of context, such language is (and has tragically been) prone to abuse and misuse; but here the hymn clearly presents this "force" not at all as a violation against the speaker, but rather as a love drawing him home, where he belongs, away from the death-dealing of his wandering. This is a love which draws her children close in an embrace to protect them from harming themselves further.

And crucially, for our purposes here, the speaker's allusion in the last two lines of this stanza to Peter's somewhat hasty reply to Jesus in John 6, serves as a reminder of Jesus' own perplexing teachings. After Jesus tells the crowds gathered at the synagogue, "'I am the bread of life. Whoever comes to me will never be hungry, and whoever believes in me will never be thirsty," (Jn 6:35 NRSVUE), many of his close followers said to themselves, "This teaching is difficult, who can accept it?" and promptly abandoned him (Jn 6:60-66). Much more could be said about how this illuminates the nature of discipleship in Wesley's hymn, but at the very least this allusion suggests that the hymn itself, through its difficult teachings, might be imitating the only One who is capable of bringing true freedom. And again, as we have seen, it is a freedom *within* not *from* true fellowship with the Father by the power of the Spirit's life-giving water.

In case there was any doubt, Stanza 7 reiterates this theme and the central framework we've already discussed in Stanza 6: Christ's resignation on the cross for the sake of humanity.

To rescue me from woe,
  Thou didst with all things part,
Didst lead a suffering life below,
  To gain my worthless heart:

My worthless heart to gain,
  The God of all that breathe
Was found in fashion as a man,
  And died a cursed death.

One might notice here the repetition and inversion of the phrase "to gain my worthless heart," and "my worthless heart to gain" in this stanza that reveal's God's incarnation and death to transform the author's heart.

Christ first resigns himself to death, enabling humanity to do the same, and, in turn, to receive the freedom of salvation. Lunn writes, "The helpless heart needs Christ to rescue it from the struggle and torment it experiences."[25] We can also note in this stanza the second mention of the state of Wesley's heart as, "worthless heart."[26]

In Stanza 8, Wesley resolutely declares his own resignation ("I yield, I yield!") even as he admits, "I sink by dying love compell'd, / And own thee Conqueror." Likewise, in Stanza 9 he forsakes all, "my friends, my life" in resignation to his "Gracious Redeemer." But the second half of stanza 9 again employs a move that is nonsensical in a culture of autonomy, as Wesley implores Christ to "possess" him—indeed, "settle" in him and "fix" his "wav'ring soul" with the "weight" of his love. Put differently, the stanza implies that sin is a state of being unsettled, dispossessed, and unmoored. And within the scope of the poem and Wesley's own biography, this clearly suggests a condition of captivity—far from the freedom found in being enveloped by the weightiness of God's love.

Stanzas 10 and 11 bring the hymn's arc to a close and also complete the tripartite description of the author's heart with the phrase: "Enter and keep my heart."[27] We also see in this phrase the final pneumatological descriptor: the indwelling of the Holy Spirit.

10 My one desire is this,
  Thy only love to know,
To seek no other bliss,
  No other good below.

My life, my portion thou,
  Thou all-sufficient art,
My hope, my heavenly treasure now,
  Enter and keep my heart.

11 Rather than let it burn
  For earth, O quench its heat,

[25]Lunn, *Theology of Sanctification and Resignation*, 67.
[26]Stanzas 4, 7, and 10.
[27]Stanza 10.

Then, when it would to earth return,
  O let it cease to beat.

Snatch me from ill to come,
  When I from thee would fly,
O take my wand'ring spirit home,
  And grant me then to die![28]

Here Lunn notes celestial themes to describe the author's transformation: first, the revelation of a "new horizon" for Wesley, as he uses celestial descriptors "to tear my soul from earth away," and again in stanza 11 where he asks that his heart not burn or beat for "earth."[29] Second, Lunn uses the phrase "the orbit of resignation," to describe the call and response, and repeated pattern we see as Wesley encounters Christ's salvation through the Spirit.[30] These celestial metaphors support the expanded viewpoint—or new horizon—in Wesley's creative process.

In summary, the hymn charts this orbit of resignation in Wesley's life, emphasizing that the author's freedom is found in rootedness in the love of Christ through the use of words like "constraint," "kept," and "weight of love," alongside the metaphor of the new horizon, or expanded view, from which the artist now writes. Additionally, and crucially, we note all three of our pneumatological themes at play in the hymn: the Spirit bringing revelation, purification, and indwelling to the author. The reader—and better yet, the singer—of the hymn will note dialectical companion themes in each stanza, seeming at first as paradox, but in reality as an invitation to mental, and ultimately, spiritual expansion. Wesley writes this hymn, as he does most, in the first person, and on the lips of the singer the words become our own. As Wesley is able to hold conflicting ideas in tension, we are welcomed to do the same, thereby igniting our own imaginations and inviting us into our own call-and-response relationship to the Holy Spirit.

---

[28]*Hymns and Sacred Poems* (London: Strahan, 1740), 76-79.
[29]Lunn, *Theology of Sanctification and Resignation*, 68.
[30]Lunn, *Theology of Sanctification and Resignation*, 68.

This study of Charles Wesley's work, I believe, offers productive links between Wesleyan pneumatology and artmaking for believers today. In examining the Wesleyan themes of revelation, purification, and indwelling in Wesley's creative process, we see a man who chooses an "active resignation" to these works of the Holy Spirit, and a subsequent new horizon of freedom in his practice is made possible. This freedom finds its anchor most fundamentally in the love of God. Rather than succumbing to aimlessness or becoming overwhelmed, we can view our Christian call as artists through a freedom of a "life resigned to God." A blank canvas, under this light, both in artmaking and in life, begins to feel less daunting when the artist's freedom is rooted not in absolute autonomy but in a deep knowledge of saving God's love.

11

THE COMFORTING AND DISRUPTING SPIRIT

THE HOLY SPIRIT AND TERRENCE MALICK'S *THE TREE OF LIFE*

David W. McNutt and Wesley Vander Lugt

Come, spirit. Help us sing the story of our land. You are our mother. We, your field of corn. We rise from out of the soul of you.

THIS OPENING INVOCATION FROM Terrence Malick's film *The New World*, spoken by Pocahontas over the image of a peaceful body of water, might serve as a kind of summary of his entire filmmaking. Malick, whose other films include *Badlands*, *Days of Heaven*, *The Thin Red Line*, *The Tree of Life*, *To the Wonder*, *Knight of Cups*, and *A Hidden Life*, employs a style that creates space for the work of the Holy Spirit. While the contemporary moviemaking landscape is often dominated by the likes of Marvel movies, Michael Bay's explosions, or the latest entry in the *Star Wars* franchise, Malick changes tack. Long shots. Ample voiceover. Less attention to chronological narrative. Open-ended resolutions. All of these artistic choices are on display in Malick's films, which we will argue can evoke the presence and work of the Spirit, calling viewers into a transformative encounter. Through his films, we are invited to be both comforted and disrupted by the presence of the Holy Spirit.

Perhaps none of Malick's films to date have demonstrated his unique style as much as *The Tree of Life* (2011), starring Brad Pitt, Jessica Chastain, and Sean Penn. The film tells the story of the O'Brien family living in Waco, Texas, during the 1950s: Mr. O'Brien (Pitt), a frustrated musician who works at the local plant; Mrs. O'Brien (Chastain), a devoted wife and mother; and their three boys: Jack, R. L., and Steve. Malick depicts for viewers the complexities of marriage, full of both love and tension, as well as the joys and struggles of growing up. He follows the three boys out the screen door, through the backyards of the neighborhood, along the stream, and across the fields as their insouciant childhood freedom is juxtaposed with a growing awareness of risk and the consequences of their choices. But the O'Brien family's seemingly peaceful (mostly White) suburban life is shattered by the news of the death of their middle son, R. L., at age nineteen. Later, an older Jack (Penn), now an unsettled architect in Houston, looks back on his youth on the anniversary of his brother's death with disquiet and unanswered questions.

We discover, though, that the narrative of the O'Brien family is only part of the story. Malick has set them within his ambitious vision of a much larger context: God's creation of the world and humanity's place within it. Indeed, the film opens with a quotation from Job 38:4-7, part of God's response to Job, who lamented his suffering: "Where were you when I laid the foundations of the earth? . . . When the morning stars sang together, and all the sons of God shouted for joy?" (NKJV). This suburban family, then, becomes a microcosm of the entire human condition. Malick's filmmaking style—eschewing some traditional elements of film, emphasizing others—evokes the movement of the Spirit.

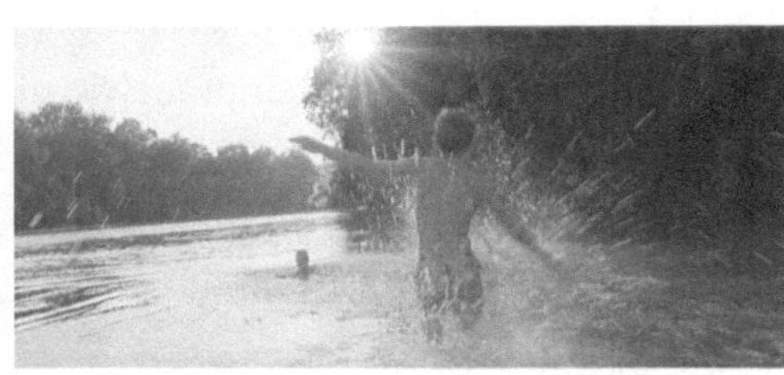

Figure 11.1. Comfort and disruption in the O'Brien family

In what follows, we will first explore the role of the Spirit as both comforter and disrupter, two dimensions of the Spirit's identity and action that are mutually informative and transformative. Next, we will introduce Malick's filmmaking by considering it in light of the transcendental style, which some filmmakers have employed in an effort to evoke a spiritual experience, and then highlighting various features of Malick's unique style that make it particularly suitable for evoking the Spirit's movement. Finally, we will explore specific elements and scenes within *The Tree of Life* that create opportunities for viewers to experience the Spirit's comfort and disruption.

The Spirit as Comforter and Disrupter in the Biblical-Theological Witness

In the biblical witness, the presence of the Spirit both comforts and disrupts. As comforter, the Spirit comes alongside people with God's presence, provision, and peace. As disrupter, the Spirit calls people out into new and demanding realities. The comforter-Spirit is one with the Father God, who is for us (Rom 8:31), and the Son, who is with us always (Mt 28:20), giving us everything we need to be conquerors and fearless disciples. At the same time, the disrupter-Spirit comes not merely to improve our lives but to completely remake them, stirring up new desires and calling us into new commitments. Much like the wind, therefore, the Spirit can be both a refreshing breeze and a gale that reshapes the whole landscape of our lives. Highlighting both the comforting and disrupting aspects of the Spirit's work is crucial in creating a robust account of how the Spirit freely moves in and through creation and works of art.

The Spirit as comforter. In the Old Testament, comfort (*nāḥam*) comes from God and by implication from the Spirit (*rûaḥ*) of God. The comfort of God is often delivered to the wandering, divided, and exiled people of God through the prophets, which includes prophecies of the coming Messiah, the one anointed by the Spirit to bring greater comfort to those who mourn (Is 61:1-2), like a mother comforts her child (Is 66:13). Likewise, central to the promises of a new covenant is the comfort God will bring to the redeemed and restored people of God (Jer 31:13; Zech 1:17).

In the New Testament, the "God of all comfort" (2 Cor 1:3) is the one who sent Jesus the Son as the first comforter (1 Jn 2:1), who then sends the Spirit as "another comforter" (Jn 14:16, ASV). The word John uses in these passages—*paraklētos* in Greek—has been variously translated as "comforter" (ASV, KJV), "advocate" (NIV, NRSV), "helper" (ESV, NKJV, NASV), and "counselor" (RSV). While some commentators favor the translation "advocate," given the legal origin of the term as someone who speaks on behalf of the accused, many commentators note that John uses *paraklētos* in broader and diverse ways, and thus they prefer to keep the word transliterated as "Paraclete."[1] Despite contemporary commentators preferring transliteration or other translations of *paraklētos* besides "comforter," we believe this title communicates an important aspect of the Spirit's role as described in Jesus' Farewell Discourse and elsewhere.[2] *Paraklētos* can be literally translated "called alongside," which suggests multiple and complementary meanings of how the Spirit is called alongside disciples of Jesus to defend (advocate), assist (helper), guide (counselor), and console (comforter). In keeping with the promises of the Old Testament, therefore, the incarnation of Jesus and the descent of the Spirit are the fulfillment of God's promise to bless and give eternal comfort to those who mourn (Mt 5:4; 2 Thess 2:16).

The comfort of the Spirit is thus situated within God's triune identity and action. Believers receive the comfort of God through union with Christ (2 Cor 1:5) and the indwelling of the Spirit (Rom 8:9-11). As such, Orthodox theologian Sergei Bulgakov speaks of the "bi-comforthood" of Christ and the Spirit, which we observe in their mutual role of interceding for believers (Heb 7:25; Rom 8:26).[3] At the same time, it is fitting to identify the Spirit as the primary divine comforter given to believers after the ascension of Jesus, just as he had promised.

In Jesus' Farewell Discourse as recorded in John's Gospel, he explains the coming Spirit as the one who will be called alongside the disciples to

[1]For example, Gary Burge insists on "*advocate*," given the legal undertones. See Gary Burge, *John*, *NIV Application Commentary* (Grand Rapids, MI: Zondervan, 2000), 395. Commentators who stress that *paraklētos* extends beyond the legal sphere and prefer to keep the word transliterated as "Paraclete" include D. A. Carson, *The Gospel According to John*, Pillar New Testament Commentary (Grand Rapids, MI: Eerdmans, 1991), 499; Colin G. Kruse, *John*, Tyndale New Testament Commentary (Downers Grove, IL: InterVarsity Press, 2017), 352; George R. Beasley-Murray, *John*, Word Biblical Commentary (Grand Rapids, MI: Zondervan Academic, 1987), 256; and Marianne Meye Thompson, *John: A Commentary*, New Testament Library (Louisville, KY: Westminster John Knox, 2015), 319.

[2]"Farewell Discourse" is the title commonly given to Jesus' teaching to his disciples at the conclusion of the Last Supper in Jerusalem as recorded in Jn 13:31–17:26.

[3]Sergius Bulgakov, *The Comforter*, trans. Boris Jakim (Grand Rapids, MI: Eerdmans, 2004), 166. Given the unity of divine action, we could also speak of the tri-comforthood of Father, Son, and Spirit.

comfort them through presence, provision, and peace. First, the Spirit is called alongside disciples to dwell in them and be with them forever (Jn 14:16-17). To be with the Spirit is to be with Jesus, a reality that will comfort the disciples once he is gone. Second, the Spirit is called alongside disciples to provide for their needs, specifically their need to remember and embody Jesus' teaching in love (Jn 14:26). The Spirit who comforts is therefore the Spirit of truth who bears witness to Jesus and empowers disciples to be faithful witnesses (Jn 15:26-27; 16:13; Acts 1:8).[4] Third, the Spirit is called alongside disciples as the peace of God, freeing them from fear, critique, and judgment (Jn 14:27). The Spirit convicts the world but comforts those who are in Christ (Jn 16:7-11).

To be a disciple of Jesus today is to walk "in the comfort of the Holy Spirit" (Acts 9:31, ASV), who is the one called alongside us as a companion for the journey, and to comfort one another with the same comfort we have received (2 Cor 13:11).

The Spirit as disrupter. The Spirit who is called alongside as the comforter also calls us out as the disrupter, the one who unsettles old identities, realities, and relationships and transforms them into new ones. The Spirit's hovering over the waters at the beginning of the biblical narrative (Gen 1:2) points to the presence and activity of the Spirit in the generative, divine work of creation, which shapes the formless void by bringing about life. As the story of God's creation continues to unfold, the Spirit sometimes does this shaping work in unexpected and disruptive ways. For example, the promise of the Spirit's outpouring through the prophet Joel presents a disruptive event in which all people irrespective of age, sex, or social standing will receive the Spirit, expanding the Spirit's power beyond anointed leaders. This event is also linked to "wonders in the heavens and on earth" of an apocalyptic nature and cosmic scale, and only those who are called out will be saved (Joel 2:28-32). The fulfillment of Joel's prophecy at Pentecost was, as we might expect, a disruptive, revolutionary event to which people responded with either incredulity or repentance (Acts 2:1-41). As Willie James Jennings observes, "The Book of Acts speaks of

[4]Thompson contends that "'Spirit of truth' virtually defines 'Paraklete' in the Gospel [of John]" (*John*, 313).

revolution. We must never forget this. It depicts life in the disrupting presence of the Spirit of God."[5] The work of the Spirit as recorded in Acts creates a community of "called-out ones" (literal translation of *ekklēsia*, usually rendered as "church"), whose identities, lifestyles, and allegiances are disrupted and transformed by the Spirit of God.[6]

On a personal level, the Spirit disrupts by calling people out from their old existence into an entirely new existence by grace through faith (Jn 3:5-8). The Spirit convicts and calls us to die to the old self before freeing us for new life in Christ (Rom 8:1-2). Commenting on the theology of Karl Barth, George Hunsinger calls this "disruptive grace," which "does not mean continuity but radical discontinuity, not reform but revolution, not violence but nonviolence, not the perfecting of virtues but the forgiveness of sins, not improvement but resurrection from the dead."[7] The grace of God given to us by "the Spirit of grace" (Heb 10:29), therefore, is "as unsettling as it is comforting."[8] Upon receiving this disruptive grace, we are called to "walk in the Spirit" (Gal 5:16), a journey that involves being called out from fleshly desires and familiar comforts to join Jesus' path of suffering and cross bearing. Walking in the Spirit also means being available and receptive to divine surprises, promptings, disruptions, and invitations (Acts 8:39; 16:6-7; 20:22). As Steven Guthrie writes, "The Spirit often disrupts settled plans already in place. What is more, the Spirit also brings about *new* and altogether *unexpected* states of affairs."[9]

On a social and political level, the Spirit is the disrupter of familiar kinships and commitments, drawing together a new community of sinners, misfits, and enemies.[10] The outpouring of the Spirit in Acts

---

[5]Willie James Jennings, *Acts* (Louisville, KY: Westminster John Knox, 2017), 1.

[6]This literal translation should not be overemphasized, however, as in context *ekklēsia* refers most directly to a group of people who are called together into a particular assembly. Frederick W. Danker, Walter Bauer, William F. Arndt, and F. Wilbur Gingrich., *Greek-English Lexicon of the New Testament and Other Early Christian Literature*, 3rd ed. (Chicago: University of Chicago Press, 2000), 303.

[7]George Hunsinger, *Disruptive Grace: Studies in the Theology of Karl Barth* (Grand Rapids, MI: Eerdmans, 2000), 16.

[8]Hunsinger, *Disruptive Grace*, 17.

[9]Steven Guthrie, *Creator Spirit: The Holy Spirit and the Art of Becoming Human* (Grand Rapids, MI: Baker Academic, 2011), 10.

[10]On the role of the Spirit as comforter and disrupter in an ethnically hostile and homogenizing world, see Rodolfo Galvan Estrada III, *A Pneumatology of Race in the Gospel of John: An Ethnocritical Study* (Eugene, OR: Pickwick, 2019).

created not only a new personal life but a whole new social reality: Jews and Gentiles worshiping and eating together, the rich sharing with the poor, slaves eating with masters, women leading alongside men. As Jennings puts it, "Luke gives us sight of a holy wind blowing through structured and settled way of living and possessing and pulling things apart."[11] Out of this disruptive force emerges the beautiful body of Christ in all its diverse ethnicities, gifts, and locations. What binds the one body together is the one Spirit of God, who enables each member to confess Jesus as the one and only Lord (Eph 4:4; 1 Cor 12:3).

The comforting and disrupting aspects of the Spirit's identity and action frequently go hand in hand. The biblical witness reveals how the Spirit's comfort is often preparation for experiences of disruption and how the Spirit's disruption can clear the way for deeper and renewed comfort. In other words, the Spirit's comfort has a way of disrupting our natural modes of consolation, and the Spirit's disruption can comfort us with new and surprising realities. Consequently, when the Spirit whispers and whips through our lives, we can be simultaneously refreshed and reshaped, settled and unsettled, assured and stretched beyond what we could ever expect, control, or imagine.

A Spiritual Style of Film?

The Spirit comforts and disrupts in many ways and through various media, including film. That being said, we want to be clear: the Holy Spirit does not *need* film. The Spirit, the eternal third person of the triune God who hovered over the waters at creation (Gen 1:2), breathed life into Adam's nostrils (Gen 2:7), empowered Jesus' ministry (Lk 4:14-21), and was poured out on the disciples at Pentecost (Acts 2:1-12), is not dependent on human artists and their creativity to act, to be present, to bring both comfort and disruption. Yet the Spirit often works with, in, and through human agents: unworthy prophets are called to deliver God's word; a miraculous conception takes place in a virgin's womb; Peter, who had denied Jesus three times, converts thousands. If the Spirit chooses, then, filmmakers and their

[11]Jennings, *Acts*, 40.

work might participate in the activity of the Spirit as well. Moreover, we must confess that the Spirit can be at work in any style or genre of film, whether popular or "artistic," drama or comedy, black and white or color. The Holy Spirit, who like the wind "blows wherever it pleases" (Jn 3:8), is not bound to the walls of church or any one style of film.

At the same time, one might ask, is there a style of film that is more suited to evoking the presence and movement of the Holy Spirit? Some filmmakers have thought so. Employing a minimalist style, some have sought to convey a sense of the spiritual. For example, American filmmaker Paul Schrader argues that the transcendental style, which he identifies with the films of Yasujiro Ozu, Robert Bresson, and Carl Dreyer, is particularly suited to evoking what he describes more generally as the holy or the transcendent. According to Schrader, who wrote the screenplays for several films directed by Martin Scorsese, including *Taxi Driver*, *Raging Bull*, and *The Last Temptation of Christ*, and who has also himself directed films such as *American Gigolo*, *Affliction*, and *First Reformed*, the transcendental style is characterized by sparseness. Rather than emphasizing what Schrader, borrowing from French Catholic philosopher Jacques Maritain, terms "abundant means" (e.g., attention to narrative, a conscious working within time, seeking to reflect reality), the transcendental style intentionally employs "sparse means" (e.g., limited camera movement and minimal musical accompaniment). For Schrader, this sparseness is a strength because it leaves room for an encounter with the spiritual: "The abundant means sustain the viewer's (or reader's or listener's) physical existence, that is, they maintain his interest; the sparse means, meanwhile, elevate his soul."[12]

Of course, things can go wrong. For Schrader, excessively "religious" films—think of DeMille's *The Ten Commandments*—are "overabundant," whereas experimental films that lack any elements to engage the audience are "oversparse." Schrader clarifies that both abundant and sparse means are present in "any piece of art, particularly sacred works of art." So, Ozu's *Tokyo Story*, Bresson's *A Man Escaped*, and Dreyer's *Ordet* still employ more traditional aspects of filmmaking. The artist who wants to express the holy

[12]Paul Schrader, *Transcendental Style in Film: Ozu, Bresson, Dreyer* (Berkeley: University of California Press, 1972), 155.

or enable an encounter with the transcendent, Schrader argues, cannot ignore either the abundant or the sparse but "must know their priority."[13]

But how exactly is that achieved in film? Schrader points to three steps that are integral to the transcendental style: (1) an attention to the everyday, or "a meticulous representation of the dull, banal commonplaces of everyday living"; (2) disparity, a crack in the everyday, "an actual or potential disunity between man and his environment which culminates in a decisive action"; and (3) stasis, "a frozen view of life which does not resolve the disparity but transcends it," which he maintains is the trademark of all religious art.[14] The end result of this minimalist filmmaking, which employs "plain, unflashy production values," is "a decidedly austere look and feel" in which explicitly religious content is optional.[15]

How does Malick's style compare with the transcendental style?

Like many works of art, his films resist a straightforward interpretation.[16] Yet there are both striking parallels to—and departures from—the transcendental style in his work. Malick does often use "sparse means" in *The Tree of Life*. For example, his focus is not on foregrounding a chronologically straightforward narrative. As viewers, we move from a single family to the creation of the universe and back to the family. Sequences of young Jack are interspersed with images of older Jack, sometimes quite quickly. In addition, Malick often prefers to have little sound or only natural, diegetic sound that originates within the world of a film (as opposed to sound that is added later). So, what Schrader said of Bresson's use of sound could apply to Malick: "The sound track consists primarily of natural sounds: wheels creaking, birds chirping, wind howling."[17] In the case of Malick's films, we might add running water, noisy crickets, and blowing curtains.

---

[13]Schrader, *Transcendental Style in Film*, 162-67, 155.

[14]Schrader, *Transcendental Style in Film*, 39, 42, 49.

[15]Richard Goodwin, *Seeing Is Believing: The Revelation of God Through Film* (Downers Grove, IL: IVP Academic, 2022), 32.

[16]Some commentators have preferred to note the influence of Martin Heidegger's philosophy, which Malick studied at Harvard and Oxford, on his work (he even published a translation of Heidegger's *Vom Wesen des Grundes*). See, for example, Marc Furstenau and Leslie MacAvoy, "Terrence Malick's Heideggerian Cinema: War and the Question of Being in *The Thin Red Line*," in *The Cinema of Terrence Malick: Poetic Visions of America, ed.* Hannah Patterson (London: Wallflower, 2003), 173-85.

[17]Schrader, *Transcendental Style in Film*, 69.

At the same time, Malick's films can hardly be described as austere or plain, like the films of Bresson or Dreyer, and certainly not in the case of *The Tree of Life*. It is aesthetically rich, saturated with arresting images that not only help us understand the complexities of the O'Brien family but might even suggest a divine presence. When viewing this film, one is both reminded of the fundamental nature of the medium of film—a series of images shown over time to create the appearance of movement (i.e., motion pictures)—and confronted by the possibility that the images might evoke something more. Peter Leithart describes Malick's style as "an art of reticence" because the juxtaposed images push the drama to the background.[18] But even if the narrative is somewhat obscured in his films, it is still a feature of his work. Moreover, Malick's complex use of nondiegetic music and voiceover resists the sonic austerity of many transcendental films. Most striking in *The Tree of Life* are the use of "Lacrimosa" from Polish composer Zbigniew Preisner's *Requiem for My Friend* in the creation sequence (composed in memory of his friend, director Krzysztof Kieslowski) and "Agnus Dei" by Hector Berlioz at the close of the film, both of which add stunning complexity to the viewer's experience.[19] In this respect, then, Malick's films are undoubtedly abundant.

All of this suggests that Malick has developed his own style, a kind of improvisation on the transcendental style, which both embraces some traditional elements of filmmaking and eschews others. With their unique combination of spareness and abundance, Malick's films evoke the presence of the Spirit and create a cinematic world in which viewers can experience the Spirit's comfort and disruption.

Comfort and Disruption in *The Tree of Life*

Many of Malick's films have been noted for the sense of calm and tranquility they elicit within viewers, especially through his extended attention to

---

[18]Peter J. Leithart, "The Divine Reticence of Terrence Malick," in *Theology and the Films of Terrence Malick, ed.* Christopher B. Barnett and Clark J. Elliston (London: Routledge, 2017), 49. See also Leithart, *Shining Glory: Theological Reflections on Terrence Malick's Tree of Life* (Eugene, OR: Cascade, 2013).

[19]Peter M. Candler Jr., "*The Tree of Life* and the Lamb of God," in Barnett and Elliston, *Theology and the Films*, 211.

images of the natural world. His works offer "stunning visual representations of nature, especially shots of light filtered through high dense trees, water, long grass shaped by wind, the play of the sun on the landscape, and exotic fauna and flora."[20] In *The Tree of Life*, the mise-en-scène is often overtaken by images of the wind (e.g., waving grass, flowing curtains, rustling trees, clouds moving across the sky, birds flocking), water (e.g., raindrops, waterfalls, rivers), light (coming through windows, breaking through treetops), and repeated uses of a flame or fire, all of which allude to the Spirit without needing to employ a voiceover reading of Acts 2. Importantly, the images relate to the story of the O'Brien family while also reflecting something akin to a quasi-sacramental presence. Christopher B. Barnett argues, for example, that Malick's use of wind imagery has theological significance, for it "is something natural, which, paradoxically, is capable of communicating the supernatural."[21]

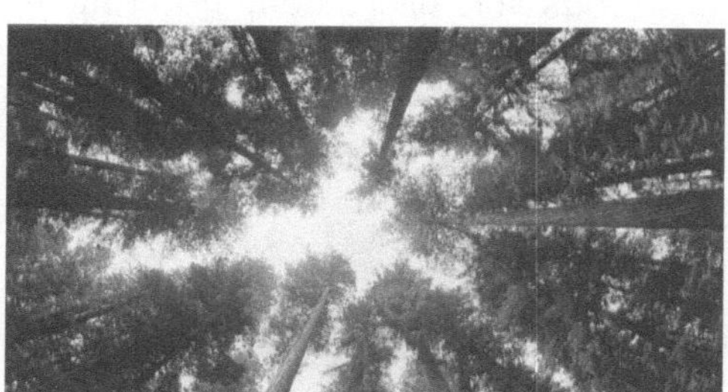

Figure 11.2. Nature evokes calming and comforting role of the Holy Spirit

In addition, Malick's depiction of suburban life in Waco, Texas, which is conveyed primarily through the experiences of the three O'Brien boys, often elicits a sense of nostalgia, peace, and comfort. These are days spent kicking a can, rolling in the grass, and running with friends. Here Malick certainly seems to embrace the first aspect of Schrader's transcendental style: attention to the everyday. Throughout these scenes, there is an abiding sense of innocence, still free from the troubles of the world—an almost Edenic experience. Moreover, all of these images of the natural world and a carefree childhood are juxtaposed against the scenes of older Jack, who finds himself in the world of downtown high-rise buildings, sharp angles, and unnatural light. A tree growing in the midst of the city stands out, almost beckoning him back to a life and relationships he has left behind.

[20] David Davies, "Terrence Malick," in *The Routledge Companion to Philosophy and Film*, ed. Paisley Livingston and Carl Plantinga (London: Routledge, 2008), 572.

[21] Christopher B. Barnett, "Spirit(uality) in the Films of Terrence Malick," *Journal of Religion and Film* 17, no. 1 (April 2013): 18.

The most stunning images of the natural world in *The Tree of Life*, though, are found in the extended sequence of the creation of the world. With images of galaxies, volcanoes, cells, and more, Malick offers a vision of the beginning of life. Here viewers encounter "nothing less than Malick's imagining of the first emergence of the universe . . . the cosmos in both its vastness and its particularity."[22] Viewers are transported from the origins of the material world to the arrival of animals, including dinosaurs, until finally we encounter the advent of humanity—in the very particular form of the O'Briens' oldest son, Jack. The extended sequence is unlike anything in contemporary cinema. Recall that the opening chapters of Genesis tell us that the Holy Spirit is present and active in God's work of creation, "hovering over the waters" (Gen 1:2) and breathing life into Adam (Gen 2:7). From the very beginning of the film, with a flickering flame, the Spirit is a character—indeed, one of the main protagonists—in this story.

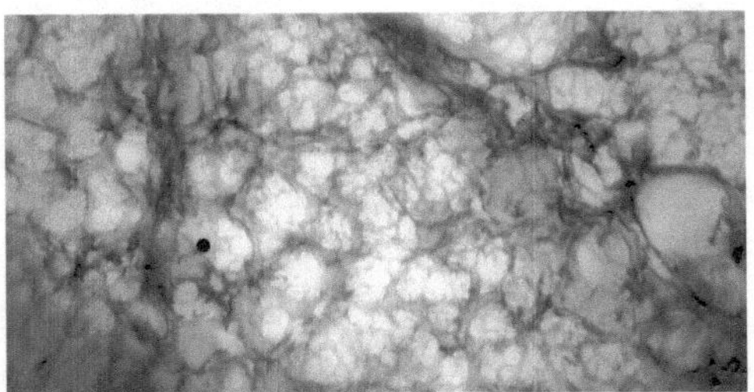

Figure 11.3. Creation and the O'Brien's place in it

Alongside these invocations of the Spirit's comforting and life-giving presence, though, are examples of disruption. If as viewers we are surprised by this, well, we should have known what we were getting ourselves into. The title of the film refers to one of the two trees found in the middle of the Garden of Eden: the tree of life and the tree of the knowledge of good and evil (Gen 2:9). The consequences of the rupture of the relationship between God and humanity as a result of Adam and Eve's transgression by eating fruit from the latter tree include their exclusion from the tree of life (Gen 3:22-24).

The reality of humanity's condition—a beloved creature made in God's image, yet fallen—is played out in the O'Brien household. In an early sequence, Mrs. O'Brien reflects on the two paths of life:

> The nuns taught us there are two ways through life: the way of nature and the way of grace. You have to choose which one you'll follow. Grace doesn't

[22]Steven Rybin, *Terrence Malick and the Thought of Film* (Lanham, MD: Lexington Books, 2013), 173.

> try to please itself, accepts being slighted, forgotten, disliked, accepts insults and injuries. Nature only wants to please itself, get others to please it too, likes to lord it over them, to have its own way; it finds reasons to be unhappy, when all the world is shining around it and love is smiling through all things. They taught us that no one who loves the way of grace ever comes to a bad end. I will be true to you, whatever comes.

The family must navigate these different visions of life and the world: Mr. O'Brien, with his warnings about the world to his sons, his rules not to go into the neighbor's yard, and his outbursts of violence, reflects nature; Mrs. O'Brien, whose tenderness envelops her children, reflects grace. This is a domestic struggle set against a cosmic drama. As the film progresses, the innocence of childhood gives way to temptation and transgression. Jack sneaks into a neighbor's house to steal a girl's dress. He hurts his brother with a BB gun. He witnesses family strife in other neighborhood homes. In a pivotal scene, a boy drowns, leading Jack to ask in a Job-like prayer or a Spirit-led groan (Rom 8:26), "Where were you? You let a boy die. You let anything happen."

But within the film, the greatest disruption (or, to borrow the term from Schrader's second step, the greatest disparity) is the death of R. L., the middle O'Brien son. Immediately after the end of Mrs. O'Brien's opening soliloquy about nature and grace, she receives news of R. L.'s death. We are never told of the exact cause of his death, as if Malick wants to tell us that those details do not matter as much as the loss itself. This tragedy elicits expressions of both faith and lament from Mrs. O'Brien. In response to a minister who attempts to comfort her by saying, "He's in God's hands now," she replies, "He was in God's hands the whole time, wasn't he?" But she also offers a Job-like lament in a whisper: "Lord, why? Where were you? Did you know? Who are we to you? Answer me."

Of course, not all disruptions are the work of the Holy Spirit. But one might still ask, where is the Spirit in the midst of this loss?

The Spirit Who Remakes by Comforting and Disrupting

The Tree of Life has been both lauded (it won the Palme d'Or at the 2011 Cannes Film Festival, and it earned three Academy Award nominations, including Best Picture, Best Director, and Best Cinematography) and panned. The experience of viewing the film, especially for those who are unfamiliar with Malick's style, can be challenging. In particular, the lengthy creation sequence can be disruptive to our collective film-viewing habits, which have become accustomed to short scenes and straightforward narratives. More importantly, the film poses difficult questions about human existence, the reality of suffering, and the meaning of life. In response to the juxtaposition of the creation of the world and the death of R. L., one reviewer posed, "What, these images ask, is the death of one boy seen through so wide a lens?"[23]

It is noteworthy that *The Tree of Life* is the most autobiographical of Malick's films to date. It is clearly informed by (if not directly reflective of) his youth spent in Waco while growing up as the oldest of three brothers. Like R. L. in the film, who received his father's gift for music, Malick's youngest brother, Larry, was a guitarist. After moving to Spain to study under Andrès Segovia, he broke his hands and died of an apparent suicide.[24] Throughout the film, Mrs. O'Brien and Jack both address God directly, reminiscent of Augustine's prayers throughout *Confessions*.[25] In this regard, *The Tree of Life*, then, might be regarded as "a Christian aesthetic theodicy," Malick's prayerful response not only to his own brother's death but to the entire conundrum of the human condition.[26]

Sometimes the Spirit disrupts our lives, agitating our seeming peace to bring transformation. When Jack hurts R. L. with the BB gun, he is struck with guilt. Echoing Paul's words from Romans 7:19, R. L. says: "What I want to do I can't do. I do what I hate." In a form of Spirit-led repentance, he says to R. L., "You can hit me if you want." But R. L. demonstrates Christlike grace and forgives him, which leads not only to an apology from Jack but

[23]Christopher Orr, "'The Tree of Life': A Beautiful, Lyrical Mess," *The Atlantic*, June 3, 2011, www.theatlantic.com/entertainment/archive/2011/06/the-tree-of-life-a-beautiful-lyrical-mess/239858/.

[24]David Sterritt. "Days of Heaven and Waco: Terrence Malick's *The Tree of Life*," *Film Quarterly* 65, no. 1 (Fall 2011): 55.

[25]See Peter M. Candler Jr., "The Tree of Life and the Lamb of God," in Barnett and Elliston, *Theology and the Films, 205-17.*

[26]Robert Sinnerbrink, *Terrence Malick: Filmmaker and Philosopher* (London: Bloomsbury Academic, 2019), 160.

a change in Jack's perspective.[27] Later, he prays, "What was it you showed me? I didn't know how to name you then. But I see it was you. Always you were calling me." Similarly, Mr. O'Brien, whose personal disappointment made him harsh with his wife and children, expresses remorse after the death of R. L.: "I wanted to be loved because I was great. A big man. I'm nothing. Look at the glory around us: trees, birds. I lived in shame. I dishonored it all and didn't notice the glory. I'm a foolish man." At times the Spirit works by disrupting, agitating, and refining God's creatures.

But the Spirit is also revealed to be the comforter. Two final scenes point to this theme. In the first, Jack envisions a heaven-like landscape—a wind-swept beach—where people are reunited with those they love. Here, in the new creation, bodies are raised from the ground, old Jack meets young Jack, Mr. O'Brien raises R. L. in his arms, and Mrs. O'Brien embraces her son again. This eschatological sequence is akin to a visual fulfillment of Revelation 2:7: "Let anyone who has an ear listen to what the Spirit is saying to the churches. To everyone who conquers, I will give permission to eat from the tree of life that is in the paradise of God" (NRSV).[28] Though the film lacks an explicit affirmation that such restoration can come about only through the life, death, and resurrection of Jesus Christ, it nevertheless affirms the comforting work of the Spirit, who does not work apart from the Son.[29] So, despite the fallenness of humanity—summarized in the broken lives of the O'Brien family—creation is revealed to be an expression of God's grace, "a continuous outpouring of light and order ex nihilo, out of nothing save God's desire to communicate himself and his nature in love."[30] The tree of life in the Garden of Eden finds its complement in the eternal, heavenly tree of life.

---

[27]Brett McCracken, "Why 'The Tree of Life' Is the Best Christian Film Ever Made," The Gospel Coalition, October 23, 2018, www.thegospelcoalition.org/article/tree-life-best-christian-film-ever-made/.

[28]Chris E. W. Green offers a different interpretation of this scene, viewing it not as a heavenly vision but as the reconciliation of Jack's present with his past through his memories. See Green, "The Move of the Spirit: Pneumatology and Temporality in Malick's Cinema," in *The Spirit and the Screen: Pneumatological Reflections on Contemporary Cinema*, ed. Chris E. W. Green and Steven Félix-Jäger (Lanham, MD: Lexington Books/Fortress Academic, 2023), 13.

[29]Malick's forthcoming film on the life of Jesus, tentatively titled *The Way of the Wind*, may develop these themes further.

[30]Thomas Gardner, *Lyric Theology: Art and the Doctrine of Creation* (Waco, TX: Baylor University Press, 2022), 78.

At the end of the film, Mrs. O'Brien finds rest in God's comfort. In a closing scene, she is flanked by two angelic figures. The scene might point, on the one hand, to Schrader's third and final step of the transcendental style (stasis), but the fluid movement of the camera is more suggestive of the activity of the Spirit. Despite her profound loss, she declares, "I give him to you. I give you my son." Here she echoes not the lament of Job but the faithfulness of two other biblical figures: Hannah, who prayed that God would give her a son despite her barrenness, and when she gave birth to Samuel dedicated him to the Lord (1 Sam 1:27-28); and Mary, who, when confronted with the astounding news of Jesus' Spirit-enabled conception and miraculous birth, replied, "Here am I, the servant of the Lord; let it be with me according to your word" (Lk 1:38 NRSV). Like these two biblical women, she has found comfort in the presence, provision, and peace of the Spirit. Importantly, this comfort comes not through the presence of an amorphous, impersonal "holy" or numinous spirit but only through the Holy Spirit, who is, in the words of the Nicene Creed, the giver of life who is worshiped and glorified with the Father and the Son.

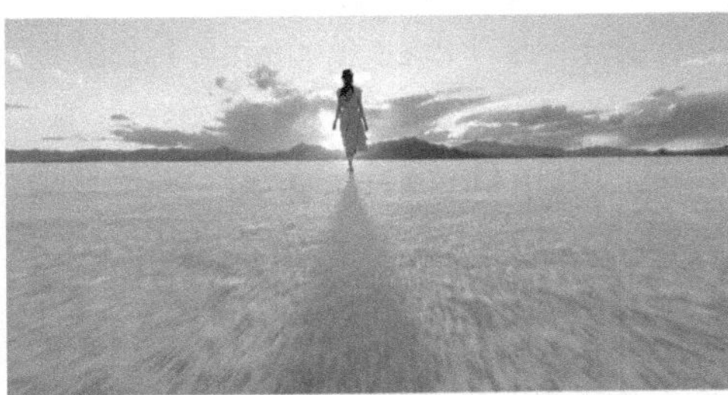

Figure 11.4. Heaven-like reunion and restorative grace of God

Rather than asking us, then, to disregard the death of one boy when seen through the wide lens of creation, *The Tree of Life* leads us to see the radical, particular grace of God in both the disruption and the comfort of the Spirit. Yes, even from the broadest perspective possible, this boy, this family, this world is loved by God. By evoking the presence and work of the Spirit, Malick's film can become a way in which the Spirit works in us: disrupting us, comforting us, and ultimately remaking us.

Come, Holy Spirit.

12

THE PARTICULARIZING SPIRIT

ON THE ART OF LANDSCAPE ARCHITECTURE

Jennifer A. Craft and W. David O. Taylor

Because [gardening] is guided by the commitments to nurture, protect, and celebrate the gifts of life, it can serve as a model for how people might frame and focus their creative activity in the world more generally.

NORMAN WIRZBA, *THIS SACRED LIFE*

Maker of heaven and earth
of time and season
Thinker-upper of soil
of autumn decay, and rot
and roots drawing nutrients
whatever they are
that feed and sustain
the beauty of the lilies, and the violets
Imagineer of variety
Puller-offer of the impossible
breaking our hearts
every spring day
with greater magnolia blossom
finer, more delicate red bud.

JOHN TERPSTRA, "IMAGINEER OF VARIETY"

In 2015, an ecumenical retreat center located in the Texas Hill Country on the banks of the Frio River, itself situated within the Edwards Plateau ecoregion, began a renovation project that would dramatically change the landscape of the place as well as people's relationship to that place. Prior to this project, guests at the Laity Lodge would have driven their cars out of the shallow East Frio riverbed and wound their way up a narrow gravel road, bordered by mountain cedar (*Juniperus ashei*) and Lacey oak (*Querus laceyi*) trees, in order to arrive at the carefully manicured grounds of the lodge, marked by neatly mowed St. Augustine grass, poured concrete paths, and tidy flowerbeds.

After the project had been completed, guests found themselves in a much stranger but also much more natural space. Instead of using non-native species, resulting in the reduction of biodiversity, the creation of imbalance, and the diminishment of robustness, the lodge chose to use native species, which served to improve water and air quality, provide wildlife habitat, reduce maintenance needs, and create a proper sense of place. This included, for example, the use of Texas beargrass plants, bur oak trees, and Spanish lavender shrubs.

Additionally, on the winding path that led to the main gathering room, perched steeply over the river, a guest no longer was afforded an undisturbed view of the lawn. Now that it was enveloped by tall native grasses, especially in the early summer months, a guest would find herself instead invaded and perhaps even inconvenienced by these grasses on her way to dinner—catching in the hair, brushing against cheeks, entangling the ankles.

The goal, as the leadership saw it, was to connect human beings more meaningfully to creation.[1] The built and natural environments would now talk to each other rather than be at odds with or at a distance from each other. This landscape would no longer hide people from creation but immerse them in it. The artfully shaped landscape would assert its personality in relation to the guests rather than be sequestered from them, and

[1]Special thanks are owed to Steven Purcell, director of the Laity Lodge; Grant Shellhouse, the lodge's program operations manager at the time of our inquiry; and Kevin Wessels, the lodge's director of stewardship, for the generous gift of their time in a personal tour of the property.

creation would no longer be domesticated through artificially curated media but would be stewarded and repaired. Species would be allowed to develop in novel ways. *Brown* would become the new *green*; the beauty of flowers would be interrogated and reconceived; and invasive species would be uprooted, while fences would be installed in order to keep the deer population from destroying this experiment in rewilding.

In short, a categorically new relationship would be created between the natural and built environments, with both promise and challenge for the people who occupied them. A host of theological questions would also present themselves as rich veins for investigation. The chief question our chapter seeks to investigate is this one: How might a doctrine of the Holy Spirit as Particularizer both inform and emerge from the landscape architecture of the Laity Lodge postrenovation? The argument of the chapter is that the Spirit's work of particularizing a people and a place is vividly witnessed in the lodge's decision to let human beings and the local ecology be "implicated in each other," to allow the native species to propagate in often-unpredictable ways, and to free the flora and fauna to be "truly themselves"—their wild, indigenous selves—within this particular region of central Texas.

Scare quotes are used liberally here on purpose. The terms of the discussion are anything but self-evident, so great care must be taken in order to make a clear and cogent case for the ways in which the landscape architecture of the lodge and the Spirit's work as Particularizer stand in mutually illumining relation. And while both the process and final result presented serious ethical challenges, we believe the project represents a case study that lends itself to a fruitful pneumatological exploration of how creation and culture might be rightly related in the artful arrangement of land. Our hope, finally, is that readers will be inspired to adopt new architectural practices that might bear witness to the particularizing work of the Spirit in the world as a testament to the shalom of God not only in this particular tract of cultivated land but also elsewhere where such construction projects are engaged.

Practically, our chapter aims to bring a detail-rich description of specific spaces on the property into conversation with Colin Gunton's cluster of ideas about the Spirit as Particularizer.[2] Our descriptive work here should be seen not as comprehensive or exhaustive but as representative and illustrative of the whole project; it functions, that is, as a microcosm of the larger plan of the lodge. With respect to Gunton's ideas, we treat, first, the idea of particularity, second, the idea of novel development, and, third, the idea of constitutive relationality. We conclude the chapter by raising a number of ethical questions that rightly demand our attention but whose full resolution lies beyond the scope of this chapter. Before proceeding to the descriptive work, however, we wish briefly to situate Gunton's pneumatology.

Gunton's Pneumatology: Summarized

In Colin Gunton's book *The One, the Three and the Many*, the Holy Spirit plays a decisive role in God's work of creaturely renewal within the sin-warped relationship between the one (the individual) and the many (the community).[3] On the one hand, against a tendency for the one to smother the many, Gunton argues that it is the Spirit who preserves the particularity of individual things in God's world.[4] On the other hand, against a tendency for the many to suppress the one, Gunton contends that the Spirit frees the many to be in right relation to each other in order to be truly harmoniously together. Gunton argues, finally, that the Spirit's particularizing work that we witness in the life and ministry of Jesus can be regarded as the decisive pattern for the Holy Spirit's work in creation at large, and that pattern points to the name of Spirit as Particularizer.

With these doctrinal ideas in mind, then, our goal is to propose a pneumatological construal of Laity Lodge's project on the conviction that what is needed is not simply creation care principles, or wise land management

[2]The doctrinal ideas of this chapter are developed more fully in W. David O. Taylor, "Mother Tongues and Adjectival Tongues: Liturgical Identity and the Liturgical Arts in a Pneumatological Key," *Worship Journal* 92 (2018): 54-70.

[3]Colin Gunton, *The One, the Three and the Many: God, Creation and the Culture of Modernity* (Cambridge: Cambridge University Press, 1993), esp. chaps. 7-8; see also Jeremy S. Begbie, *Resounding Truth: Christian Wisdom in the World of Music* (Grand Rapids, MI: Baker Academic, 2007), esp. chaps. 8-9.

[4]Gunton, *One, the Three and the Many*, 190.

practices, or philosophically green architectural strategies, but also serious theological reflection that ought to inform such approaches to the art of landscape architecture.

We begin, then, with the particularizing work of the Spirit in creation.

Becoming Native to the Place

"Our becoming native," writes agriculturalist Wes Jackson, "will depend on our emerging consciousness of how we are to use the gifts of the creation. We must think in terms of different relationships."[5] The leadership at Laity Lodge take up this call in their own restoration work, seeking to renegotiate the spaces provided to native and nonnative tree species, which includes managing for invasives and cultivating a more sensitive and resilient environment for the flourishing of biodiverse native species in the existing landscape. What Jackson does not say directly, however, but gestures toward throughout his work with the Land Institute is that such work is always an exercise in particularity. To become conscious of the gifts of creation is to attend to the diverse particularity of the individual members of the ecological community of a place and the often complicated relationships that result.

In the case of the new landscape architecture of Laity Lodge, and the reimagined system of land management that accompanied it, one goal was to responsibly make space for the tree species to be themselves. The new system encouraged belonging within the whole while still allowing the plants to speak for themselves. This in turn created a cooperative system grounded in the notion of maintaining particularity without creating an environment of extreme competition. The leadership invited guests to become native to creation by managing for particular species that serve the place in more holistic ways. This would include, for example, the inclusion of American sycamore, bald cypress, flame leaf sumac, and escarpment black cherry trees; the planting of big bluestem, Lindheimer's senna, and Texas beargrass plants; and the insertion of agarita, esperanza, fragrant sumac, and Spanish lavender shrubs onto the property.

---

[5]Wes Jackson, *Becoming Native to This Place* (Louisville: University of Kentucky Press, 1994), 99.

This prioritization of cooperative particularity connects to Gunton's assertion that the Spirit, as the Lord and giver of life, is the divine person who maintains the unique character of all things in creation: "the cabbages, mountains, statues and melodies that surround us."[6] What we witness in God's creation, accordingly, is not timeless ideals but rather a celebration of creation's particularity: not generic cabbages but napa and Savoy cabbages, not any kind of mountains but volcanic and plateau ones, not homogenous statues but freestanding or relief sculptures, and not the same melody across human cultures but rather Celtic and sub-Saharan melodies, each very much a one-of-a-kind species.[7] Indeed, this is the mystery of existence: not that everything is the same, Gunton writes, but "that everything is what it is and not another thing."[8] On this account, the Spirit ought to be seen not only as the divine person who in the beginning animates and who in the end reanimates or perfects creation but also as the one who in this present age secures each thing in being.

For Gunton, it is the Spirit who enables each thing in creation to be fully "its own thing," in its own proper place.[9] As relates to the lodge's project, this means that a truly Spirited work of landscape architecture will prioritize managing native over nonnative species and will actively extirpate invasive species and exclude overpopulated species.[10] Yet this is never a straightforward affair; it is instead an often complicated,

---

[6]Gunton, *One, the Three and the Many*, 196.

[7]Gunton, *One, the Three and the Many*, 207. Alexander Schmemann makes a similar point in *For the Life of the World: Sacraments and Orthodoxy* (Crestwood, NY: St Vladimir's Seminary Press, 1973), 76.

[8]Gunton, *One, the Three and the Many*, 206.

[9]Relatedly, the calling of the Christian in this light, to borrow the language of essayist Cynthia Ozick, is "to distinguish one life from another; to illuminate diversity; to light up the least grain of being, to show how it is concretely individual, particularized from any other; to tell, in all the marvel of its singularity, the separate holiness of the least grain." Ozick, *Art and Ardor* (New York: Knopf, 1983), 248.

[10]It should be noted that this is not because native species should always be planted in exclusion of nonnative. In the particular case of the Laity Lodge project, though, leadership sought to return the land to its most natural conditions, even if it was acknowledged that this condition had indeed also been cultivated by years of human dwelling in the region, including Indigenous management of the land before White settlers emerged there. An ecology of nativeness, in other words, is always time-bound; the landscape changes and adapts to the communities it accommodates. This, of course, relates to the following two points regarding the Spirit's work and its relation to patterns of creation.

tension-filled matter. In theological terms, particularity is never an end in itself, never for its own sake alone. It is for the sake of an ecology of right relatedness, whose true shape may be properly perceived only eschatologically. As such, a great deal of wisdom and even grit is needed in order to negotiate horticulturally and ethically complex territory for the sake of prudent decision-making and a comprehensive vision of flourishing for botanical species in a shared ecology.

To put this point in more concrete terms, the prolific reproduction of the Chinese pistache shows the tensions inherent in building an ecology of the place. In its native environment the Chinese pistache does not contribute to systems-level collapse, but displaced from its ecological home, it tends to crowd out other plants for resources. Deemed an invasive due to its competitive overuse of both resources and space, Laity Lodge regularly removes the trees for the sake of the thriving of diverse species.[11]

The mountain cedar trees, on the other hand, sometimes called ashe or blueberry juniper, are native, but not to the degree in which they populate the existing landscape. Historically controlled by fire and affected by animal populations, they now live in the ecological community in ways that have become adaptive to the current use case by humans, a world where fire in the landscape is limited and animal populations that help control the environment have been altered through human presence. Their native place in the landscape must be managed, as it has been through human encounter for thousands of years, even if the tree generally desires

---

[11]The larger discussion surrounding nonnative and native species, along with the question of what belongs or is accepted into the environment, is one that draws out all sorts of complicated questions regarding how we engage these categories in human terms. Of course, that discussion is largely outside the scope of this essay, but it deserves note that in both ecological and human social usage, the discussion surrounding native and nonnative belonging, invasive management, and (dis)placement of native species reveals the tensions inherent in both language about place and actual placed practice. Some of the ethical dimensions of this conversation will be addressed at the conclusion of this essay. For a larger discussion of the diverse methodologies and tensions inherent within restoration ecology, see William Throop, ed., *Environmental Restoration: Ethics, Theory, and Practice* (Lanham, MD: Rowman & Littlefield, 2000). Additionally, see the Environmental Protection Agency's literature on invasives management in watersheds ("Invasive Non-native Species," United States Environmental Protection Agency, July 26, 2024, www.epa.gov/watershedacademy/invasive-non-native-species) versus a more negative view of native-species restoration in Mark A. Davis et al., "Don't Judge Species on Their Origins," *Nature* 474, nos. 153-54 (2011), https://doi.org/10.1038/474153a.

to make its home there. This management of even the native species reveals the ways that what we consider wild space is almost always touched by human culture, even if those effects remain invisible to the uninitiated.

While healthy competition is a backbone of ecological health and diversity, overextension of a species's dominance on the landscape is ruinous. Empowering freedom for the variety of occupants to live well in the place means the imposition of some boundaries and interventions to enable each member of the ecological community to exercise its life on the landscape in particular, relational, and ultimately nondamaging ways. Belonging, in other words, is fostered not simply on the grounds of one's being native or nonnative but rather in one's being noncompetitive to the degree that a singular species' existence does not overly stifle or dominate to exclusionary and deterministic ends. This means, as well, that for humans to belong within the community of the trees, they must learn how to adapt their presence in ways that are helpful for the whole, sometimes making a place for and sometimes displacing what is harmful, in order for the whole ecological community to thrive in diverse particularity.

Gardeners at Laity Lodge, for example, chose to plant agarita shrubs and Mexican buckeye bushes, both native to the region, and installed a fence around the nineteen-hundred-acre property in order to keep out feral hogs, mountain goat, and white-tailed deer populations, which overeat the habitat within the property. They also trap brown-headed cowbirds, which, while native to the region, have overpopulated the land on account of the absence of bison and have outcompeted other native bird species, in order to preserve this new harmony of land and animal relation. Land managers dispossess specific animal species such as white-tailed deer or brown-headed cowbirds in this way not because the *haecceity* (the "thisness") of those species falls afoul of the loving work of the Spirit of God to sustain all creaturely things in life; rather, they manage *this* place is *this* way because those species do not properly belong to this particular ecological region or because they threaten to undermine the reparative work that this project seeks to accomplish within this unique space.[12]

[12]The term *haecceity* is taken from medieval philosopher Duns Scotus, who coined it in order to underscore the irreducible particularity of all things in creation. Late nineteenth-century English

This work of dispossession and replacement ought also to be seen, we assert, as Spirit-authored, Spirit-discerned work. Making a space for particularity to flourish, in other words, is intimately tied up in the expression of diversity, a theological point underscored by both the Spirit's active and particularizing presence in creation and in the practical principles of ecological land management. Importantly, this diversity is actively managed in ways that impose limits on freedom even as it empowers the expression of one's own particularity.

Serendipitous Discoveries

Another key aesthetic-ecological change revealed in the newly renovated landscape of Laity Lodge is the presence of more "wild space" over and above spaces of anthropocentrically oriented artificial order. The lawn by the Great Hall, for example, along with patches of ground surrounding the new limestone pathways between structures, rather than being pristinely mowed St. Augustine grass, is now occupied by native wildflowers, the results of which both constrain and open up new spaces of seeing. The leadership of the project remarks: "Each of us has visited places where a preponderance of signs prevents any sense of expectation or unfolding mystery. Our aim is different: we want to heighten guests' anticipation—and even invite a little serendipitous discovery—by scaling back the types and number of signs around the Lodge." While in certain seasons, this change may seem uncontroversial (when the flowers are in full display), at other seasons, some will experience the change as an eyesore and an aesthetic assault on the order of the place. One guest, we were told during our visit to the property, remarked dismissively that the lawn had been overrun by sunflowers and that the space lacked beauty on account of the dominance of this heliotropic, heat-tolerant but rather gangly and "common" flower (*Helianthus annuus*). Because the flowers had been allowed to reseed themselves, their numbers were not determined in the same way as more closely managed and planted species of flowers. At the height of their flower, this freedom to be wild also imposes limits on both visitors' vision

poet Gerard Manley Hopkins developed this at great length in his poetry; see, e.g., "As Kingfishers Catch Fire," in *Poetry and Prose* (London: Penguin Classics, 1953), 51.

and their experience of perambulation. The flowers create boundaries for guests (they now cannot walk through thickly vegetated spaces that were once open), even as they open up new spaces for nonhuman life to thrive.

In theological terms, such limits ought not to be seen as unfortunate limitations but as blessed gifts that result from working with the God-ordained *givens* of the land. The species are now afforded their own relative freedom and cannot be fully predicted in advance; they will do so, we contend, in Spirit-authored "wild" fashion.

This point relates to Gunton's second assertion, namely that the Spirit's particularizing work enables things in creation to unfold in truly novel ways. Drawing on Gunton's line of thought, Jeremy Begbie puts the point this way: "With respect to creation at large, if the Son or Word through whom all things are created is associated with the dynamic stability of reality, the Spirit is active 'to enable new possibilities, to empower freedom to live in the abundance that is given.'"[13] It goes against the character of the Spirit of God, that is, to deny the creature the freedom to be just what it is in its creaturely life. In the Spirit, there is a place for each thing in creation; this place is a gift and it is a grace, and it is a place for the creature to go of itself rather than to be governed by irresistible forces; it is a place, finally, for the creature to go anew, more fully and richly itself, rather than to be governed by metaphysically impersonal or deterministic forces.[14]

Creaturely life is governed instead by the third person of the Trinity, who, in the case of nonhuman creatures, neither squelches genuine development or new growth, nor, in the case of the human creature, underwrites autonomously construed ventures into novelty or self-determinative pursuits of freedom. As with particularity, novelty in creation is never an end in itself, for it too is caught up in the eschatological purposes of God for all of creation.[15] And as with all things in the triune economy this side

---

[13]Jeremy Begbie, *Theology, Music and Time* (Cambridge: Cambridge University Press, 2000), 242; see also 223-24, 241-45.

[14]Colin Gunton, *The Triune Creator: A Historical and Systematic Study* (Grand Rapids, MI: Eerdmans, 1998), 86.

[15]Drawing on similar theological traditions, Daniel Hardy and David Ford, in *Jubilate* (London: Darton, Longman & Todd, 1984), 119, explain this dynamic further when they write that God "respectfully addresses, shapes, and proportions reality, giving it its inner, non-equilibrial balance

of the eschaton, the Holy Spirit's restorative work in creation stands over against all entropic and sin-infected forces that would undermine God's good purposes for the world that he so loves in Christ Jesus, in whom all things in creation hold together and through whom the telos of the cosmos is properly discerned.[16]

The vocation of humans, accordingly, is to partner with the Spirit by helping creaturely things, such as flowers and insects, to unfold both as they are and as they might be, rather than by forcibly foreclosing the possibility of genuine development and unforeseen novelty. On this point, the lodge's director of stewardship, Kevin Wessels, admits that he cannot yet predict how the land will change over the coming years. A time will come when difficult decisions will need to be made about what stays and what gets uprooted or excluded. At present, the variables are greater than the constants, and there is a way that the flora and fauna may well propagate in unpredictable, perhaps even "counterproductive" or "destructive" ways.

This is the risk, and indeed the adventure, of the project; it is the adventure of letting a place be a verb with a mind of its own, to borrow Marlene Creates's language. Grasses may spread profligately; flowers of one species may colonize the flowers of another; trees intimately tied to the architectural space may suddenly die or inconveniently block out the light of the sun; waterways may carve channels into the earth that unevenly distribute nourishment to bushes and trees in the immediate area.

In addition to a nondeterministic growth pattern for the wildflower species, the process of reseeding asks that visitors reassess their conceptions of beauty. When the various flowers that carpet the lawn die, they are allowed to remain in place to seed out into the soil, resulting in a brown, ostensibly dead landscape but one that will in another season resurrect new life. Death is a key feature of the new ecological experience of beauty in the place. The beauty that a guest experiences now is one of true freedom and ecological life cycle, allowing for innovation and

---

in movement. . . . It refuses all pigeon-holing, allows no self-sufficient closed systems, and, positively, it is the dynamic stability of reality, allowing freedom but also embodying constraints."

[16]The pneumatological grammar of Romans 8 may be especially helpful to this point, where Paul describes the Spirit as the one who heals creation in the face of creation's experience of waiting, futility, bondage, and groaning.

outcomes that cannot be foreseen in advance. Sometimes, for instance, the sunflowers overrun the lawn; at other times the bee balm bushes dip into the path to reveal a buzzing, humming community of insects that visitors may find unwelcome.

But in allowing the flowers to educate us in their own particular beauty, we re-attune our loves to the patterns of creation, where each thing is uniquely itself, free to become that which was conceived before only in possibility. Such re-attunement clarifies the Spirit-empowered human vocation to live responsively to the patterns and powers of creation rather than ignorantly or dismissively of them. This, again, is the promise and peril of the human vocation to till and to keep the earth, in the lodge's case by way of gardening and architectural labors.

"There's a Tree in My Shower"

These movements toward particularity and freedom for the ecology of the place are also met with a profound reimagination of how a guest relates to nature. With respect to the newly renovated Cedar Break guest rooms, for example, a guest is invited to share a space not just with fellow guests but with characters who reveal a different kind of dwelling, one more permanent and yet more fragile. In the past, guests would occupy multiple but sometimes disparately connected spaces. The guest rooms at the time were warm and inviting, the open lawn by the Great Hall good for lounging, and the concrete paths meandering but open enough to feel a relative freedom to explore. In the new renovation, regular bathroom showers, for example, were traded for the company of redbud trees, which, while not in bloom during our April visit to the property, would be a spectacular sight of purple in another season as one washed the day's dirt away.

The trees in the shower are just one signal of the ways that our own human rituals would be drawn together with those of nature. Rather than being seen as invasive of a guest's space, the trees offer guests an invitation to live cooperatively with them, and in this way they thicken a guest's sense of being an earthling, a creature *of* the earth, not *above* or *beyond* the earth.

This brings to light Gunton's final assertion, namely that the Spirit's particularizing work enables particular things in God's creation to be fundamentally relationally constituted.[17] This means that things in creation are not merely connected. It means that things in creation "mutually constitute each other, make each other what they are."[18] As Gunton explains, "Everything may be what it is and not another thing, but it is also what it uniquely is by virtue of its relation to everything else."[19] What trinitarian love accomplishes, on this thinking, is a constitutive relationality whereby things and persons in creation are opened out to one another without any loss of particular identity. It is because of the Spirit's work in creation that the one and the many need not be in zero-sum competition with each other. The one can remain fully and uniquely one while also being harmoniously related to the many.[20]

In negative terms, both absolute mutability (with a corresponding loss of concrete identity) and absolute changelessness (or ossified permanence) are to be rejected, as are all form of reductionistic difference and flattening homogeneity. In more positive terms, the one remains semiporously open to the many rather than opaque or wholly porous, and in this way becomes more richly itself without any loss of unique identity. In specifically theological terms, the Spirit preserves the integral identity of the one in relation to the integral identity of the many, and does so in ways that remain commensurate to the distinctive telos of human and nonhuman creatures—Christlikeness for the former, full flourishing for the latter.

Informed by the idea of *biophilia,* or the love of place, the lodge's landscape architects sought to help guests reimagine their relationship to the land in a host of ways. Buildings, for example, were no longer to be seen as separate from the surrounding cedar forests but rather enveloped and defined by them; they were to be built in proportion to the size of the trees rather than be allowed to loom over against the trees; and they were to be designed in conversation with the actual beauty of the trees, bushes, and soil rather than by making them artificially beautiful, impervious to the shape, texture, color, and line of the local habitat itself. Another goal of the

---

[17]Gunton, *Triune Creator*, 170.

[18]Gunton, *Triune Creator*, 169.

[19]Gunton, *Triune Creator*, 173.

[20]Gunton, *Triune Creator*, 161-62, 224.

architects was to remove the poured concrete paths. While this might make it less convenient for guests to travel from A to B, it would invite them to slow down, to attend more purposefully to the details of creation in their immediate vicinity, and to experience a "purposeless" meandering through a space rather than traversing a path in the most efficient manner possible.

The hope, according to the leadership, was that on the other side of an apparent inconvenience might lie a blessing: a quieting of the mind, a reordering of bodily passions, a nourishment of the heart, and a repair of the imagination. By enmeshing guests more richly into the landscape, the hope was that the land might reconcile guests more fully to their amphibious identity, as dust-formed creatures made in the image of God, and thereby rehumanize them. The hope was that such an experience might disrupt deeply ingrained and dehumanizing consumerist, productivist, or individualist tendencies, and invite guests to feel their mutually constitutive relationship to the earth more deeply. This, too, we suggest, is the work of the particularizing Spirit, who in Christ reconciles all things in creation to their true identity to the glory of the Father.

Nowhere is this more apparent than in the water that shapes the land and sustains life for its inhabitants. The landscape architecture asks now that we walk among permeable limestone pathways to quiet ourselves to the sound of the water itself, moving us to be shaped and molded through attentive presence, to be joined together with the place itself. Check dams, for instance, made of cedar sticks interrupt the landscape at varying intervals, slowing the flow of water over stone and soil. Limestone rocks not only form small spaces for water to pool and filter but also provide spaces of contemplation as visitors walk through the natural landscape.

Both of these human-placed but natural features of the landscape architecture reveal the ways that our situatedness in the land comes at a cost that must be borne by all inhabitants. The lodge has made the choice to conserve, redirect, and responsibly manage the water and soil in a way that centers the canyon itself as an active participant in the place. The canyon, with its ecological requirements, thus asks that we retrain our vision to see the place as a refuge—not only for guests in need of spiritual retreat but also for the variety of nonhuman members of the ecological community it accommodates.

On this point, Holy Scripture reflects a God-people-place relationship that suggests we are mutually intertwined with the rest of God's creation, an entanglement that constitutes not only our outcomes of action but also our identity itself. This being so, we argue that attention to the landscape of Laity Lodge and its systems of relatedness can show us something significant about the Spirit's work in the world. We live within systems of entanglement that reflect, as Norman Wirzba suggests, "the symbiotic character of life."[21] This kinship with one another does not suggest a dissolution of borders when it comes to place and its communities but rather a reframing of the way that things belong to one another within hospitable border arrangements. As this case study illustrates, the Spirit works to join together communities in their shared difference without abrogating particularity. In addition to this, we as human beings become more truly ourselves on account of this enmeshment with creation. On the pneumatological terms of this chapter, we are not disinterested spectators of landscape architecture; we are instead redefined by the botanical life and, in consequence of our bodily entanglement with it, made more alive.[22]

Principles of robustness, balance, nativeness, and diversity have been prioritized in all these spaces elaborated above, and the aesthetic and ecological choices of Laity Lodge reflect the leadership's ongoing interest in caring for the larger creational order of things as well as balancing hospitality toward its guests with responsible ecological stewardship and aesthetic sensitivity. Love of creation characterizes all these choices in the landscape, and visitors are invited into a love of the place for its own sake as well as a new form of neighbor love. But love is never neutral, either horticulturally or theologically, and the place teaches us that sometimes exclusion and displacement, along with the granting of freedom for creation to be itself, is required for holistic flourishing. A beauty that is properly "placed" and that invites diverse belonging must also sometimes exclude,

[21]Norman Wirzba, *This Sacred Life: Humanity's Place in a Wounded World* (Cambridge: Cambridge University Press, 2021), 63.

[22]Wirzba, *This Sacred Life*, 213-14.

manage, or otherwise intervene. This, of course, generates a variety of ethical questions, which we raise here in the final section of the chapter.

Ethical Questions

Projects such as these are never uncontested, and the choices made by the leadership at Laity Lodge open up questions for their own ongoing conservation work as well as larger considerations for theologically minded visitors. First, it may be helpful to consider the questions the project brings up on a more local level. The project interrogates the ways that financial, aesthetic, and ecological questions become further complicated when the mission of the organization is brought into view. How are we to balance the desire for Christian ministry to a variety of participants with the ideological interests expressed in the project? Beauty always comes at a cost, for example, but how expensive is too expensive when a project like this is undertaken? In what ways were competing interests and tensions handled regarding these issues, and what may remain unresolved?

For Laity Lodge, these questions are both practical and theological. Hospitality and stewardship sometimes present themselves at odds with each other.[23] For instance, the family and youth camps have playing fields for children, but those fields are managed with nonnative grasses and with more financial and ecological expense. Or trees that have been long loved at the camps, such as the Chinese pistache, must be evaluated for whether the sense of place (grounded, in this case, in a misconstrued notion of what belongs) should outweigh the ecological impact of letting such an invasive species remain.

While a singular tree may not seem consequential, it stands for the ways that one's sense of place might be interrogated by a theology of

[23]On the language of stewardship, Norman Wirzba cautions against an overreliance on the term, noting, in personal correspondence, how the managerial overtones can easily go awry. See Wirzba, *The Paradise of God: Renewing Religion in an Ecological Age* (Oxford, Oxford University Press, 2003), esp. chap. 4. He recommends in its stead the language of "study and service," which he believes gets more closely to the Genesis command to "till and keep." "Practically," he writes, "this means that more emphasis falls on the need to continually learn through engagement and labor what the land recommends. Consulting the genius of the place has contemplative dimensions, but above all it is about working with the land and in that work discerning what is good or not to do."

creation that seeks to understand the relationality of the whole. How might we adjust our own conveniences and loves to meet the needs of a robust, diverse creation of particular species? How might we also adjust our ideological expectations for the immediate benefit of populations in need of loving care (in this case, children and families visiting the camps)? The answers to those questions are never singular and invariably require inquiry into additional theological loci.[24]

Second, regarding finances, questions of cost come to bear on both aesthetic and ecological choices. The architectural choices (e.g., the use of expensive materials such as natural stone), plant choices (more expensive native versus nonnative species), and management choices (labor-intensive weeding by hand rather than labor-light mowing by machine) all reveal the ways that certain notions of beauty come at a higher cost. Additionally, the organization sought to treat the property as a place of refuge in an exemplary way, and so the financial costs incurred in renovating are justified through the way that they offer ongoing healing, support, and sabbath retreat for both human and nonhuman creatures.

While the financial considerations are no less real, one may find an analogy in the great cathedrals of Europe. Abbot Suger, thinking theologically about the sumptuous art of the Abbey Church of St. Denis in France, acknowledged "great cost and much expenditure for their gilding as was fitting."[25] Both the expense and the beauty of the great cathedral were fitting to the divine presence it housed. Similarly, the beauty that is prioritized in the landscape of Laity Lodge may be said to befit an encounter

---

[24]The landscape architecture of the lodge, on this account, is a specific species of culture-making and should be distinguished, we suggest, from a national park, such as Big Bend or Yellowstone in the US, and a manicured garden, such as Queen Elizabeth Park in Vancouver, British Columbia. A primary purpose of a national park is to preserve its wildness, while a primary purpose of such a garden is to entertain and to delight visitors in the aesthetic pleasure of flowers, bushes, and trees. With the lodge, the primary purpose of the design and management of plant species is to serve the purpose of human rest and retreat. There is a more direct service of the landscape, we propose, to the goals of human hospitality at the lodge, which would not necessarily be the case with a national park or public garden.

[25]Abbot Suger, *Abbot Suger on the Abbey Church of St. Denis and Its Art Treasures*, 2nd ed., ed. and trans. Erwin Panofsky and Gerda Panofsky-Soergel (Princeton, NJ: Princeton University Press, 1979), 47.

with the beauty of God in the landscape and the beauty of hospitality in the activities of rest and retreat.[26]

Third, these more locally relevant questions bring up more expansive theological and ethical questions as well. The notion of the beautiful, along with its relationship to competing senses of place and attitudes of belonging, raises a much larger theological conundrum. How ought we to think about things that a community regards as beautiful or believe should belong in a place but that might not be the best for the place and its communities?[27] How, in this case, might the disordered love of place, warped by sin, be construed and resolved? The doctrine of the Spirit elaborated here may help resolve these concerns. If the Spirit educates us in a love of particularity, then the reordering of our love of place and its multitudinous beauties must begin with an attentive listening to the Spirit. While our love of place might be bent askew by the power of sin, we suggest that the Spirit works to "make straight" our ways of seeing, re-forming our affections to better understand the whole creational vision of God for the world.

The Spirit does so not through solipsistic musings but rather through the work of communal discernment, which in the case of the lodge includes ongoing conversation with the communion of saints, such as Wendell Berry and A Rocha, and the communion of wise experts, such as master naturalists, wildlife conservationists, and skilled gardeners. In doing so, the Spirit does not reveal a homogenous experience of place to which we must conform but instead opens up a vision of affective relatedness through which we may understand our experience to be both committed and reconfigured in noncompetitive particularity. Our vision of both beauty and place, in other words, becomes reoriented to new horizons of seeing, where

[26]While much more could be said on this account, ethical judgments of the lodge's landscape decisions must be rendered within the larger mission of the H. E. Butt Foundation.

[27]One relevant point of application here is the way Western notions of beauty have often been used to wield control and power over places and people. Willie James Jennings, for instance, observes the ways that Western conceptions of beauty become oppressive to both places and people, along with the ways those aesthetic values have been tied to theological evaluation in the colonial Christian imagination. While this is not a matter we can properly address here, it reveals the ways that these discussions, even as they regard particular patterns of placemaking in local landscapes, have much larger cultural implications. See Willie James Jennings, "The Aesthetic Struggle and the Ecclesial Vision," in *Black Practical Theology*, ed. Dale P. Andrews and Robert London Smith Jr. (Waco, TX: Baylor University Press, 2015), 163-85.

our conceptions of power and dominion are replaced by the dispositions of mutual submission within the whole community of creation.

This uncovers a final set of ecological and theological questions for which we may offer only glimpses of a possible future direction of inquiry. We have highlighted the ways that the renovation project at Laity Lodge enabled the construction of a new sense of place that indeed may be more fitting for the land, animal, and human populations that find themselves in the Frio River canyon in Texas Hill Country. But this newly constructed sense of place came, at least in part, through a process of displacement and exclusion.

One may ask: Is the displacement of things (or people) always an absolute wrong or evil? How do we think theologically about the necessary displacement of trees or grasses or flowers for the sake of re-implacement, whether this involves the "unfortunate" destruction of a species that has made its home there or the positive destruction of a species that is invasive to a particular region (e.g., the ashe juniper in central Texas)? How, more challengingly, might the narratives of Scripture that recount various placements and displacements theologically inform our practices of placemaking today?[28] And, equally crucial, how might the work of master naturalists and conservationists inform and interrogate our own—perhaps naive or narrow—theological ideas of displacement?

These are not easy questions with easy answers, and the ecological and theological answers may reveal conflicting concerns. For instance, ecological conservation would suggest a far more unproblematic evaluation of the question of displacement—namely, as that which serves the most regenerative and self-sustaining community of the particular place (what is kept) and that which stifles the thriving of local species and biodiverse landscapes (what is removed). Certainly, these questions may seem easier when we consider whether to cultivate local sunflowers versus nonnative grasses, but what happens when we apply the concept to human populations of any kind?

[28]Narratives such as Abraham's displacement and promised re-implacement, the wandering placemaking of Israel in the desert, the conquest of the land of Canaan, Christ's own refugee status in the land of Egypt for a time, and the calling of the disciples out of their homes and families and to the ends of the earth—how do these stories of placement and displacement reveal the wider goals of God for his creation, along with the way displacement can function both destructively and restoratively?

Does a more robust doctrine of the Spirit's particularizing work decenter humanity to the point of a diminished theological anthropology? Certainly not, but the questions, it seems, do become more complicated when one ventures into less carefully defined generalities. And while we cannot necessarily offer a full-scale interpretation of what it means that God might choose to displace some creatures for others, the landscape architecture project of Laity Lodge does suggest ways that a misconstrued sense of place does often need a manner of displacement in order to be made whole and holy.

Conclusion

If our sense of place is warped by the many wrong turns to which sin has directed us, then the Spirit's particularizing work may precisely be the work of displacement *for the sake of* re-implacement, redirecting our gaze to that which is illuminated by the constitutive relationality the Spirit offers. And while this constitutive relatedness multiplies its own set of questions related to competition for resources that we see in both nature itself and our relation to it, we must at the end of the day place our trust in the divine vision that Christ himself embodies in his vulnerable self-offering to creation. Because of Christ's cosmic vision of redemption, fulfilled life is possible for all, but it may be so only within the eschatological vision of place offered in the new creation.

Nature may show us a vision for such life, while at the same time deeply questioning it. And our hopeful aspirations for the particularizing work of the Spirit may remain unfulfilled even as we work toward justice and peace for all God's creatures in their places. What we have hopefully offered in this brief survey of Laity's Lodge's landscape restoration project, however, is a creative example of how humans may become more aligned with, related to, and indeed changed by their relationship to the natural world. In being so aligned, related, and changed, the hope is that guests at the lodge might be inspired and compelled to live similarly in their own local places. Finally, if these practices of refuge-making and creation care offer us any hope for a future of deeper relation to God and his creation, then they move us closer to the particularizing vision of the Spirit for and in the world.

ACKNOWLEDGMENTS

More than any other published project we've undertaken, the creation of this book has been communal from start to finish. The essays shared here are a product of a community of scholars that was nurtured over the course of many years, gathering together in various locations throughout the United States, editing and listening to each other's work, and graciously challenging one another to produce our very best. Our community, however, is itself a living testament to a network of communities, organizations, and institutions who have made this possible.

In particular we wish to thank the McDonald Agape Foundation for its generous financial support of the project, without which none of our work would have been possible. We thank the leadership of Duke Divinity who have eagerly championed its cause. Steven Purcell and the entire staff at the Laity Lodge were especially generous in their hospitality in the early stages of this project, inviting us into new spaces and rhythms which nurtured our thinking as much as our friendships. Similarly, the Creative Arts Coalition of Belmont University in Nashville not only extended incredible hospitality as the project drew to a close but has also encouraged us to continue dreaming about what *might* be possible in years to come.

We wish to acknowledge the various academic institutions across the United States that provided both funding and time for the many scholars represented here. We are most especially thankful to the families and friends surrounding these scholars who made this work possible. We wish we could name each of you in turn, but we acknowledge the many sacrifices you have made and appreciate your steadfast encouragement along the way.

We extend our gratitude to the community at InterVarsity Press for their support of this project. Chief among these is Zachary Gordon, who has graciously steered its publication throughout the whole process and has been a great source of encouragement and wisdom.

Lastly, it is no exaggeration to say that this project would be inconceivable without Jeremy Begbie. Jeremy has worked tirelessly throughout his career to build institutions in the UK and the US that would nurture the kind of scholarship that is presented here. Many of the scholars in this group, in fact, studied under Jeremy or in programs he helped create, and his own scholarship has served as a model for the work we've sought to foster through this project. He has championed the cause when necessary, offered sage advice where needed, and never wavered in his belief that this sort of work could serve the Spirit's ongoing work of renewing and transforming the world.

For all of these, and so many more, we give thanks.

LIST OF CONTRIBUTORS

Devon Abts (PhD, King's College London) is a theologian whose work explores the intersections of modern theology, Christian ethics, and the arts, with special expertise in literature. She holds a PhD in theology from King's College London, and an MA in religion and literature from Yale. Devon currently serves as Director of Research and Operations for The Clemente Course in the Humanities. Prior to Clemente, she was interim director of the Henry Luce III Center for the Arts and Religion in Washington, DC. She holds a visiting fellowship in theology at King's and is a contributor to multiple transatlantic research collaborations in her field.

Phil Allen, Jr. (PhD, Fuller Theological Seminary) is a theologian and ethicist who researches and writes on social structures, healing racial trauma, and fostering racial solidarity. He is the author of *Open Wounds: A Story of Racial Tragedy, Trauma, and Redemption* (Fortress Press 2021) and *The Prophetic Lens: The Camera and Black Moral Agency From MLK to Darnella Frazier* (Fortress Press 2022). He is also a professor (Fuller Theological Seminary), poet, and documentary film producer. He is also founder and president of the nonprofit Racial Solidarity Project based in Pasadena, CA.

Christina Carnes Ananias (PhD, Duke Divinity School) is the Lilly Endowment Faculty Fellow in the School of Theology and Christian Ministry at Belmont University, where her research and teaching focuses on contemporary applications of Scripture and theology. She received her master's and doctoral degrees at Duke Divinity School, where her scholarship centered on discovering parallels between patristic Christology and modernist visual artwork. At Belmont, she teaches various classes on Scripture, theology, and the arts, while comanaging a suite of research and programming titled *In Every Generation*, an initiative aimed at nurturing intergenerational friendships in the church through the arts.

Jonathan A. Anderson (PhD, King's College London, University of London) is the Eugene and Jan Peterson Associate Professor of Theology and the Arts at Regent College (Vancouver, BC). He is the author of *The Invisibility of Religion in Contemporary Art* (2025), *Modern Art and the Life of a Culture: The Religious Impulses of Modernism* (with William Dyrness, 2016), and many articles and book chapters on related topics. For more info, see jonathan-anderson.com.

Justin Ariel Bailey (PhD, Fuller Theological Seminary) is professor of theology at Dordt University. He is the author of two books, *Reimagining Apologetics* and *Interpreting Your World* and hosts the *In All Things* podcast. He is married and has two teenage children in northwestern Iowa.

Jennifer Allen Craft (PhD, University of St Andrews) is professor of theology and humanities at Point University in West Point, GA, where she teaches classes in theology, culture, and the arts. She is the author of *Placemaking and the Arts: Cultivating the Christian Life* (IVP Academic, 2018), and her current research centers on the relationship between place and displacement in Christian theology, the arts as they relate to the work of justice, and the ecological/aesthetic dimensions of our life in place.

Steven Guthrie (PhD, University of St Andrews) is professor of theology and religion and the arts at Belmont University and is Senior Fellow of the Creative Arts Collective for Christian Life and Faith. He is the author of *Creator Spirit: The Holy Spirit and the Art of Becoming Human* (Baker Academic, 2011) and is the cogeneral editor of the *Oxford Handbook of Music and Christian Theology* (Oxford University Press, 2026). He continues to work as a professional musician, performing and recording in the Nashville area.

Joelle A. Hathaway (ThD, Duke Divinity School) is assistant professor of theological studies at Bethany Theological Seminary, where she directs the MA: Theopoetics and Writing. She is a double graduate of Duke Divinity School, where she completed her MTS and then ThD in theology and the arts. Joelle's research and teaching examines the intersection of Christian theology, the arts, and the built environment. Of particular interest is what insights the arts can offer to practices of theological, spiritual, racial, and ecological formation. She lives outside Indianapolis with her spouse Brent Smith and their daughters Lillian and Vivian.

Amy Whisenand Krall (ThD, Duke University Divinity School) is assistant professor of religion at Hope College. She is the author of *Singing Reconciliation: Inhabiting the Moral Life According to Colossians 3:16.* Her research and publications focus on the intersection of New Testament studies, ethics, music-making, and worship practices.

Wesley Vander Lugt (PhD, University of St Andrews) is a pastor-theologian, writer, educator, nonprofit leader, and arts advocate. He teaches theology and directs the Leighton Ford Initiative in Theology, the Arts, and Gospel Witness at Gordon-Conwell Theological Seminary in Charlotte, NC, and is the Co-Founder of Kinship Plot, a community of learning and practice cultivating resonant relationships of every kind. Wes holds a PhD in Theology, Imagination, and the Arts from the University of St Andrews, and his latest books are *Beauty is Oxygen: Finding a Faith that Breathes* (Eerdmans, 2024) and *A Prophet in the Darkness: Exploring Theology in the Art of Georges Rouault* (IVP Academic, 2024).

David W. McNutt (PhD, University of Cambridge) is senior acquisitions editor at Zondervan Academic, an imprint of HarperCollins Christian Publishing, and associate lecturer of Core Studies at Wheaton College, where he teaches courses in systematic theology, theology and the arts, and theology and film. He is also an ordained minister in the Presbyterian Church, the coauthor of *Know the Theologians*, and the cofounder of McNuttshell Ministries, which seeks to serve both the church and the academy.

Julian Davis Reid (MDiv, Candler School of Theology) is a child of God, husband, father, son, brother, and Black artist-theologian of Chicago. His academic and musical work focuses on rest and Black music as eschatological hope and lived reality. Alongside having founded Notes of Rest, Julian is a consultant with Fearless Dialogues and a touring musician. He has projects out with his own ensemble Circle of Trust and with the jazz-electronic fusion group he cofounded, The JuJu Exchange. Julian's work has been covered in *The New York Times* and *Sojourners*. He hopes his offering helps you listen deeper still.

Erin Shaw (MFA, University of Oklahoma) is a painter and visual storyteller. As a Chickasaw-Choctaw artist, she creates in a state of tension, suspended between two worlds where both solemnity and humor pervade her art. She finds that truths are revealed in unanticipated ways. The artist earned her BFA in studio art from Baylor University and her MFA from the University of Oklahoma. She has twenty-five years of educational experience as an international speaker, artist, and a featured artist in Visual Voices: Contemporary Chickasaw Art, among other exhibits in the United States.

Shannon Sigler (PhD candidate, University of Manchester, UK) serves as the Executive Director for Fuller Seminary's Brehm Center for Worship, Theology, and the Arts. Her art and research center around a Wesleyan paradigm for the arts, as well as explorations supporting the spiritual health of artists. Shannon previously served as the Associate Director for CIVA | Christians in the Visual Arts. She lives in Seattle with her husband, Matt, and son, Elijah.

Chelle Stearns (PhD, University of St Andrews) has taught theology at The Seattle School of Theology & Psychology for sixteen years and has a broad interest in theological engagement with the arts, with her primary research in music and theology. Her book *Handling Dissonance: A Musical Theological Aesthetic of Unity* is an exploration of a theology of unity through Arnold Schoenberg's compositional philosophy and Colin Gunton's trinitarian theology. Her writing can be found in publications by IVP Academic, Lexington, Cascade, Cambridge University Press, and Oxford University Press. Chelle is currently researching and writing a book on music, trauma studies, and theology.

W. David O. Taylor (ThD, Duke Divinity School) is associate professor of theology and culture at Fuller Theological Seminary and the author of several books, including *A Body of Praise* (Baker Academic, 2023) and *Glimpses of the New Creation* (Eerdmans, 2019). His editing work includes *The Art of New Creation* (IVP Academic, 2022) and *Contemporary Art and the Church* (IVP Academic, 2017). He has published articles in the *Calvin Theological Journal*, *Christian Scholars Review*, *Worship*, and *Theology Today*, among others. An Anglican priest, he has lectured widely on the arts, from Thailand to South Africa.

Daniel Train (PhD, Baylor University) is assistant teaching professor of the practice of theology and the arts at Duke Divinity School, where he serves as the associate director of Duke Initiatives in Theology and the Arts (DITA). He is the coeditor of *The Art of New Creation and The Saint John's Bible and Its Tradition: Illuminating Beauty in the Twenty-First Century.*

Taylor Worley (PhD, University of St Andrews) is visiting associate professor of art history at Wheaton College and directs a research project on art and contemplation. He is an alumnus of the Institute for Theology, Imagination, and the Arts at the University of St Andrews and author of *Memento Mori in Contemporary Art: Theologies of Lament and Hope* (2020).

Wesley Vander Lugt (PhD, University of St Andrews) is a pastor-theologian, writer, educator, nonprofit leader, and arts advocate. He teaches theology and directs the Leighton Ford Center for Theology, the Arts, and Gospel Witness at Gordon-Conwell Theological Seminary in Charlotte and is the Co-Founder of Kinship Plot, a community of learning and practice cultivating resonant relationships of every kind. Wes holds a PhD in Theology, Imagination, and the Arts from the University of St Andrews, and his latest books are *Beauty is Oxygen: Finding a Faith that Breathes* (Eerdmans, 2024) and *A Prophet in the Darkness: Exploring Theology in the Art of Georges Rouault* (IVP Academic, 2024).

Amos Yong (PhD, Boston University) is professor of theology and mission at Fuller Theological Seminary and the author or editor of dozens of volumes, three of which may be of interest to readers of this book: *Renewing Christian Theology: Systematics for a Global Christianity*, images and commentary by Jonathan A. Anderson (Waco, TX.: Baylor University Press, 2014); *Mission after Pentecost: The Witness of the Spirit from Genesis to Revelation*, Mission in Global Community (Grand Rapids, MI: Baker Academic, 2019); and *Revelation*, Belief: A Theological Commentary on the Bible series (Louisville, KY: Westminster John Knox Press, 2021).

GENERAL INDEX

SCRIPTURE INDEX

DITA Duke Initiatives in THEOLOGY & THE ARTS

Established at Duke Divinity School in 2009 under the leadership of Professor Jeremy Begbie, Duke Initiatives in Theology and the Arts (DITA) promotes a vibrant, two-way engagement between Christian theology and the arts. Committed to training leaders who will implement and extend its vision, DITA seeks not only to have a transformative influence in the academy but also in local churches and the community at large. Through events, teaching, and research, DITA is dedicated to showing how the arts can be enriched by theology, and theology in turn renewed through the arts.

www.ingramcontent.com/pod-product-compliance
Lightning Source LLC
LaVergne TN
LVHW091127080826
845145LV00008B/2072

9781514013489